SELF-INSTRUCTION PEDAGOGY

SELF-INSTRUCTION PEDAGOGY

How to Teach Self-Determined Learning

By

DENNIS E. MITHAUG
Teachers College Columbia University

DEIRDRE K. MITHAUG
St. John's University

MARTIN AGRAN
University of Wyoming

JAMES E. MARTIN
University of Oklahoma

MICHAEL L. WEHMEYER
University of Kansas

CHARLES C THOMAS • PUBLISHER, LTD.
Springfield • Illinois • U.S.A.

Published and Distributed Throughout the World by

CHARLES C THOMAS • PUBLISHER, LTD.
2600 South First Street
Springfield, Illinois 62704

© 2007 by CHARLES C THOMAS • PUBLISHER, LTD.

ISBN 978-0-398-07722-8 (hard)
ISBN 978-0-398-07723-5 (paper)

Library of Congress Catalog Card Number: 2006051430

With THOMAS BOOKS *careful attention is given to all details of manufacturing
and design. It is the Publisher's desire to present books that are satisfactory as to their
physical qualities and artistic possibilities and appropriate for their particular use.*
THOMAS BOOKS *will be true to those laws of quality that assure a good name
and good will.*

Printed in the United States of America
UB-R-3

Library of Congress Cataloging-in-Publication Data

Mithaug, Dennis E.
  Self-instruction pedagogy : how to teach self-determined learning / by Dennis E. Mithaug
... [et al.].
    p. cm.
  Includes bibliographical references and index.
  Contents: Direct instruction vs. self-instruction: what's the difference? -- Your instruction
teacher-or student-directed? -- How students develop learner control -- How students adjust
to learner control -- How students direct their learning -- How self-determined learning
increases at school and work -- Why teachers are reluctant to choose choice -- Will you
choose self-instruction pedagogy?
  ISBN 978-0-398-07722-8 (hc) -- ISBN 978-0-398-07723-5 (pbk.)
    1. Learning, Psychology of. 2. Autonomy (Psychology) 3. Self-culture. 4. Instructional
    systems--Design. I. Title.
LB1060.M58 2007
370.15'23--dc22   2006051430

PREFACE

For decades we have known that students who are good self-regulators do better in school and are more successful in life than students who are not. In the 1960s, for example, Walter Mischel provided the first evidence of this when he used the now famous Marshmallow Test to assess levels of self-control in four-year-olds. He found that some children were able to resist the impulse to grab marshmallows when they were available and other children were not. The first group became known as "waiters" and the second as "grabbers." In a follow-up of these children more than a decade later, Mischel found that the grabbers who were poor self-regulators were seen by others as being stubborn, overactive, envious, jealous, easily upset, and troubled with low self-esteem, whereas the waiters who were good self-regulators were seen as competent, self-assertive, socially adjusted, adaptable in difficult situations, dependable, and academically successful (Mischel, Shoda, & Rodriguez, 1989). Recently, *New York Times* editorial writer David Brooks reported on this study again, this time suggesting that educators and policymakers had ignored its implication for solving the education crisis.

> ... children who waited longer [to get marshmallows] went on to get higher SAT scores. They got into better colleges and had, on average, better adult outcomes. The children who rang the bell quickly [to get marshmallows] were more likely to become bullies. They received worse teacher and parental evaluations 10 years on and were more likely to have drug problems at age 32
>
> ... Young people who are given a series of tests that demand self-control get better at it over time. This pattern would be too obvious to mention if it weren't so largely ignored by educators and policy makers. ... Walter Mischel tried to interest New York schools in programs based on his research. Needless to say, he found almost no takers. (Brooks, 2006)

Since this study, we have learned much about the nature of self-regulation, how it affects learning, and what can be done to develop it in all learners. Indeed, hundreds of studies on self-control, self-management, and self-instruction have reported robust adjustment gains when children and adults develop this capability. Nonetheless, as Brooks suggests, most educators and policymakers, including those in special education, are unaware of this work. In the book we address this oversight by identifying some reasons special educators resist the use of self-instruction strategies when teaching students with disabilities. Then we present a four-step pedagogical strategy for empowering students to become self-directing, self-determined learners before they leave school.

The first two chapters argue that special educators are reluctant to use self-instruction strategies when they teach because they believe direct control of student responding as prescribed by pedagogies of direct instruction is the best way to guarantee learning. They are also reluctant to empower students to learn on their own because of the belief that controlling all aspects of the learning process is necessary for students who lack self-control to learn on their own.

Chapter 1 on *Direct Instruction vs. Self-Instruction: What's the Difference?* challenges the first claim by comparing the theoretical, empirical, and practical advantages of self-instruction pedagogy over direct instruction and then concluding that although the two are comparable in some ways, self-instruction pedagogy is superior because it teaches students to regulate their own adjustments to any learning challenge and hence become better prepared for the self-determined learning challenges they face once they leave school.

Chapter 2 on *Is Your Instruction Teacher- or Student-Directed* provides evidence for the second claim that teachers like yourself are reluctant to adopt student-directed methods of control because of a strong preference for controlling all functions of the teaching-learning process for students with disabilities, which include (a) identifying their needs and disabilities, (b) setting of goals to meet those needs, (c) developing instructional plans to meet those goals, (d) implementing instructional plans, (e) evaluating student progress, and (f) adjusting goals and plans based on evaluations. The chapter presents evidence indicating that when general and special education teachers rate their control levels for these functions, they report significantly higher ratings for teacher- than for student-control during their instruction and in their curriculum.

Chapters 3–6 present a four-step pedagogical strategy for shifting this agency of learner control to students. Chapter 3 on *How Students Develop Learner Control* describes the first step in the shift showing that when students develop the capacity to self-record, self-evaluate, and self-reinforce when completing work, they exhibit the self-control needed for self-determined learning. For example, when students learn self-monitoring strategies, they learn to control what they are doing when adjusting to a new challenge. When they learn to self-evaluate, they learn to control the accuracy and appropriateness of their behavior in these situations, and when they learn to self-reinforce, they learn to control the rewards they receive for the work they complete.

Chapter 4 on *How Students Adjust to Instructional Control* describes the second step in this shift in agency of control. It builds on the previous chapter by showing how students learn to engage in repeated episodes of goal setting, choice making, self-recording, self-evaluating, and self-adjusting until they accomplish what they set out to do. During this phase of their assumption of control, students self-regulate by comparing their results with their expectations for gain and then changing their expectations, choices or behaviors as needed to improve the match between them during subsequent learning attempts. This step yields remarkable gains in students' adaptive capabilities across behaviors, settings, and time.

Chapter 5 on *How Students Direct Their Learning* presents the last step in this shift of control. It teaches a pattern of self-regulated goal setting, planning, acting, and adjusting that satisfies students' self-identified needs and interests. The step introduces three interconnected problem-solving strategies that students implement using 12 self-instructions. The first sets goals that are consistent with what students choose to learn. The second provokes self-engagement to discover what they want to know, and the third sustains recursive problem solving until students meet their goal and discover what they want to know.

Chapter 6 on *How Self-Determination Increases at School and Work* describes a curriculum designed to teach students to develop their own IEPs and to direct their own school-to-work transitions. The curriculum is based on three learning-to-learn self-questions: "What do I want to know? What is my plan for finding out? Have I learned what I want to know?" The chapters show how use of picture-cued forms that regulate searches for answers to these questions helps students with disabilities learn by adjusting to the challenges posed in their self-directed IEPs and during their school-to-work transitions.

Chapter 7 on *Why Teachers Are Reluctant to Choose Choice* addresses the question posed earlier as to why teachers prefer teacher- to student-directed pedagogies when they teach. The chapter describes studies showing that preservice teachers tend to persist in teacher-directed methods even when instructed in the use of student-directed strategies. The chapter concludes that in order for teachers to consider adopting a self-directed learning pedagogy, they need to understand its theoretical, empirical, and practical advantages over direct instruction as explained in Chapter 1, the directedness of their own teaching as indicated in Chapter 2, and the four-step shift toward student control as described in Chapters 3–6.

Chapter 8, *Will You Choose Self-Instruction Pedagogy*, concludes with a review of the four principles that promote self-determined learning: the choice principle, the self-instruction principle, the matching principle, and the persistence principle. The *choice principle* predicts that opportunities to choose motivate learners to select the opportunity that best matches their interests and capabilities, which in turn provokes them to self-engage, adjust and learn from their adjustment. The *self-instruction* principle describes the remarkable effects of strategy use when regulating expectations, choices, and actions to adjust to new learning opportunities. The *matching principle* describes the effects of matching expectations to results, which provokes learner persistence in adjusting and hence learning from new opportunities. And the *persistence principle* predicts that the more frequent and persistent the learner's adjustments to challenge, the more likely that learning will maximize.

The main claim of this book is that when the four principles are fully incorporated in teaching as they are in self-instruction pedagogy, the engagement of challenging choice opportunities is provoked, the resulting adjustments to those opportunities generalize across settings and time, and the learning that results from those adjustments maximizes.

REFERENCES

Brooks, D. (May, 7, 2006). Marshmallows and Public Policy. In *The New York Times: Opinion*. New York: New York.

The Marshmallow Test, http://www.cde.state.co.us/ssw/pdf/SSWConf2005_Caselman_Tonia_Marshmallow.pdf.

Mischel, W., Shoda, Y., & Rodriguez, M. L. (1989). Delay of gratification in children. *Science, 244*, 933–938.

CONTENTS

Page

Preface v

Chapter

   1. Direct Instruction vs. Self-Instruction:
      What's the Difference? 3
      Dennis E. Mithaug

   2. Is Your Instruction Teacher- or Student-Directed? 31
      Dennis E. Mithaug and Deirdre K. Mithaug

   3. How Students Develop Learner Control 45
      Martin Agran

   4. How Students Adjust to Learner Control 66
      Deirdre K. Mithaug

   5. How Students Direct Their Learning 88
      Michael L. Wehmeyer

   6. How Self-Determination Increases at School
      and Work 106
      James E. Martin, Lori Y. Peterson, and
      Chauncey D. Goff

   7. Why Teachers Are Reluctant to Choose Choice 130
      Deirdre K. Mithaug

   8. Will You Choose Self-Instruction Pedagogy? 150
      Dennis E. Mithaug and Deirdre K. Mithaug

ix

Appendix A: Research on Self-Instruction and Direct
Instruction Pedagogies 159

Appendix B: Instruction and Curriculum Scales
for Self-Determined Learning 179
Dennis E. Mithaug and Deirdre K. Mithaug

Name Index 217

Subject Index 229

SELF-INSTRUCTION PEDAGOGY

Chapter 1

DIRECT INSTRUCTION VS. SELF-INSTRUCTION: WHAT'S THE DIFFERENCE?

DENNIS E. MITHAUG

The most effective pedagogies for educating students with disabilities offer contrasting approaches to improving their adjustments and learning. Direct instruction, arguably the most widely-used pedagogy in special education today, prescribes teacher control of student learning, whereas the less widely-used self-instruction pedagogy prescribes student control of adjustments. This chapter compares the two to give you a basis for deciding how best to teach your students. We believe that after considering these differences you will choose the latter because it promises the greatest long-lasting benefits for students.

However, in presenting these comparisons, we recognize that adopting this approach to teaching may be difficult given the pervasive view among special educators that direct instruction is the only viable method of teaching students with significant learning problems. To illustrate this perspective, consider Lewis and Doorlag's (2003) comparison of direct instruction with other teaching methods in their introductory text, which claimed that instruction should consist of:

> . . . selecting the desired student behavior, arranging instructional antecedents, and providing consequences such as feedback regarding performance accuracy. . . .
>
> [These authors claimed] it is important to differentiate between direct (or explicit) instruction and an alternative approach, discovery learning. In discovery learning, information and skills are not taught directly. Instead, the teacher arranges the learning environment and students explore that environment as they attempt to discover the facts, concepts, principles, and skills that make up the school curriculum. Discovery approaches are considered constructivists because students are expected to construct their own knowledge by building on prior knowledge they bring to the learning task. . . .

Unfortunately, [they claim] some students do not succeed in programs in which discovery learning is the norm (Gersten & Dimino, 1993). Students with mild disabilities and others at risk for academic learning problems are more likely to succeed when instruction is presented using the principles of direct teaching. (King-Sears, 1997; Vergason & Anderegg, 1991)

Beliefs like these reflect a long-standing dominance of direct instruction that Heshusius (1991) described more than a decade ago.

The measurement and control procedures of CBA/DI [curriculum-based instruction/direct instruction] are wide ranging. First, these techniques offer a framework for teacher preparation.... A survey of the methodological content of teacher training programs in learning disabilities (Pugach & Whitten, 1987) showed that up to 69% of programs surveyed fell into related categories of CBA, DI, and DBI.

Second, CBA offers a set of procedures to use for student referral for special education services (Blankenship, 1985, p. 238). Third CBA/DI provide the methodology for research to show that a certain program "Works" (to name a few studies and overviews of research. (see, e.g., Bursuck & Lessen, 1987; Fuchs et al., 1984; Gersten, Carnine, & Woodward, 1987; Jones & Krause, 1988; Moore, 1986; Peterson, Heistad, Peterson, & Reynolds, 1985)

Finally, it has been proposed that school psychologists master CBA as a way to save school psychology from sliding into the background – particularly in the light of the Regular Education Initiative and the resultant lessening of relevance of testing. (See Reschly, 1988.)

The CBA/DI literature portrays its constructs and procedures as near-scientific tools to solve many of our assessment, instruction, student referral, and research problems. (p. 316)

Ramsey and Algozzine (1991) reported the same pattern of pedagogical dominance in their survey of 15 state competency tests. They found that knowledge of behavior theory and direct instruction was required for state certification in special education. Indeed, for most states in the survey, knowledge of behavior theory was required in the areas of behavior modification procedures (14 states), primary reinforcers (13 states), secondary reinforcers (13 states), schedules of reinforcement (14 states), punishment techniques (14 states), contingency management (14 states), backward chaining (10 states), and discrimination principles (10 states). Most states also required knowledge of direct instruction in such areas as task analysis and criterion measurement (14 states), task difficulty levels (14 states), learning rates (13 states), intentional learning and memory procedures (13 states), and massed and distributed practice effects (13 states). By contrast, only six of the 15 state tests required knowledge of self-instruction pedagogy.

This institutionalization of direct instruction methods in special education practice is also evident in introductory texts published today. Our review of 12 such texts, for example, indicated greater coverage of direct instruction methods than coverage of student-directed methods (Friend & Bursuck, 2002; Gargiulo, 2003; Hallahan & Kaulfman, 2003; Hardman, Drew & Egan, 2002; Heward, 2003; Hunt & Marshall, 2002; Kirk, Gallagher, & Anastasiow, 2003; Lewis & Doorlag, 2003; Smith, 2001; Turnbull, Turnbull, Shank, Smith, & Leal, 2002; Vaughn, Bos, & Schumm, 2003).

This chapter presents the theoretical, empirical, and practical reasons for direct instruction's dominance in special education. It compares these factors with equally robust theoretical, empirical, and practical reasons for adopting self-instruction pedagogy. The chapter concludes that self-instruction pedagogy would be the preferred approach among educators like yourself were they aware of its long-term, sustainable impact on students' prospects for self-determined learning and achievement in school and beyond.

What's the Theoretical Difference?

But before getting to this conclusion, we should remember that theoretical support for direct instruction was already in place long before the Education of All Handicapped Children's Act of 1975 required individualized instructional programs for every student with a disability. By then, the effects of direct instruction on student learning had been established by advocates of operant learning theory who used the theory's discrimination and reinforcement principles to develop teacher-directed methods of instruction (Holland & Skinner, 1961; Haring & Phillips, 1962; Bereiter & Engelmann, 1966; Englemann, Osborn, & Engelmann, 1969; Haring & Lovitt, 1967; Hewett, Taylor, & Artuso, 1969; Homme, deBaca, Cottingham, & Homme, 1968; Lindsey, 1964.

These innovative applications of the theory prescribed direct *control* of all components in a student's individualized program, which included (a) the presentation of salient instructional cues to increase correct responding, (b) immediate reinforcement of correct responses and correction of incorrect responses, and (c) continuous monitoring of response rates to evaluate the effects of that control on learning. These prescriptions in turn became central dictates of direct instruction. Figure 1.1 illustrates this correspondence between operant learning theory, applied behavior analysis research methods, and direct instruction. The first panel presents the operant theory claim that when discriminative stimuli provoke new responses and when reinforcing stimuli follow, future responding to those events is likely. The second panel presents that causal paradigm to describe applied behavior analysis research. The third panel presents the same defining sequence for direct instruction.

Looking back, it appears that these straightforward links between theory, research, and practice were imminently more useful for teachers than anything

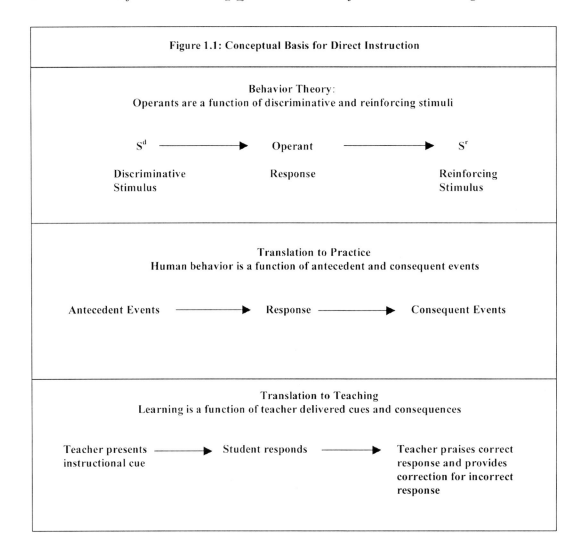

Figure 1.1: Conceptual Basis for Direct Instruction

available at the time, including self-instruction pedagogy. This was especially evident during the decade of the 1960s when direct instruction advocates were forging functional connections between theory and practice and self-instruction pedagogy was little more than a backup to be used occasionally. During this early period, self-instruction had no comparable theoretical backing for its role in developing self-directed learning. Contemporary theories by Luria (1960) that focused on language development in children, and by Miller, Gallanter, and Pribaum (1960) that focused on internal reinforcement mechanisms offered little help nor did the self-regulation models developed in subsequent decades (Jackson & Boag, 1981; Jeffrey & Berger, 1982; Kanfer, 1971; Carver & Scheier, 1983; Corno & Mandinach, 1983; Pesut, 1990).

Figure 1.2 illustrates the problem, with a solid line between direct instruction and operant learning theory indicating robust theoretical support and a broken line between self-instruction and theories of Luria (1960) and Miller et al. (1960) on the right indicating weak theoretical support. Perhaps this explains why direct instruction became institutionalized in special education and self-instruction did not. It had more robust justifications for use with students exhibiting significant learning problems. Moreover, direct instruction's emphasis on direct control of learning seemed to be exactly what some students needed in order to learn.

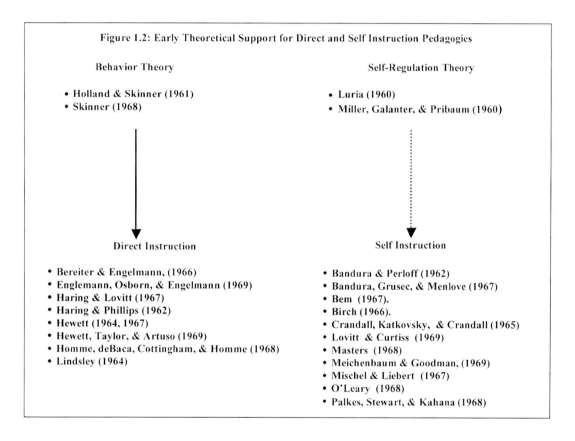

Figure 1.2: Early Theoretical Support for Direct and Self Instruction Pedagogies

Behavior Theory

- Holland & Skinner (1961)
- Skinner (1968)

Direct Instruction

- Bereiter & Engelmann, (1966)
- Englemann, Osborn, & Engelmann (1969)
- Haring & Lovitt (1967)
- Haring & Phillips (1962)
- Hewett (1964, 1967)
- Hewett, Taylor, & Artuso (1969)
- Homme, deBaca, Cottingham, & Homme (1968)
- Lindsley (1964)

Self-Regulation Theory

- Luria (1960)
- Miller, Galanter, & Pribaum (1960)

Self Instruction

- Bandura & Perloff (1962)
- Bandura, Grusec, & Menlove (1967)
- Bem (1967).
- Birch (1966).
- Crandall, Katkovsky, & Crandall (1965)
- Lovitt & Curtiss (1969)
- Masters (1968)
- Meichenbaum & Goodman, (1969)
- Mischel & Liebert (1967)
- O'Leary (1968)
- Palkes, Stewart, & Kahana (1968)

Self-Determined Learning Theory

Fortunately, direct instruction's theoretical advantage ended when self-determined learning theory was constructed to explain the relationship between self-regulation, adjustment, and learning (Mithaug, Mithaug, Agran, Martin, & Wehmeyer, 2003). According to this account, learners learn by regulating their adjustments to unusual circumstances, and the adjustments that result are what they learn. This explanation was significant for self-instruction pedagogy because it explained how student use of various self-instruction strategies increased their control of adjustments and hence *their ability to learn.*

The theory was significant for other reasons as well. One was that it explained what operant theory and other theories could not, namely the relationship between opportunities to learn and the persistence, maximization, and generalization of learning across environments and time. It explained why learning occurs in the absence of instruction, as well as how instruction can improve a learner's capacity to adjust and learn in any environment. Other insights into the learning-teaching process were that: (a) learning is a function of adjustments to change, and that producing new adjustments requires self-regulation; (b) learners who improve their ability to self-regulate, improve their ability to adjust and to learn; and therefore that (c) when instruction improves the ability to self-regulate, it improves the ability to adjust and learn across environments and time.

The founding premise of the theory is that learning occurs when unusual circumstances provoke learners to change their current adjustment, which they perceive to be inconsistent with those events. According to the theory, learners adjust differently when they perceive those circumstances to be *optimal* for changing the situation in a desirable direction. The adjustment that results from that change attempt is what they learn. The following claims summarize this account: (a) *all learning is adjustment;* (b) learners adjust and learn when they perceive an unusual or unexpected event to be a *valuable* and *doable opportunity* for gaining something by acting; and (c) learners act to change a situation by *regulating their expectations, choices,* and *actions* differently. This is how they adjust to learn. And the resulting adjustments – their *changed beliefs* about the situation, *changed feelings* about the situation, and *changed responses* to the situation – are what they learn.

According to the theory, two optimality factors explain the maximization of learning: (a) the *optimality of the opportunity* to change a situation in a desirable direction and (b) the *optimality of adjustment* that results from the change attempt. When these factors approach the optimal, learning approaches the maximum. To illustrate, consider the first factor's effect on engagement, the *opportunity* to gain something by changing a situation. When a situation presents an *optimal opportunity* for gain, the learner has judged it to be both *valuable* and *doable*. The learner has judged it to be valuable because changing the situation promises to produce a desired result, and she has judged it to be doable because she knows how to make that change. This is how situations vary in optimality. When learners perceive them to be both valuable and doable, they are optimal for acting to produce a desirable result. But when learners perceive situations to be unimportant, difficult, or unimportant and difficult, they are suboptimal for taking action. Therefore, the closer to optimal a situation is perceived to be, the more likely the learner will act on it to produce a desirable change: the more likely she will engage the opportunity.

Now consider the second factor that affects learning: the adjustment that results from the change attempt, which is learner engagement. It, too, varies in optimality. Adjustments are optimal to the extent learners *regulate* their expectations, choices, and actions as effectively as possible to produce the change they expect. This occurs when learners have expectations that are consistent with the situation (adaptive expectations), make choices that are consistent with those expectations (rational choices), take actions that are consistent with those choices (efficient actions), and produce results that are consistent with their expectations (successful results). Under these four conditions, adjustments optimize.

Table 1.1 presents the theory, which claims two factors - the optimality of opportunities and the optimality of adjustments - determine how much is learned in any situation. When both are optimal, learning maximizes, and when both are suboptimal, learning minimizes. The four propositions of the theory describe the net effects of these factors on learning. The first proposition explains the effects of optimal opportunities on self-regulation. The second proposition explains the effects of self-regulation on adjustments. The third proposition explains the effects of optimal adjustments on feelings of control and learning. And the fourth proposition concludes that as opportunities optimize, learning maximizes. In other words, as opportunities become valuable and doable (optimal), and as self-regulated adjustments to those circumstances become effective (optimal), learning maximizes.

Table 1.1: Self-Determine Learning Theory:
How Optimal Opportunity Maximizes Engagement, Sense of Control, and Learning

1. The closer to optimal the opportunities for experiencing gain, the more likely the regulation of expectations, choices, and actions to produce gain.
2. The more often the regulation of expectations, choices, and actions to produce gain, the more likely that adjustments optimize as expectations, choices, actions, and results become adaptive, rational, is efficient, and successful.
3. The closer to optimal the adjustments to an opportunity, the more persistent is the engagement to produce gain, the greater is the feeling of control over gain production, and the closer to maximum is the learning from that adaptation.
4. Therefore, the closer to optimal the opportunities for experiencing gain, the more persistent is the engagement, the greater is the sense of control, and the closer to maximum is the learning (Mithaug, Mithaug, Agran, Martin, & Wehmeyer, 2003, p. 14).

Key Theoretical Differences

The main differences between operant and self-determined learning theories are the control factors claimed by each, as Figure 1.3 illustrates. The top panel presents the control factors central to the operant explanation, which are the *discriminative*

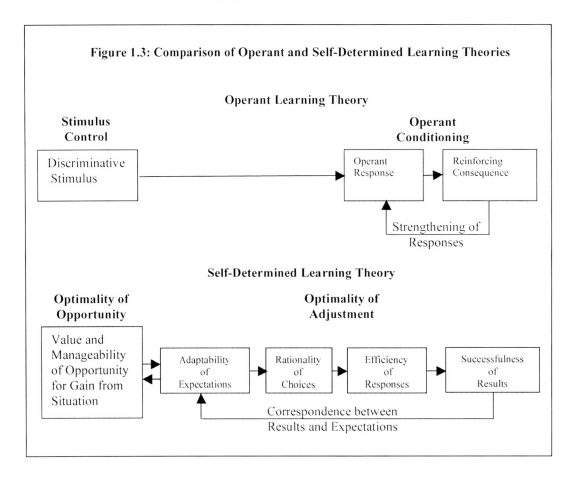

Figure 1.3: Comparison of Operant and Self-Determined Learning Theories

stimuli that provoke operant responding and the *reinforcing events* that strengthen associations between stimuli and responses. Here learning occurs when responses are contingent upon discriminative stimuli and reinforcing events are contingent upon responses. In other words, the locus of cause is *external* to the learner. The lower panel presents the control factors central to the self-determined learning theory. Here learning occurs when *opportunities* for gain provoke *adjustments* to produce that gain, and the locus of cause is internal to the learner.

These differences have significant implications for instruction in that teachers following prescriptions suggested by operant theory arrange antecedent cues and reinforcing consequences to produce learning *in students*, whereas teachers following prescriptions suggested by self-determined learning theory present opportunities that provoke adjustments and learning *by students*. Also, teachers of direct instruction script cues and consequences to maximize control of responding, whereas teachers of self-instruction present choice opportunities that provoke students to regulate new adjustments to those circumstances. Finally, teachers of direct instruction strive for *errorless learning*, whereas teachers of self-instruction strive for *self-determined* learning.

Figure 1.4 presents these differences from yet another point of view, using the now familiar three-term contingency identified with operant learning theory. The first panel presents the three-term contingency, the second panel presents direct instruction pedagogy, and the third panel presents self-instruction pedagogy. The last panel breaks the three-term contingency into self-instructional parts to show how learners direct their learning *from an operant perspective*. Note that this break-down covers all features of effective instruction: from knowing the needs, interests, and abilities of the learner (question 1), to setting goals to meet those needs (question 2), developing plans to meet goals (question 3), taking action to implement

Figure 1.4: Correspondence between Behavior Theory's Causal Model, Direct Instruction, and Self-Instruction

Behavior Theory's Causal Model

Antecedents → Responses → Consequences

Direct Instruction Pedagogy

Teacher Selected Cues → Student Responses → Teacher Delivered Consequences

Self-Instruction Pedagogy

Student Selected → Cues		Student → Responses	Student Delivered Consequences		

Student → Identified Interests, Needs & Capabilities:	Student → Selected Goals:	Student → Constructed Plans:	Student → Responses:	Student → Self-Monitoring:	Student → Self-Evaluation:	Student Self-Adjustment:
1. "What do I want, need, and what can I do?"	2. "How do I want the situation to change?"	3. "How can I get it to change?"	4. "What actions do I need to take now?"	5. "What am I doing?"	6. "What have I done and did I get the change I want?"	7. "What will I do next?"

plans (question 4), monitoring outcomes to track progress toward goals (question 5), evaluating outcomes (question 6), and adjusting subsequent goals and plans based on evaluations (question 7). Therefore, when students master this sequence of self-instructions, *they control the three-term contingency* and with that their adjustments and learning. They become their own "direct instruction teachers."

What's the Empirical Difference?

On the question of which approach has greater empirical support, self-instruction has a distinct advantage in that from 1960 through the 1990s, studies reporting its effects were nearly three times the number reporting direct instruction's effects. To get an idea of the scope of these differences, consider the range of studies conducted on the two pedagogies. Figure 1.5 presents a histogram for the research conducted on several variations of direct instruction, which include precision teaching and curriculum-based assessment. As indicated in the figure, most of the research has been on curriculum-based assessments. Table 1.2 classifies the research further by listing studies that focused on teacher-directed cues and consequences (column 1) and on the measurement of student responses to those interventions (column 2). As you can see, most of these studies focused on the measurement feature of the pedagogy (also see Appendix A).

Now consider the data in Figure 1.6 summarizing the accumulation of nearly 400 articles on self-instruction pedagogy during the same period (also see Appendix A). Most of this research, which is nearly three times as large, covered three areas of inquiry: self-instruction studies on use of verbal strategies to regulate

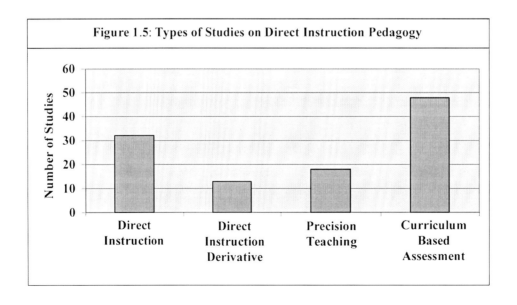

Figure 1.5: Types of Studies on Direct Instruction Pedagogy

Table 1.2: Research on Teacher-Directed Instruction from 1970-1990

Programmed Cues & Consequences	Measurement of Instructed Responses	
1970s Research	**1970s Research**	
Becker (1977)	Kunzelman (Ed) (1970)	
Becker, Englemann, & Thomas (1971)	Lindsley (1971)	
Carnine (1976)	Klausmeier & Ripple (1971)	
Carnine & Fink (1978)	Gentry & Haring (1976)	
Englemann, Granzin, & Severson (1979)	White & Liberty (1976)	
Hall (1971)	Deno & Mirkin (1976)	
Jenkins Mayhall, Peshka, & Townsend (1974)	Jenkins, Deno, & Mirkin (1979)	
Polirstok & Greer (1977)		
Tawney, Knapp, O'Reilly, & Pratt (1979)		
1980s Research	**1980s Research**	
Becker & Gersten (1982)	Blankenship (1985)	German & Tindal (1985)
Binder & Watkins (1989)	Coulter (1985)	Gickling & Thompson (1985)
Carnine (1981)	Deno (1986)	Jones & Drouse (1988)
Darch, Gersten, & Taylor (1987)	Deno (1985)	Liberty, Haring, & White (1980)
Engelmann & Carnine (1982)	Deno (1987)	Marston & Magnusson (1985)
Engelmann & Bruner (1988)	Deno & Fuchs (1987)	Marston, Mirkin, & Deno (1984)
Engelmann, Haddox, & Bruner (1983)	Deno, Marston, & Mirkin (1982)	Marston, Tindal, & Deno (1984)
Gersten, Carnine, & Woodward (1987)	Deno, Marston, Shinn, & Tindal	McDade & Olander (1987)
Gersten & Maggs (1982)	(1983)	McGreevy (1984)
Gersten & Keating (1987a)	Deno, Mirkin, & Chiang (1982)	Mercer, Mercer, & Evans (1982)
Gersten & Keating (1987b)	Deno, Mirkin, & Isson (1984)	Mirkin, Deno, Tindal, & Kuehnle
Gersten, Keating, & Becker (1988)	Ferguson & Fuchs(1991)	(1982)
Gersten, Woodward, & Darch (1986)	Fuchs (1986)	Rosenfield & Rubinson (1985)
Greer, McCorkle, & Williams (1989)	Fuchs (1988)	Shinn (1988)
Lloyd & Carnine	Fuchs, Deno, & Mirkin (1984)	Shinn & Marston (1985)
Lockery & Maggs (1982)	Fuchs & Fuchs (1984)	Shinn, Ysseldyke, Deno, & Tindal
Meyer (1984)	Fuchs & Fuchs (1986)	(1986)
Meyer, Gersten, & Gutkin (1983)	Fuchs, Deno, & Marston (1983)	Taylor, Willits, & Richards (1988)
Moore (1986)	Fuchs, Fuchs, & Deno (1985)	Tucker (1985)
White (1988)	Fuchs, Fuchs, & Hamlett (1989)	Isson, Fuchs, Tindal, Mirkin, & Deno
	Fuchs, Fuchs, & Deno (1982)	(1986)
	Fuchs, Fuchs, & MaxIll (1988)	Isson, King, & Deno (1984)
	Fuchs, Hamlett, Fuchs, Stecker,	Isson, Skiba, Sevick, King, & Deno
	& Ferguson (1988)	(1984)
		White & Haring (1980)
		White (1986)
1990s Research	**1990s Research**	
Adams & Engelmann (1996)	Binder, Haughton, & Van Eyk	Lindsley (1990a).
Becker (1992)	(1990)	Lindsley (1990b
Binder (1996)	Fuchs & Deno (1992)	Lindsley (1991)
Binder & Watkins (1990)	Fuchs, Allinder, Hamlett, &	Lindsley (1992a)
Bock, Stebbins, & Proper (1996)	Fuchs (1990)	Lindsley (1992b)
Carnine, Silbert, & Kameenui (1998)	Fuchs, Fuchs, & Hamlet (1994)	Lindsley 1995)
Donley & Greer (1993)	Fuchs, Fuchs, Hamlett, &	Potter & Wamre (1990)
Engleman & Carnine (1992)	Ferguson (1992)	Isson (1991)
Gersten (1998)	Fuchs, Fuchs, & Hamlet (1992)	
Greenwood, Carta, Arreaga-Mayer, & Rager (1991)	Fuchs, Fuchs, Hamlett, & Stecker	
Greer (1991)	(1991)	
Greer (1994)	Fuchs, Fuchs, Hamlett, &	
Greer (2002)	Allinder (1991)	
Ingham & Greer (1992)	Fuchs, Fuchs, Hamlett, Phillips, &	
Kameenui & Carnine (1998)	Benz (1994)	
Kameenui & Simmons (1990)	Heshusius (1991)	
Koorland, Keel, & Ueberhorst (1990)	Liberty & Haring (1990)	
Lamm & Greer (1991)		
Malott & Heward (1995)		
McDade (1992)		
Selinske, Greer, & Lodhi (1991)		
Stein, Silbert, & Carnine (1997)		

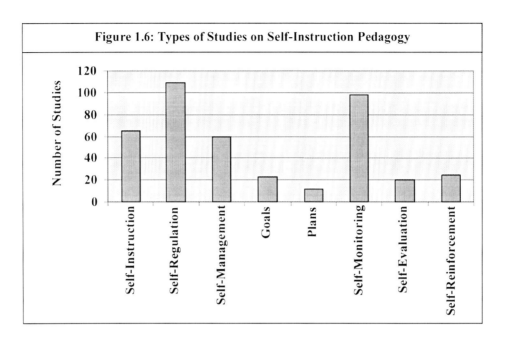

behavior, self-regulation studies on use of cognitive and behavior strategies to improve learning, and self-management strategies on use of self-monitoring, self-evaluation, and self-reinforcement to improve adjustments. The remaining studies focused on single-strategy use: goal setting, self-planning, self-monitoring, self-evaluation, or self-reinforcement. Tables 1.3-1.5 list the studies from 1970 through the 1990s that focused on student management of the cues and consequences of learning and on development of their self-regulation skills and behaviors.

As you can see, this research base is extensive, covering as it does the use of verbal and non-verbal strategies to improve self-regulation, as well as the use of strategies like goal setting, self-planning, self-monitoring, self-evaluation, and self-reinforcement and adjustment to regulate adjustments and learning. Indeed, it covers all the causal factors used to explain the self-regulated adjustments necessary for learning, as Figure 1.7 illustrates.

The left box in the figure represents the first factor – the learner's perceptions of a circumstance as being an opportunity or obstacle for producing gain – and the box on the right represents the second factor – the effectiveness of the learner's regulation of expectations, choices, and actions to produce a desired result. Interaction between the two factors is represented by the *opportunity effect* arrow connecting the opportunity box on the left with the adjustment box on the right and the *adjustment effect* arrow connecting the adjustment box with the opportunity box. When they affect each other, their optimality values change to determine what and how much is learned.

Table 1.3: 1970s Research on Student-Directed Learning

Self-Managed Cues and Consequences		Self-Regulated Behavior
Bender (1977) Blackwood (1970) Borden, Hall, & Mitts (1971) Bornstein & Quevillon (1976) Bornstein, Mungas, Quevillon, Knivila, Miller, & Holombo (1976) Brownell, Colletti, Ersner-Hershfield, Hershfield, & Wilson (1977) Burron & Bucher (1978) Camp, Blom, Herbert, & Van Doorninck (1977) Connis (1979) Flexer, Newbery, & Martin (1979) Fredericksen & Frederiksen (1975) Friedling & O'Leary (1979) Fry (1978) Glynn (1970) Gottman & McFall (1972) Hartig & Kanfer (1973) Helland, Paluck, & Klein (1976) Higa, Tharp, & Calkins (1978) Hildelbrandt, Feldman, & Ditrichs (1973) Holman & Baer (1979) Humphrey, Karoly, & Kirschembaum (1978) Hundert & Altstone (1978) Israel & Brown (1977) Israel (1978) Jones, Nelson, & Kazdin (1977) Kaufman & O'Leary (1972) Kazdin (1974) Kendall (1977) Kim & Hamner (1976) Layne, Rickard, Jones, & Lyman (1976) Lipinski & Nelson (1974) Lipinski, Black, Nelson, & Ciminero (1975) Litrownik, Cleary, Lecklitner, & Fanzini (1978) Litrownik, Franzini, Geller, & Geller (1977) Lovitt (1973) Mahonery, Moore, Wade, & Moura (1973) Mahoney, Moura, & Wade (1973) Masters & Peskay (1972). Masters (1972) Masters (1973) Masters & Christy (1974) Masters, Furman, & Barden (1977) McKenzie & Rushall (1974) Meacham (1978)	Meichenbaum & Goodman (1971) Miller, Iinstein, & Karniol (1978) Mischel & Patternson (1976) Monahan & O'Leary (1971) Nelson & Birkimer (1978) Nelson & O'Leary (1971) Nelson, Lipinski, & Black (1975) Nelson, Lipinski, & Boykin (1978) Patterson & Mischel (1975) Peacock, Layman, & Rickard (1978) Robin, Armel, & O'Leary (1975) Rosen, Diggory, Floor, & Nowakiwska (1971) Santogrossi, O'Leary, Romanczyk, & Kaufman (1973) Sawin & Parke (1979) Seymour & Stokes (1976) Shure & Spivack (1972) Sieck & McFall (1976) Spates & Kanfer (1977) Switzky & Haywood (1974) Terborg (1976) Thomas (1976) Wood & Flynn (1978) Zegiob, Klukas, & Juniger (1978)	Anderson, Fodor, & Albert (1976) Bolstad & Johnson (1972) Carter, Patterson, & Quasebarth (1979) Douglas, Parry, Marton, & Garson (1976) Drabman, Spitalnik, & O'Leary (1973) Epstein & Goss (1978) Fagen & Long (1976) Fagen & Long (1979) Frantuzzo, Harrell, & McLeoud (1979) Glenwick & Barocas (1979) Glynn & Thomas (1974) Glynn, Thomas, & Shee (1973) Goetz & Etzel (1978) Goldfried, Decenteceo, & Iinberg, (1974) Karoly & Dirks (1977) Karoly & Kanfer (1974) Kendall & Finch (1978) Kendall & Finch (1976). Kurtz & Neisworth (1976) Mahoney & Mahoney (1976) Meichenbaum (1972) Meichenbaum (1977) O'Leary & Dubey (1979) Patterson & Carter (1979) Pressley (1979) Rachlin (1974) Robertson, Simon, Pachman, & Drabman (1979) Rosenbaum & Drabman (1979) Sagotsky, Patterson, & Lepper (1978) Toner, Holstein, & Hetherington (1977) Turkowitz, O'Leary, & Ironsmith (1975) Wallace & Pear (1977) Williams & Akamatsu (1978) Zivin (1979)

Table 1.4: 1980s Research on Student-Directed Learning

Self-Managed Cues and Consequences		Self-Regulated Behavior
Ackerman & Shapiro (1984)	Nelson & Hayes (1981)	Agran, Martin, & Mithaug (1989)
Agran, Fodor-Davis, Moore, & Deer (1989)	Piersel (1985)	Bandura (1989)
Agran, Fodor-Davis, & Moore (1986)	Rhode, Morgan, & Young (1983)	Barkley, Copeland, & Sivage (1980)
Agran, Salzberg, & Stowitschek (1987)	Rooney, Hallahan, & Lloyd (1984)	Borkowski, Estrada, Milstead & Hale
Alberto & Sharpton (1987)	Rooney, Polloway, & Hallahan	(1989)
Alvarez & Adelman (1986)	(1985)	Coleman & Whitman (1984)
Ames (1984)	Rudrud, Ziarnik, & Coleman	Deshler, Schumaker, & Lenz (1984)
Anderson-Inman, Paine, & Deutchman (1984)	(1984)	Deshler & Schumaker (1986)
Beal (1987)	Rumsey & Ballard (1985)	Ellis (1986)
Blick & Test (1987)	Rusch, Martin, Lagomarcino, &	Ellis, Deshler, & Schumaker (1989)
Browder & Shapiro (1985)	White (1987)	Ellis, Lenz, & Sabornie (1987)
Childers (1987)	Rusch, McKee, Chadsey-Rusch, &	Gambrell & Bates (1986)
Christie, Hiss, & Lozanoff (1984)	Renzaglia (1988)	Garner & Alexander (1989)
Copeland (1981)	Rusch, Morgan, Martin, Riva, &	Gettinger (1985)
Crouch, Rusch, & Karlan (1984)	Agran (1985)	Grace, Cowart, & Matson (1988)
Dickerson & Creedon, (1981)	Schloss (1987)	Graham & Harris (1989a)
Dunlap & Dunlap (1989)	Schunk (1985)	Harris (1980)
Fantuzzo & Clement (1981)	Shapiro (1989)	Harris (1982)
Fantuzzo, Polite, Cook, & Quinn (1988)	Shapiro & Ackerman (1983)	Harris (1986)
Fish & Mendola, (1986)	Shapiro, Browder, & D'Huyvetters	Harris (1988)
Fowler (1984)	(1984)	Harris & Graham (1985)
Fowler (1986)	Shapiro, McGonigle, & Ollendick	Martin, Rusch, James, Decker, &
Frith & Armstrong (1986)	(1980)	Trtol (1982)
Fuchs, Bahr, & Rieth (1989)	Shaprio & Klein (1980)	Pearl (1985)
Gajar, Schloss, Schloss, & Thompson (1984)	Smith, Young, Ist, Morgan, &	Pearl (1985)
Gardner, Cole, Berry, & Nowinski (1983)	Rhode (1988)	Reid & Borkowski (1987)
Graham & Harris (1989b)	Solrs, Rusch, Connis, & Cummings	Ringel & Springer (1980)
Graham & MacArthur (1988)	(1980)	Solomon & Globerson (1987)
Graham, Harris, & Sawyer (1987)	Srikameswaran & Martin (1984)	Sowers, Verdi, Bourbeau, &
Guevremont, Osnes, & Stokes (1986)	Sugai & Rol (1984)	Sheehan (1985)
Hallahan & Sapona (1983)	Thierman & Martin (1989)	Stevenson & Fantuzzo, (1984)
Hallahan, Marshall, & Lloyd (1981)	Tollefson, Tracey, Johnson, &	Stevenson & Fantuzzo, (1986)
Hanel & Martin (1980)	Charman (1986)	Stone (1989)
Harris (1986)	Wacker & Berg (1983)	Wong, Wong, & Blenkinsop (1989)
Heins, Lloyd, & Hallahan (1986)	Wacker & Berg (1984)	Zimmerman (1989)
Hopman & Glynn (1989)	Wacker & Greenebaum (1984)	
Hughes & Hendrickson (1987)	Wacker, Berg, Berrie, & Swatta,	
Hughes & Petersen (1989)	(1985)	
Hughes, Ruhl, & Peterson (1988)	Wacker, Berg, & McMahon	
Johnston, Whitman, & Johnson (1980)	Templeman, McKinney, Swarts,	
Keogh, Faw, Whitman, & Reid (1984)	Visser, & Marquardt (1988)	
Kneedler & Hallahan (1981)	Whitman (1987)	
Leon & Pepe (1983)	Whitman & Johnston (1983)	
Lagomarcino & Rusch (1989)	Whitman, Spence, & MaxIll (1987)	
Litrownik & Frietas (1980)	Zohn & Bornstein (1980)	
Lloyd & Hilliard (1989)		
Lloyd, Bateman, Landrum, & Hallahan (1989)		
Locke, Shaw, Saari, & Latham (1981)		
Lovett & Haring (1989)		
Malott (1984)		
Mank & Horner (1987)		
Martin & Hrydowy (1989)		
Martin, Elias-Burger, & Mithaug (1987)		
McLaughlin (1983)		
McLaughlin (1984)		
McLaughlin & Truhlicka (1983)		
McNally, Kompik, & Sherman (1984)		
Moore, Agran, & Fodor-Davis (1989)		

Table 1.5: 1990s Research on Student-Directed Learning		
Self-Managed Cues and Consequences		**Self-Regulated Behavior**
Agran, Fodor-Davis, Moore, & Martella (1992) Englert, Raphael, Anderson, Anthony, Stevens, & Fear (1991) Hughes (1992) Hughes & Agran (1993) Agran, Fodor-Davis, Martella, & Moore (1992) Agran, Snow, & Swaner (1999) Ames (1992) Briggs, Alberto, Sharpton, Berlin, McKinley, & Ritts (1990) Carr & Punzo (1993) Dalton, Martella, & Marchard-Martella (1999) Davis, Brady, Williams, & Burta (1992) Digangi & Maag (1992) Dunlap, Dunlap, Doegel, & Koegel (1991) Edwards, Salent, Howard, Brougher, & McLaughlin (1995) Ferretti, Cavalier, Murphy, & Murphy (1993) Firman, Bere, & Loyd (2002) Fuchs, Fuchs, Hamelett, & Whinnery (1991) Garff & Storey (1998) Glomb & Ist (1990) Grossi & Heward (1998) Harchik, Sherman, & Sheldon (1992) Harris, Graham, Reid, McElroy, & Hamby (1994) Hinshaw & Melnick (1992) Hoff & DuPaul (1998) Hughes & Boyle (1991) Hughes, Korinek, & Gorman (1991) Hughes & Lloyd (1993) Hughes & Scott (1997) Hughes, Harmer, Killian, & Niarhos (1995) Irvine, Erickson, Singer, & Stahlberg (1992) Kern, Dunlap, Childs, & Clarke (1994) King-Sears (1999) Koegel & Koegel (1990) Koegel, Koegel, Hurley, & Frea (1992) Lenz, Ehren, & Smiley (1991) Liberty & Paeth (1990)	Maag, Reid, & DiGangi (1993) MacDuff, Krantz, & McClannahan (1993) Martella, Leonard, Marchand-Martella, & Agran (1993) Martino (1993) McAdam & Cuvo (1994) McCarl, Svobodny, & Beare (1991) McDougall & Brady (1998) Mechling & Gast (1997) Miner (1990) Misra (1992) Moxley (1998) Nelson, Smith, & Colvin (1995) Nelson, Smith, Young, & Dodd (1991) Newman, Buffington, & Hemmers (1996) Newman, Buffington, O'Grady, McDonald, Poulson, & Hemmes (1995) Newman, Ryan, Tuntigian, & Reinecke (1997) Ninness, Fuerst, & Rutherford (1991) Ninness, Ellis, Miller, Baker, & Rutherford (1995) Peterson, Young, Ist, & Peterson (1999) Pierce & Schreibman (1994) Post & Storey (2002) Prater, Hogan, & Miller (1992) Reid & Harris (1993) Reinecke, Newman, & Meinberg (1999) Sainato, Strain, Lefebvre, & Rapp (1990) Schloss & Wood (1990) Shapiro, DuPaul, & Bradley-Klug (1998) Smith, Young, Nelson, & Ist (1992) Stahmer & Schreibman (1992) Stecker, Whinnery, & Fuchs (1996) Trammel, Schloss, & Alper (1994) Trask-Tyler, Grossi, & Heward (1994) Wacker & Berg (1993) Ibber, Scheuermann, McCall, & Coleman (1993)	Bambara & Ager (1992) Collet-Klingenberg & Chadsey-Rusch (1991) Danoff, Harris, & Graham (1993) De La Paz (1999) De La Paz & Graham (1997a) De La Paz & Graham (1997b) Derry (1990) Dick & Leggett (1999) Garner (1990) Graham (1997) Graham & Harris (1993) Graham & Harris (1997) Graham, Harris, & Reid (1992) Graham, Harris, MacArthur, & Schwartz (1991) Graham, MacArthur, & Schwartz, (1995) Graham, MacArthur, Schwartz, & Page (1992) Harris & Pressley (1991) Harris (1990) Montague, Graves, & Leavell (1991) Page-Voth & Graham (1999) Paris & Winograd (1990) Sawyer, Graham, & Harris (1992) Schunk & Schwartz (1993) Sexton, Harris, & Graham (1998) Sullivan, Mastropieri, & Scruggs (1995) Torrance, Thomas, & Robinson (1991) Troia, Graham, & Harris (1999) Whitman (1990) Wong (1994) Wong, Butler, Ficzere, & Kuperis (1997)

The top left side of the figure represents research on the effects of beliefs that a situation constitutes an opportunity for producing a desirable change in those circumstances. The right side represents research on the effects of self-instruction strategies (goal setting, self-planning, self-monitoring, self-evaluation, self-reinforcement) on adjustments to those perceived opportunities for gain. The lower left side represents research on the effects of adjustment outcomes on feelings of self-efficacy, self-control, and causal agency in those situations, as well as on the

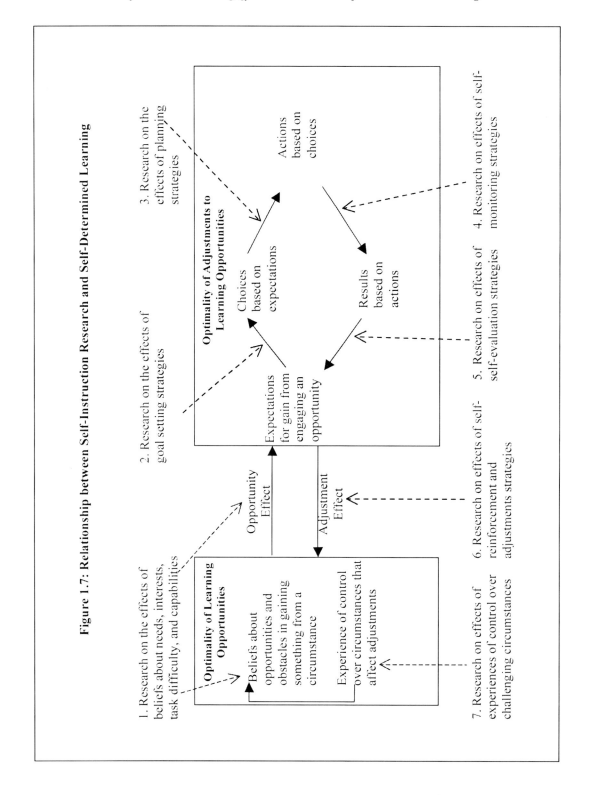

Figure 1.7: Relationship between Self-Instruction Research and Self-Determined Learning

effects of those feelings on subsequent beliefs and perceptions of the situation. The areas labeled 1-7 identify these types of studies. Research on beliefs (self-efficacy, locus of control, causal attribution) has reported on the effects of opportunities on self-regulated adjustments (1). Research on goal setting (2), self-planning (3), self-monitoring (4), self-evaluation (5), and self-adjustment/self-reinforcement (6) has reported on the effects of adjustments to new circumstances. And research on experiences of control shows that there are belief effects on the optimality of opportunities for gain (7).

What's the Practical Difference?

The two pedagogies offer substantially different educational benefits for students, as well. The main benefit of direct instruction is the efficiency of its skill development in students who need ample doses of teacher direction in order to learn. The pedagogy achieves these gains by carefully sequencing instructional cues so students perceive them to be *maximally doable* (they know what responses to emit) and as *maximally valuable* (they know reinforcement will follow). This is the central tenet of the pedagogy: to make certain students know exactly how to adjust to get the reinforcer they expect. According to self-determined learning theory, this type of teaching will maximum learning because opportunities are always optimal and adjustments to them are always optimal. This is the good news. The bad news is that this errorless adjustment-learning guarantee eliminates the need for students to deal with less optimal opportunities for gain. Which explains why they return to maladaptive behavior and marginal learning when they no longer receive this type of instruction. Although they have learned what to do when opportunities and adjustments are both optimal, they have not learned what to do when they are not. They have not learned to improve adjustments to improve situations and based on that to improve adjustments and situations again and again until they get what they want. In other words, they don't know how to engage in self-determined learning.

The Learning to Learn Benefit

But this is the main benefit of self-instruction pedagogy. Being based on a theory that explains why learning is adjustment and why improvements in self-regulation improve adjustments, the pedagogy can show how the teaching of self-regulation strategies improves student adjustments and learning in any environment. Indeed, there is research substantiating this benefit for underachieving elementary students (Fantuzzo & Clement, 1981; Stevenson & Fantuzzo, 1984; Stevenson & Fantuzzo, 1986), students with learning disabilities (Ellis, 1986; Ellis, Lenz, & Sabornie, 1987; McDougall & Brady, 1998; Peterson, Young, West, &

Peterson, 1999; Stecker, Whinnery, & Fuchs, 1996; Troia, 2002; Wong, 1994), students with mental retardation (Briggs, Alberto, Sharpton, Berlin, McKinley, & Ritts, 1990; Coleman & Whitman, 1984; Hughes, 1992; Irvine, Erickson, Singer, & Stahlberg, 1992; Mank & Horner, 1987; Schloss & Wood, 1990; Thinesen & Bryan, 1981; Trask-Tyler, Grossi, & Heward, 1994; Wacker, Berg, McMahon, Templeman, McKinney, Swarts, Visser, & Marquardt, 1988), students with autism (Pierce & Schreibman, 1994; Stahmer & Schreibman, 1992); students with behavior disorders (Epstein & Goss, 1978; Ninness, Fuerst, & Rutherford, 1991; Ninness, Ellis, Miller, Baker, & Rutherford, 1995; Rhode, Morgan, & Young, 1983; Turkowitz, O'Leary, & Ironsmith, 1975; Williams & Akamatsu, 1978); and students with severe disabilities (Agran, Salzberg, & Stowitschek, 1987; Wacker & Berg, 1984; Wacker, Berg , Berrie, & Swatta, 1985).

Viewed broadly, research like this suggests that (a) when students use strategies to regulate their expectations, choices, and actions to get what they want, their adjustments optimize and their learning maximizes; (b) when students use strategies to adjust to new challenges, they generalize what they learn across settings and time; and (c) when students learn to self-regulate during student-directed rather than teacher-directed instruction, they are more likely to adjust optimally to non-instructal situations.

To illustrate the nature of these claims about learning and its transfer, consider the work of Zimmerman and Pons (1986) who reported that high school students who use strategies to regulate their expectations, choices, and actions during schoolwork have higher achievement levels than do students who do not use self-regulation strategies, and that these differences correlate positively with membership in high and low achieving groups. In fact, use of self-regulation strategies was 93 percent accurate in predicting student membership in low or high achievement groups. Stevenson and Fantuzzo (1984; 1986) also found that underachieving elementary students who learned to use a self-regulation strategy card to regulate their homework in math transferred what they learned across all of the 15 generalization domains. In these studies, students set their own work goals, planned and monitored their work, and then evaluated and rewarded themselves for their achievements. As a result they increased their correctly completed math assignments in class and at home, which generalized across all 15 subject, behavior, setting, and time domains. Building on this work, Mithaug and Mithaug (2003a) found that young children with severe disabilities who learned to use a self-regulation strategy during student-directed instruction were more likely to engage in self-regulated adjustments to unsupervised work tasks than when they learned strategy use during teacher-directed instruction.

Studies like these lead to the conclusion that students' *self-regulatory capabilities affect their adjustments and learning.* The more effective students are at self-regulation, they closer to optimal their adjustments will be and the closer to maximum will be their learning. Conversely, the less effective students are at self-regulation, the closer to suboptimal their adjustments will be and the more marginal will be their learning. Mithaug and Mithaug (2003b) tested this prediction directly by comparing self-regulation capabilities of two groups of special and general education elementary students who regulated their expectations, choices and responses to produce results they expected from solving a computer-generated adjustment problem that required point totals to *match* goal expectations. Students solved a series of adjustment problems by *regulating* their expectations during goal setting, their task selections during choice options, time spent on tasks during work periods, and their evaluations of points gained following their work. The findings supported the prediction that there would be significant self-regulation and adjustment differences between the two groups. Students from special education were significantly less effective at regulating their expectations, choices, actions, and results and had significantly less optimal adjustments than students from general education. Hence, they produced significantly fewer point gains, too, differences that were evident for easy as well as difficult tasks. There is also evidence self-regulation deficiencies like these negatively impact students' prospects for self-determination. In a study that assessed the self-determination of more than 450 students with and without disabilities from 72 schools and programs in California and New York, Mithaug, Campeau, and Wolman (2003) found that self-determination levels were significantly lower for students with disabilities than for students without disabilities, and that these differences were due to less effective self-regulation capabilities. Students with learning disabilities, mental retardation, emotional and behaviors problems, as well as students with other disabilities, were significantly less effective in (a) setting expectations that were consistent with their needs, interests, and abilities; (b) making choices and taking actions based on their expectations; and (c) evaluating results and adjusting their expectations, choices and actions based on those evaluations. There is also evidence to suggest that these differences are present in students from other countries. Kebbeh and Mithaug (2003), for example, reported significant self-determination differences between youth with and without disabilities in schools in The Gambia, West Africa. These students also exhibited significant differences in self-regulation skills in that students with disabilities were significantly less capable self-regulators.

Fortunately, Columbus and Mithaug (2003) showed how use of self-instruction pedagogy could eliminate these deficiencies and their negative impact on students' prospects for self-determination. In this study, one group of students with severe learning and behavior problems received instruction on use of self-regulation strategies and the other with similar disabilities did not. The results indicated that the instructed group significantly improved their levels of self-determination, whereas the non-instructed group showed no improvement. Moreover, the increased levels of self-determination experienced by the instructed group were comparable to the levels reported by college students without disabilities.

Finally, the strategies prescribed by self-instruction pedagogy also help students succeed in adulthood (Martin, Mithaug, Oliphint, Husch, & Frazier, 2002), a finding that is not particularly surprising given that adults who succeed in business and industry use similar strategies. To appreciate this comparability, consider the strategy use that Napoleon Hill (1960) found among the successful in the 1920s. These superachievers used a strategy that (1) defined specific goals to be achieved, (2) systematically developed their capacity to meet those goals, (3) developed practical plans for goal attainment, (4) accumulated specialized knowledge needed to complete plans, and (5) persisted in adjusting to results as they implemented plans. More recently, others have reported on similar strategy use among the most successful. Garfield (1986) interviewed 1500 super achievers in business, science, sports, and the arts and found that they used strategies that (1) defined and pursued missions that motivated, (2) produced plans and engaged in purposeful activities directed toward achieving goals, (3) provided for self-observation and effective thinking to assure maximum performance, (4) corrected and adjusted activities to maintain a critical path to goal attainment, and (5) anticipated and adapted to major change while maintaining momentum to complete their overall plan. Finally, in the following passage Anthony Robbins (1997), former President Clinton's personal counselor, described the same pattern of strategy use by successful people:

> If you look at successful people, you'll find they follow these steps. They start with a target, because you can't hit one if you don't have one. They took action, because just knowing isn't enough. They have the ability to read others, to know what response they were getting. And they kept adapting, kept adjusting, kept changing their behavior until they found what worked. (Robbins, 1997, p. 12)

According to self-determined learning theory these strategies work because they help learners solve three types of *adjustment* problems. They help them identify what must be changed in a situation to produce a desirable result. They help them direct their behaviors toward producing that change. And they help learners determine whether their strategy produced the expected result. According to the theory, these strategies help learners adjust optimally to challenging circumstances because they focus attention on (a) setting expectations for gain that *are based* on their needs, interests, and abilities and that *are consistent* with those circumstances (adaptive expectations); (b) choosing the best approach to meet expectations for gain (rational choice making); (c) following through on choices (efficient responding); and (d) adjusting subsequent expectations, choices, and actions until there is match between results and expectations (successful results).

The Learning-to-Learn Teaching Strategy

You can teach your students these learning-to-learn strategies by following the steps suggested by the columns in Table 1.6, which move instruction from being primarily teacher-directed to being primarily student-directed. The first column

Special Education Policy IDEA Directedness Required	Moving from Pedagogies of Direct Instruction to Pedagogies of Self-Instruction				Special Education Policy IDEA Student Agency Required
	Step 1 Teaching Content Of Learning	Step 2 Teaching Self-Managed Learning	Step 3 Teaching Self-Regulated Learning	Step 4 Teaching Self-Determined Learning	
Individualized Education Program (IEP)					Student-Directed IEPs
Needs, interests, and abilities	Teacher-identified needs, interests, abilities	Teacher-identified needs, interests, abilities	Teacher-identified needs, interests, abilities	**Student**-identified needs, interests, abilities	Student identified needs, interests, abilities
Goals	Teacher Set goals to meet teacher-identified needs/interests	Teacher Set goals to meet teacher-identified needs/interests	**Student** Set goals to meet teacher-identified needs/interests	**Student** set goals to meet needs/interests based on abilities	Student set goals to meet needs/interests based on abilities
Plans	Teacher plans to meet goals	Teacher plans to meet goals	**Student** Plans to meet goals	**Student** plans to meet goals	Student selected plans to meet goals
Activities	Teacher monitored actions to follow plans	**Student**-Monitored actions to follow plans	**Student** monitored actions to follow plans	**Student** monitored actions to follow plans	Student monitored actions to follow plans
Evaluations	Teacher evaluations of results of actions and plans	**Student**-Evaluations of results of actions	**Student** Evaluations of results of actions and plans	**Student** Evaluations of results of actions and plans	Student evaluations of results of actions and plans
Adjustments	Teacher adjustments in actions and plans to improve results	**Student**-Adjustments in actions and plans to improve results	**Student** Adjustments in actions and plans to improve results	**Student** Adjustments in actions and plans to improve results	Student adjustments in actions and plans, to improve results

Table 1.6: Four Pedagogical Steps toward the Teaching of Self-Determined Learning

identifies the *functional connections* that must be present to maximize learning regardless of whether instruction is directed externally or internally. In either case, to be effective, instruction must have:(1) instructional goals that are consistent with learner needs, interests, and abilities; (2) instructional plans that are consistent with goals; (3) actions that are consistent with plans, (4) evaluations that assess the match between results and goals; and (5) adjustments that are consistent with evaluations.

The second column presents the baseline of instructional control that is likely *when you* identify your student's needs, interests, and abilities (row 2); set goals to be met based on those needs, interests, and abilities (row 3); develop plans to meet goals (row 4); act on plans during instruction (row 5); evaluate whether results meet goals (row 6); and then when you adjust subsequent goals, plans, and actions in response to your evaluations (row 7).

The third column presents the first step toward *student-directed learning*, which begins when you teach students to use the following strategies to regulate their behavior in any situation: self-monitoring, self-evaluation, and self-adjustment/reinforcement. The fourth column represents the *second step toward student-directedness.* Here you teach students to use a strategy to match *their* results with *their* expectations. The fifth column represents the *third step toward student-directedness.* Here students identify their needs and interests and then solve adjustment problems in order to satisfy them. At this level, students have mastered the strategies they need to become self-determined learners. They have strategies to identify their needs and interests, set goals based on those needs and interests, develop plans to meet goals, act on plans, evaluate results, and adjust subsequent goals, plans, and actions. Thus, they have all the tools they need to control and direct the development and implementation of their own IEPs (column 6).

CONCLUSION

The conclusions we hope you draw from these theoretical, empirical, and practical comparisons are: (a) self-instruction and direct instruction are equally robust theoretically, (b) self-instruction has a significantly greater empirical base than does direct instruction, (c) self-instruction pedagogy has a significantly greater practical benefit since it develops students' adaptive capabilities across situations and time, and therefore (d) that it should be used as much as possible because it empowers students to learn how to learn in any learning pursuit they may choose.

Self-instruction produces this empowering effect because of its focus on choice opportunities, strategy training, match contingencies, and repeated self-regulated adjustment over time. It gives students the opportunities they need to control the adjustment-learning process, which, in turn, empowers them to become self-determined learners and achievers across environments. The problem with other pedagogies is that they fail to employ all four methods at the same time. They may provide choice opportunities but not strategy instruction, reinforcement contingencies but not match contingencies, or discrete trial learning but not repeated opportunities for self-regulated adjustment. As a result, students never have the means or the opportunity to develop control over their adjustments, and never become self-determined learners.

Direct instruction pedagogy is the least empowering in this regard because of its focus on teacher control of learning as Table 1.7 illustrates. The control features prescribed by direct instruction are listed in the first two columns of the table, and the control features of self-instruction are listed in the last two columns. The numbered rows compare the pedagogies on each.

Beginning with row 1, consider how behavior theory and direct instruction pedagogy provoke and control learning, which is through antecedent events that *teachers choose* for students. Next, consider how self-determined learning theory and self-instruction pedagogy provoke and control learning, which is through *choices students make* when deciding what and how to learn something new. In both cases, provocation is effective to the extent learners perceive opportunities to be valuable and doable enough to engage. In the case of direct instruction, the teacher chooses instructional cues that have those "valuable-doable" characteristics, whereas in self-instruction, the student chooses learning options with those characteristics. Put simply, during direct instruction teachers make choices and feel in control, while during self-instruction students make choices and feel in control. In other words, the actor making the choice feels in control.

The second row presents the instructional targets of the two pedagogies. For behavior theory and direct instruction, the targets are instructional cues and consequences that control student responses; and for self-determined learning theory and self-instruction, the targets are the strategies students can use to regulate their expectations, choices, actions, and results. Again, opportunities for control reside with teachers in direct instruction and with students in self-instruction. As a result, during direct instruction students depend on their teachers' regulation of antecedent and consequent events to learn, and during self-instruction, they depend on their use of a self-regulation strategy to learn.

The third row presents the circumstances that maintain learning. For behavior theory and direct instruction, motivation to learn is a function of reinforcement contingencies established by the teacher. For self-determined learning theory and self-instruction pedagogy, motivation to learn is a function of result-expectation matches established by the student.

The last row presents the outcomes of learning. For behavior theory and direct instruction, these outcomes are changes in the *associations* between *cues, responses,*

Table 1.7: Summary of Differences between Direct and Self-Instruction Pedagogies

	Behavioral Learning Theory	Direct Instruction Pedagogy	Self-Determined Learning Theory	Self-Instruction Pedagogy
1.	Antecedent Events:	Programmed cues	Optimality of Opportunities:	Just-right choice options
2.	Behavioral Events:	Observable Responses to cues	Self-regulated Events:	Strategies to regulate expectations, choices, responses, and results
3.	Consequent Events:	Reinforcement Contingencies	Optimality of Adjustments:	Expectation-result matches
4.	Operant Learning:	Change in cue-response-consequence associations	Self-regulated Learning:	Adjustments in feelings and beliefs about the situation and in expectations, choices, and responses to the situation

and *consequences*, and for self-determined learning theory and self-instruction pedagogy, learning outcomes are the *adjusted beliefs* and *feelings* about the provocative situation as well as the new *expectations, choices, responses,* and *results* associated with those adjusted beliefs and feelings.

As this review suggests, direct instruction requires significantly lower levels of student-directedness during learning than does self-instruction. In other words, if you directly control all features of your students' instructional program right now – from identifying their needs to evaluating their progress and adjusting learning goals *for them* – then you probably require less student-directedness than what they need if they are to learn on their own. Your instruction is probably more teacher- than student-directed. Moreover, were you to adopt the pedagogical methods prescribed in this text (as we hope you do) then you would probably become more student-directed *than you are now.*

Chapter 2 will help determine where you are on this scale of instructional control. It describes a self-assessment you can use to identify the control of student learning and adjustment you *currently* exert when you teach. Our hope is that by assessing the instructional directedness and curriculum functionality of your teaching before reading chapters on how to empower students, you will know exactly what is needed to become more empowering. The methods described in chapters 3–6 outline four steps that will help you move from there to where you want your students to be, given, of course, that you want them to be self-determined learners.

REFERENCES

Agran, M., Salzberg, C. L., & Stowitschek, J. J. (1987). An analysis of the effects of a social skills training program using self-instructions on the acquisition and generalization of two social behaviors in a working setting. *Journal of the Association for Persons with Severe Handicaps, 12*, 131–139.

Bereiter, C., & Engelmann, S. (1966). *Teaching disadvantaged children in the preschool.* Englewood Cliffs, NJ: Prentice-Hall.

Blankenship, C., S. (1985). Using curriculum-based assessment data to make instructional decisions. *Exceptional Children, 52*(3), 223–238.

Briggs, A., Alberto, P., Sharpton, W., Berlin, D., McKinley, C., & Ritts, C. (1990) Generalized use of a self-operated audio prompt system. *Education and Training in Mental Retardation, 25*, 381–389.

Bursuck, W. D., & Lessen, E. (1987). A classroom-based model for assessing students with learning disabilities. *Learning Disabilities Focus, 3*(1), 17–29.

Carver, C. S., & Scheier, M. F. (1983). An information processing perspective on self-management. In P. Karoly & F. H. Kanfer (Eds.), *Self-management and behavior change: From theory to practice* (pp. 93–128). New York: Pergamon Press.

Coleman, R. S., & Whitman, T. L. (1984). Developing, generalizing, and maintaining physical fitness in mentally retarded adults: Toward a self-directed program. *Analysis and Intervention in Developmental Disabilities, 4*, 109–127.

Columbus, M.A., & Mithaug, D. E. (2003). The effects of self-regulation problem-solving instruction on the self-determination of secondary students with disabilities. In D. E. Mithaug, D. K. Mithaug, M. Agran, J. E. Martin, & M. L. Wehmeyer (Eds.) *Self-determined learning theory: Construction, verification, and evaluation* (pp. 172–187). Mahwah, NJ: Lawrence Erlbaum Associates.

Corno, L., & Mandinach, E. B. (1983). The role of cognitive engagement in classroom learning and motivation. *Educational Psychologist, 18*, 88–108.

Ellis, E. S. (1986). The role of motivation and pedagogy on the generalization of cognitive training by the mildly handicapped. *Journal of Learning Disabilities, 19*, 66–70.

Ellis, E. S., Lenz, B. K., & Sabornie, E. J. (1987). Generalization and adaptation of learning strategies to natural environments: Part 1: Critical agents. *Remedial and Special Education, 8*(1), 6–20.

Englemann, T., Osborn, K. & Engelmann, T. (1969). *Distar language: An instructional system.* Chicago: Science Research Associates, Inc.

Epstein, R., & Goss, C. M. (1978). A self-control procedure for the maintenance of nondisruptive behavior in an elementary school child. *Behavior Therapy, 9*, 109–117.

Fantuzzo, J. W., & Clement, P. W. (1981). Generalization of the effects of teacher and self-administered token reinforcers to nontreated students. *Journal of Applied Behavior Analysis, 14*, 435–447.

Friend, M., & Bursuck, W. D. (2002). *Including students with special needs: A practical guide for classroom teachers.* Boston, MA: Allyn and Bacon.

Fuchs, S., Deno, S. L., & Mirkin, P. K. (1984). The effects of frequent curriculum-based measurement and evaluation of pedagogy, student achievement, and student awareness of learning. *American Educational Research Journal, 21*, 449–460.

Garfield, G. (1986). *Peak performers: The new heroes of American business.* New York: Avon.

Gargiulo, R. M. (2003). *Special education in contemporary society: An introduction to exceptionality.* Belmont, CA: Wadsworth/Thomson Learning.

Gersten, R., & Dimino, J. (1993). Visions and revisions: A special education perspective on the whole language controversy. *Special education and Remedial Education, 14*(4), 5–13.

Gersten, R., Carnine, D., & Woodward, J. (1987). Direct instruction: A research-based approach to curriculum design and teaching. *Exceptional Children, 53*(1), 17–31.

Hallahan, D. P., & Kaulfman, J. M. (2003). *Exceptional learners: Introduction to special education.* Boston, MA: Allyn and Bacon.

Hardman, J. L., Drew, C. J., & Egan, M. W. (2002). *Human exceptionality: Society, school, and family.* Boston, MA: Allyn and Bacon.

Haring, N. G., & Lovitt, T. C. (1967). Operant methodology and educational technology in special education. In N. G. Haring & R. Scheifelbusch (Eds.), *Methods in special education.* New York: McGraw-Hill.

Haring, N. G., & Phillips, E. L. (1962). *Educating emotionally disturbed children.* New York: McGraw-Hill.

Heshusius, L. (1991). Curriculum-based assessment and direct instruction: Critical reflections on fundamental assumption. *Exceptional Children, 57*(4), 315–328.

Heward, W. (2003). *Exceptional children: An introduction to special education.* 7th ed. Columbus, OH: Merrill Prentice-Hall.

Hewett, F. M. Taylor, F. D., & Artuso, A. K. (1969). The Santa Monica Project: Evaluation of an engineered classroom design with emotionally disturbed children. *Exceptional Children, 35*, 523–529.

Hill, N. (1960). *Think and grow rich.* New York: Fawcett Crest.

Holland, J. G., & Skinner, B. F. (1961). *The analysis of behavior: A program for self-instruction.* New York: McGraw-Hill Book Co., Inc.

Homme, L., deBaca, P.C., Cottingham, L., & Homme, A. (1968). What behavioral engineering is. *The Psychological Record, 18*, 425–434.

Hughes, C. (1992). Teaching self-instruction utilizing multiple exemplars to produce generalized problem-solving by individuals with severe mental retardation. *American Journal on Mental Retardation, 97*, 302–314.

Hunt, N., & Marshall, K. (2002). *Exceptional children and youth.* Boston, MA: Houghton Mifflin Company.

Irvine, B. A., Erickson, A. M., Singer, G., & Stahlberg, D. (1992). A coordinated program to transfer self-management skills from school to home. *Education and Training in Mental Retardation, 27*(3), 241–254.

Jackson, H. J., & Boag, P. G. (1981). The efficacy of self-control procedures as motivational strategies with mentally retarded persons: A review of the literature and guidelines for future research. *Australian Journal of Developmental Disabilities, 7*, 65–79.

Jeffrey, D. B., & Berger, L. H. (1982). A self-environmental systems model and its implications for behavior change. In K. R. Blankstein and J. Polivy (Eds.), *Advances in the student of communication and affect, Volume 7: Self-control and self-modification of emotional behavior* (pp. 29–69). New York: Plenum Press.

Jones, E. D., & Krause, J. P. (1988). The effectiveness of data-based instruction by student teachers in classrooms for pupils with mild learning handicaps. *Teacher Education and Special Education, 11*(1), 9–19.

Kanfer, F. H. (1971). The maintenance of behavior by self-generated stimuli and reinforcement. In A. Jacobs & L. B. Sachs (Eds.). *The psychology of private events: Perspectives on covert response systems* (pp. 41–59). New York: Academic Press.

Kebbeh, A. S., & Mithaug, D. E. (2003). Assessing self-determination prospects of students with and without disabilities in The Gambia, West Africa. In D. E. Mithaug, D. K. Mithaug, M. Agran, J. E. Martin, & M. L. Wehmeyer (Eds.) *Self-determined learning theory: Construction, verification, and evaluation* (pp. 89–103). Mahwah, NJ: Lawrence Erlbaum Associates.

King-Sears, M. E. (1997). Best academic practices for inclusive classrooms. *Focus on Exceptional Children, 29*(7), 1–22.

Kirk, S. A., Gallagher, J. J., & Anastasiow, N. J. (2003). *Educating exceptional children.* Boston, MA: Houghton Mifflin Company.

Lewis, R. B., & Doorlag, D. H. (2003). *Teaching special students in general education classrooms.* Columbus, OH: Merrill Prentice Hall.

Lindsey, O. R. (1964). Direct measurement and prosthesis of retarded children. *Journal of Education, 147*, 62–81.

Luria, A. R. (1960). Verbal regulation of behavior. In M. A. B. Brazier (Eds.), *The central nervous system and behavior*, (pp. 359–379). New York: Josiah Macy, Jr. Foundation.

Mank, D. M., & Horner, R. H. (1987). Self-recruited feedback: A cost effective procedure for maintaining behavior. *Research in Developmental Disabilities, 8*, 91–112.

Martin, J. E., Mithaug, D. E., Oliphint, J. H., Husch, J. V., Frazier, E. S. (2002). *Self-directed employment: A handbook for transition teachers and employment specialists.* Baltimore, MD: Paul H. Brookes Publishing Co.

McDougall, D., & Brady, M. P. (1998). Initiating and fading self-management interventions to increase math fluency in general education classes. *Exceptional Children, 64*(2), 151–166.

Miller, G. A., Gallanter, E., & Pribaum, K. H. (1960). *Plans and the structure of behavior.* New York: Holt, Rinehart and Winston.

Mithaug, D. E., & Mithaug, D. K. (2003b). Assessing adjustment gains of students in general and special education. In D. E. Mithaug, D. K. Mithaug, M. Agran, J. E. Martin, & M. L. Wehmeyer (Eds.) *Self-determined learning theory: Construction, verification, and evaluation* (pp. 121–137). Mahwah, NJ: Lawrence Erlbaum Associates.

Mithaug, D. E., Campeau, P. L., Wolman, J. M. (2003). Assessing self-determination prospects among students with and without disabilities. In D. E. Mithaug, D. K. Mithaug, M. Agran, J. E. Martin, & M. L. Wehmeyer (Eds.) *Self-determined learning theory: Construction, verification, and evaluation* (pp. 61–76). Mahwah, NJ: Lawrence Erlbaum Associates.

Mithaug, D. E., Mithaug, D. K., Agran, M., Martin, J. E., & Wehmeyer, M. L. (2003). *Self-determined learning theory: Construction, verification, and evaluation.* Mahwah, N. J. Lawrence Erlbaum Associates.

Mithaug, D. K., & Mithaug, D. E. (2003a). The effects of choice opportunities and self-regulation training on the self-engagement and learning of young children with disabilities. In D. E. Mithaug, D. K. Mithaug, M. Agran, J. E. Martin, & M. L. Wehmeyer (Eds.) *Self-determined learning theory: Construction, verification, and evaluation* (pp. 141–157). Mahwah, NJ: Lawrence Erlbaum Associates.

Moore, J. (1986). Direct instruction: A model for instructional design. *Educational Psychology, 6*(3), 201–230.

Ninness, H. A. C., Fuerst, J., & Rutherford, R. D. (1991). Effects of self-management training and reinforcement on the transfer of improved conduct in the absence of supervision. *Journal of Applied Behavior Analysis, 24*, 499–508.

Ninness, H.A. C., Ellis, J., Miller, W.B., Baker, D., & Rutherford, R. (1995). The effect of a self-management training package on the transfer of aggression control procedures in the absence of supervision. *Behavior Modification, 19*, 464–490.

Pesut, D. J. (1990). Creative thinking as a self-regulatory metacognitive process: A model for education, training and further research. *Journal of Creative Behavior, 24*(2), 105–110.

Peterson, J., Heistad, D., Peterson, D., & Reynolds, M. (1985). Montevideo individualized prescribe instructional management system. *Exceptional Children, 52*(3), 239–243.

Peterson, L.D., Young, K.R., West, R.P., & Peterson, M.H. (1999). Effects of student self-management on generalization of student performance to regular classrooms. *Education and Treatment of Children, 22*, 357–372.

Pierce, K. L., & Schreibman, L. (1994). Teaching daily living skills to children with autism in unsupervised settings through pictorial self-management. *Journal of Applied Behavior Analysis, 27*, 471–481.

Pugach, M., & Whitten, M. E. (1987). The methodological content of teacher education programs in learning disabilities: A problem of duplication. *Learning Disability Quarterly, 10*(1), 291–299.

Ramsey, R. S., & Algozzine, B. (1991). Teacher competency testing: What are special education teachers expected to know? *Exceptional Children, 57*(4), 339–350.

Reschly, D. J. (1988). Special education reform: School psychology revolution. *School Psychology Review, 17*(3), 459–475.

Rhode, G., Morgan, D. P., & Young, K. R. (1983). Generalization and maintenance of treatment gains of behaviorally handicapped students from resource rooms to regular classrooms using self-evaluation procedures. *Journal of Applied Behavior Analysis, 16*, 1781–187.

Robbins, A. (1997). *Unlimited power.* New York: Fireside.

Schloss, P., & Wood, C. E. (1990). Effect of self-monitoring on maintenance and generalization of conversational skills of persons with mental retardation. *Mental Retardation, 28,* 105–113.

Smith, D. D., (2001). *Introduction to special education: Teaching in an age of opportunity.* Boston, MA: Allyn and Bacon.

Stahmer, A.C., & Schreibman, L. (1992). Teaching children with autism appropriate play in unsupervised environments using a self-management treatment package. *Journal of Applied Behavior Analysis, 25,* 447–459.

Stecker, P. M., Whinnery, K. W., & Fuchs, L. S. (1996). Self-recording during unsupervised academic activity: Effects on time spent out of class. *Exceptionality, 6*(3), 133–147.

Stevenson, H. C., & Fantuzzo, J. W. (1984). Application of the "generalization map" to a self-control intervention with school-aged children. *Journal of Applied Behavior Analysis, 17,* 203–212.

Stevenson, H. C., & Fantuzzo, J. W. (1986). The generality of social validity of a competency-based self-control training intervention for underachieving students. *Journal of Applied Behavior Analysis, 19,* 269–276.

Thinesen, P. J., & Bryan, A. J. (1981). The use of sequential pictorial cues in the initiation and maintenance of grooming behaviors with mentally retarded adults. *Mental Retardation, 5,* 247–250.

Trask-Tyler, S.A., Grossi, T.A., & Heward, W.L. (1994). Teaching young adults with developmental disabilities and visual impairments to use tape-recorded recipes: Acquisition, generalization, and maintenance of cooking skills. *Journal of Behavioral Education, 4,* 283–311.

Troia, G. A., (2002). Teaching writing strategies to children with disabilities: Setting generalization as the goal. *Exceptionality, 10*(4), 249–269.

Turkowitz, H., O'Leary, K. D., & Ironsmith, M. (1975). Generalization and maintenance of appropriate behavior through self-control. *Journal of Consulting and Clinical Psychology, 43,* 577–583.

Turnbull, R., Turnbull, A., Shank, M., Smith, S., & Leal, D. (2002). *Exceptional lives: Special education in today's schools.* 3rd Ed. Columbus, OH: Merrill Prentice-Hall.

Vaughn, S., Bos, C., & Schumm, J. S. (2003). *Teaching exceptional, diverse, and at-risk students in the general education classroom.* 3rd Edition. Boston, MA: Allyn and Bacon.

Vergason, G. A., & Anderegg, M. L., (1991). Beyond the Regular Education Initiative and the resource room controversy. *Focus on Exceptional Children, 23*(7), 1–7.

Wacker, D. P., & Berg, W. K. (1984). Training adolescents with severe handicaps to set up job tasks independently using picture prompts. *Analysis and Intervention in Developmental Disabilities, 4,* 353–365.

Wacker, D. P., Berg, W. K. , Berrie, P., Swatta, P. (1985). Generalization and maintenance of complex skills by severely handicapped adolescents following picture prompt training. *Journal of Applied Behavior Analysis, 14,* 329–336.

Wacker, D. P., Berg, W. K., McMahon, C., Templeman, M., McKinney, J., Swarts, V., Visser, M., & Marquardt, P. (1988). An evaluation of labeling-then-doing with moderately handicapped persons. Acquisition and generalization with complex tasks. *Journal of Applied Behavior Analysis, 21,* 369–380.

Williams, D. Y., & Akamatsu, T. J. (1978). Cognitive self-guidance training with juvenile delinquents: Applicability and generalization. *Cognitive Therapy and Research, 2,* 285–288.

Wong, B. Y. L. (1994). Instructional parameters promoting transfer of learned strategies in students with learning disabilities. *Learning Disability Quarterly, 17,* 110–120.

Zimmerman, B. J., & Martinez-Pons, M. (1986). Development of a structured interview for assessing student use of self-regulated learning strategies. *American Educational Research Journal, 23,* 614–628.

Chapter 2

IS YOUR INSTRUCTION TEACHER-
OR STUDENT-DIRECTED?

DENNIS E. MITHAUG
DEIRDRE K. MITHAUG

Did you know that the control and content of your teaching affects whether your students will become determined to learn how to learn on their own? This chapter describes an instrument that assesses these instructional and curricular factors in your teaching. You can use it now to rate your instructional approach and then compare it with that of 250 experienced teachers whose teacher-directed control is consistent with Bickel and Bickel's (1986) prescription for teachers to take:

> . . . an active, direct role in the instruction of . . . students. These educators give many detailed and redundant instructions and explanations when introducing a new concept. . . . They give ample opportunity for guided practice with frequent reviews of student progress. . . . They check for understanding, using such techniques as questioning, consistent review of homework, and review of previous day's lessons before moving on to new areas. Such teachers move among students when they are involved in practice seatwork. Feedback is provided frequently and with meaningful detail. Effective teachers use feedback strategies for positive reinforcement of student success. Feedback also provides the basis for reteaching where necessary. Effective teachers take an active role in creating a positive, expectant, and orderly classroom environment in which learning takes place. To accomplish these climate objectives, effective teachers actively structure the learning process and the management of time, building in such things as signals for academic work and maintaining student attention by group alerting and accountability techniques and through variation in educational tasks . . . (Bickel & Bickel, 1986, 492–493)

Of course, if your teaching is substantially different from that approach, it may be closer to the one advocated by Ellis (1986) who foresaw problems with too much teacher control:

. . . classroom structures which provide little daily and weekly opportunity for students' input or selection of instructional goals, activities and rule setting can subtly reinforce an external locus of control, e.g., classroom environments which are highly structured, assignments are predetermined by the teacher without considering the students' goals, little opportunity for students to participate in the decision-making process regarding their education, little opportunity for the student to verbally state what is being learned and why. In short, efforts by some teachers to run highly organized and tightly structured classrooms may inadvertently reduce student opportunities to learn and use metacognitive skills of self-structuring and monitoring. While satisfying the need to help students by frequently acting as a controlling agent and too frequently or unnecessarily offering help, teachers can be training their students to be more dependent on the instructor for problem solving, guidance, and feedback. (Ellis, 1986, p. 67)

On the other hand, if your teaching matches neither of these models, you are not alone either in that Mithaug, Agran, Martin, and Rusch (1988) foresaw the need for both teacher- and student-directedness during instruction, but for different reasons:

The immediate and long-term needs of our students pull in opposite directions. Upon entry into special education many students need structure, direction, and external management, especially if they lack the internal control necessary to function effectively in the mainstream. Students with learning difficulties are unable to learn on their own. Teacher direction in learning and management will help increase basic skills and reduce behaviors incompatible with learning.

But students also need to become independent. They must be able to think critically, solve problems independently, make choices, set their own goals, decide what to do, initiate action, evaluate their work and adjust accordingly. They need frequent opportunities practicing these behaviors in as many situations as possible. (Mithaug, Agran, Martin, & Rusch, 1988, pp. 40–41)

This chapter allows you to find out where your teaching is on questions of control and curricular emphasis. We believe that once you know your own baseline on these factors, you will also know how to judge the importance of the teaching methods we describe in upcoming chapters.

The first step in establishing this baseline is to use the *Instruction and Curriculum Scales for Self-Determined Learning* to rate your teaching approach. The second is to summarize the instructional-directedness and curricular functionality of those ratings. The third is to compare your ratings with those of a test sample of teachers to determine whether you also favor teacher-controlled instruction of basic skills. The last step is to use your own baseline of instruction to decide whether to shift some of that control to students. The chapter ends with a plan for helping you decide whether to make this shift toward empowering students to learn how to learn on their own.

Step 1: Assessing the Control and Content of Your Instruction

To establish your instruction and curriculum baseline for teaching, use the *Instruction and Curriculum Rating Scale for Self-Determined Learning* (see Appendix A for details). This instrument consists of 48 teaching statements, which are rated on a four-point scale to indicate how often you teach that way, with 0 indicating never, 1 almost never, 2 sometimes, 3 almost always, and 4 indicating always. You can complete that assessment now by answering the 48 questions presented in Table 2.1.

Step 2: Score the Functional Directedness of Your Teaching

The next step is to enter the rated items in Table 2.1 in the scale columns for instructional-directedness in Table 2.2 and the scale columns for curricular functionality in Table 2.3. For example, to calculate instructional-directedness scores enter the Table 2.1 ratings for items: 1, 6, 9, 13, 21, 23, 27, 31, 32, 35, 37, and 45 in the teacher-directedness column of Table 2.2, total them and then divide by 12 to get your average teacher-directedness. Do the same with the student-directedness ratings in Table 2.1. Enter the Table 2.1 ratings for items 3, 11, 15, 17, 19, 25, 29, 34, 38, 40, 43, and 47 in the student-directedness column of Table 2.2, total them and then divide by 12 to get your average student-directedness.

To calculate curricular functionality scores enter Table 2.1 ratings for items 4, 5, 10, 12, 16, 18, 24, 26, 33, 41, 42, and 48 in the basic skills column of Table 2.3, total them and divide by 12 to get your average basic skills score. Do the same to get an applied skills score. Enter Table 2.1 ratings for items 3, 11, 15, 17, 19, 25, 29, 34, 38, 40, 43, and 47 in the applied skills column of Table 2.3, total them and divide by 12 to get your average applied skills score. The average scores for teacher-directedness, student-directedness, basic skills, and applied skills constitute your teaching baseline for this instruction and curriculum assessment.

Step 3: Compare Yourself with Others

The next step is to evaluate your approach by comparing it with the instructional-directedness and curricular functionality scores of 253 other experienced special and general education teachers who rated themselves on the same instrument. This group included 28 experienced special education teachers from the West Indies, 31 experienced general education teachers from the U.S., and 194 experienced special education teachers from the U.S. The next section presents the self-assessment ratings for these three groups. After reviewing these results, you will have an opportunity to compare your baselines with theirs.

Table 2.1: Assessing the Applied Directedness of Your Instruction and Curriculum
0=Never, 1=Almost Never, 2=Sometimes, 3=Almost Always, 4=Always

1. I learn what my students like so I can make decisions based on their preferences.	0 1 2 3 4
2. My students learn to read words to solve everyday problems.	0 1 2 3 4
3. There are instructional opportunities for students to adjust their plans frequently and repeatedly in order to improve their results.	0 1 2 3 4
4. My students learn to add numbers during drill and practice exercises.	0 1 2 3 4
5. My students learn to write words at their developmental level.	0 1 2 3 4
6. I learn what students can do so that I can make decisions based on their abilities.	0 1 2 3 4
7. My students learn to add numbers to solve everyday problems.	0 1 2 3 4
8. My students learn to write words that solve everyday problems.	0 1 2 3 4
9. I set goals for students based on what they need or want and what they are able to do to satisfy those needs and wants.	0 1 2 3 4
10. My students learn to subtract numbers during drill and practice exercises.	0 1 2 3 4
11. There are instructional opportunities for students to act independently on their plans to meet their learning goals.	0 1 2 3 4
12. My students learn to read phrases at their developmental level.	0 1 2 3 4
13. I make plans for how students will meet learning and behavior goals.	0 1 2 3 4
14. My students learn to subtract numbers to solve everyday problems.	0 1 2 3 4
15. There are instructional opportunities for students to construct plans to meet their learning and behavior goals.	0 1 2 3 4
16. My students learn to divide numbers during drill and practice exercises.	0 1 2 3 4
17. My students monitor their results by comparing them with goals in order to determine whether their plans are working.	0 1 2 3 4
18. My students learn to write and read English compositions at their developmental level.	0 1 2 3 4
19. There are instructional opportunities for students to set goals for what they want to learn and what they want to do.	0 1 2 3 4
20. My students learn to divide numbers to solve everyday problems.	0 1 2 3 4
21. I use my evaluations of student results to adjust their goals, plans, and actions so that they will improve next time.	0 1 2 3 4
22. My students learn to adjust to signs in their communities.	0 1 2 3 4
23. I have frequent opportunities to set goals for what students need and want to learn.	0 1 2 3 4
24. My students learn to multiply numbers during drill and practice exercises.	0 1 2 3 4
25. My students learn by adjusting to their results until they know what choices and actions produce the results they want.	0 1 2 3 4
26. My students learn science concepts at their developmental level.	0 1 2 3 4
27. I learn about my students by adjusting to results repeatedly until I know what decisions and actions produce the results I want for them.	0 1 2 3 4
28. My students learn to multiply numbers to solve everyday problems.	0 1 2 3 4
29. There are instructional opportunities for students to discover for themselves what they like, what they want, and what they can do to satisfy their interests and needs.	0 1 2 3 4
30. My students learn how to improve their adjustments at home.	0 1 2 3 4
31. There are instructional opportunities for me to discover what students like, what they want, and what they can do to satisfy their interests and needs.	0 1 2 3 4
32. I monitor students' results by comparing them with their goals in order to determine whether my plans are working for them.	0 1 2 3 4
33. My students learn social studies at their developmental level.	0 1 2 3 4
34. My students use their evaluations of results to adjust their plans to improve next time.	0 1 2 3 4
35. There are instructional opportunities for me to construct plans for students to meet their learning goals.	0 1 2 3 4
36. My students learn how to improve their adjustments at work.	0 1 2 3 4
37. There are instructional opportunities for me to follow through on plans I construct for students to meet their learning goals.	0 1 2 3 4
38. My students make their own plans to meet their goals.	0 1 2 3 4
39. My students learn to recognize phrases that solve everyday problems.	0 1 2 3 4
40. My students learn to set goals based on what they need or want and what they are able to do to satisfy their needs and wants.	0 1 2 3 4
41. My students learn to spell words at their developmental level.	0 1 2 3 4
42. My students learn to solve reading, math, and science problems at their developmental level.	0 1 2 3 4
43 My students learn what they can do so they can make choices based on their abilities.	0 1 2 3 4
44. My students learn to spell words that solve everyday problems.	0 1 2 3 4
45. There are instructional opportunities for me to adjust student plans frequently and repeatedly in order to improve their results.	0 1 2 3 4
46. My students learn how to adjust to different situations in the community.	0 1 2 3 4
47. My students learn what they like so they can make choices based on that knowledge.	0 1 2 3 4
48. My students learn to read words at their developmental level.	0 1 2 3 4

Q#	Teacher Directedness	Your Rating	Q#	Student Directedness	Your Rating
	Table 2.2: Score the Directedness of Your Instruction				
1	I learn what my students like so I can make decisions based on their preferences.		3	There are instructional opportunities for students to adjust their plans frequently and repeatedly in order to improve their results.	
6	I learn what students can do so that I can make decisions based on their abilities.		11	There are instructional opportunities for students to act independently on their plans to meet their learning goals.	
9	I set goals for students based on what they need or want and what they are able to do to satisfy those needs and wants.		15	There are instructional opportunities for students to construct plans to meet their learning and behavior goals.	
13	I make plans for how students will meet learning and behavior goals.		17	My students monitor their results by comparing them with goals in order to determine whether their plans are working.	
21	I use my evaluations of student results to adjust their goals, plans, and actions so that they will improve next time.		19	There are instructional opportunities for students to set goals for what they want to learn and what they want to do.	
23	I have frequent opportunities to set goals for what students need and want to learn.		25	My students learn by adjusting to their results until they know what choices and actions produce the results they want.	
27	I learn about my students by adjusting to results repeatedly until I know what decisions and actions produce the results I want for them.		29	There are instructional opportunities for students to discover for themselves what they like, what they want, and what they can do to satisfy their interests and needs.	
31	There are instructional opportunities for me to discover what students like, what they want, and what they can do to satisfy their interests and needs.		34	My students use their evaluations of results to adjust their plans to improve next time.	
32	I monitor students' results by comparing them with their goals in order to determine whether my plans are working for them.		38	My students make their own plans to meet their goals.	
35	There are instructional opportunities for me to construct plans for students to meet their learning goals.		40	My students learn to set goals based on what they need or want and what they are able to do to satisfy their needs and wants.	
37	There are instructional opportunities for me to follow through on plans I construct for students to meet their learning goals.		43	My students learn what they can do so they can make choices based on their abilities.	
45	There are instructional opportunities for me to adjust student plans frequently and repeatedly in order to improve their results.		47	My students learn what they like so they can make choices based on that knowledge.	
	Total for Your Teacher Directedness			**Total for Your Student Directedness**	
	Total divided by 12 is Your Teacher-Directedness Average			**Total divided by 12 is Your Student-Directedness Average**	

Teaching Profiles of the Comparison Sample

This section describes the teaching profiles of this comparison group by identifying significant differences in the directedness of their instruction and in the functionality of their curriculum. The first analysis showed that for the entire 253-teacher sample, instruction was significantly more teacher-directed and the curriculum was significantly more basic skills focused. The second analysis focused on the instruction

	Table 2.3: Scoring the Functionality of Your Curriculum				
Q#	Basic Skills Content	Your Rating	Q#	Applied Skills Content	Your Rating
4	My students learn to add numbers during drill and practice exercises.		2	My students learn to read words to solve everyday problems.	
5	My students learn to write words at their developmental level.		7	My students learn to add numbers to solve everyday problems.	
10	My students learn to subtract numbers during drill and practice exercises.		8	My students learn to write words that solve everyday problems.	
12	My students learn to read phrases at their developmental level.		14	My students learn to subtract numbers to solve everyday problems.	
16	My students learn to divide numbers during drill and practice exercises.		20	My students learn to divide numbers to solve everyday problems.	
18	My students learn to write and read English compositions at their developmental level.		22	My students learn to adjust to signs in their communities.	
24	My students learn to multiply numbers during drill and practice exercises.		28	My students learn to multiply numbers to solve everyday problems.	
26	My students learn science concepts at their developmental level.		30	My students learn how to improve their adjustments at home.	
33	My students learn social studies at their developmental level.		36	My students learn how to improve their adjustments at work.	
41	My students learn to spell words at their developmental level.		39	My students learn to recognize phrases that solve everyday problems.	
42	My students learn to solve reading, math, and science problems at their developmental level.		44	My students learn to spell words that solve everyday problems.	
48	My students learn to read words at their developmental level.		46	My students learn how to adjust to different situations in the community.	
	Total for Your Basic Skills Focus			Total for Your Applied Skills Focus	
	Total divided by 12 is Your Basic Skills Focus Average			Total divided by 12 is Your Applied Skills Average	

and curriculum patterns of each group in the sample. For example, West Indies teachers were found to be significantly more teacher-directed and their curriculum significantly more basic skills focused; and special and general education teachers from the U.S. were found to be significantly more teacher-directed and their curriculum to be equally basic and applied skills focused. The third analysis focused on differences between the three groups on instruction and curriculum patterns. Here, special education teachers from the U.S. were found to be significantly more teacher-directed than were special education teachers from the West Indies. General and special education teachers in the U.S. were found to be significantly more student-directed than were special education teachers from the West Indies. And the curriculum used by West Indies and U.S. general education teachers was found to be significantly more basic and applied skills focused than was the curriculum used by special education teachers from the U.S. In other words, special education from the U.S. rated curricular tasks in general less frequently than did the other two groups.

Sample Profile. Figure 2.1 presents mean ratings for the 253 teachers in the sample. It shows the group to be significantly more teacher- than student-directed during instruction ($t_{103} = 12.31$; $p < .000$) and significantly more basic than applied skills focused ($t_{103} = 3.13$; $p < .002$).

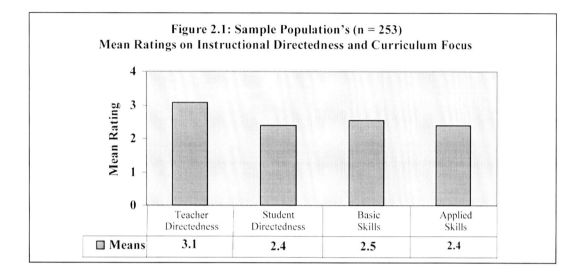

Figure 2.1: Sample Population's (n = 253) Mean Ratings on Instructional Directedness and Curriculum Focus

	Teacher Directedness	Student Directedness	Basic Skills	Applied Skills
Means	3.1	2.4	2.5	2.4

Group Profiles. Figure 2.2 presents the instruction and curriculum profiles of the West Indies teachers. It shows that the instruction of this group to be significantly more teacher- than student-directed ($t_{27} = 8.51$; $p < .000$) and the curriculum to be significantly more basic than applied skills focused ($t_{27} = 3.13$; $p < .000$).

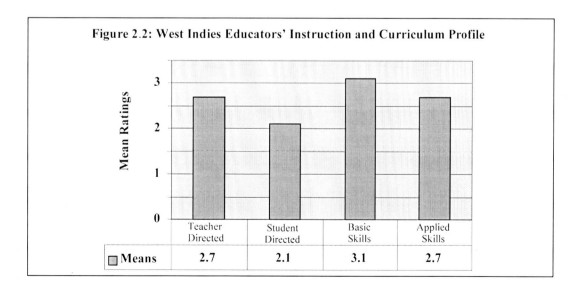

Figure 2.2: West Indies Educators' Instruction and Curriculum Profile

	Teacher Directed	Student Directed	Basic Skills	Applied Skills
Means	2.7	2.1	3.1	2.7

Figure 2.3 presents the instruction and curriculum profiles for general education teachers in the U.S. It shows this group's instruction to be significantly more teacher- than student-directed ($t_{30} = 4.155$; $p < .000$), and the curriculum used to be equally applied and basic skills focused ($t_{30} = .594$; $p < .557$).

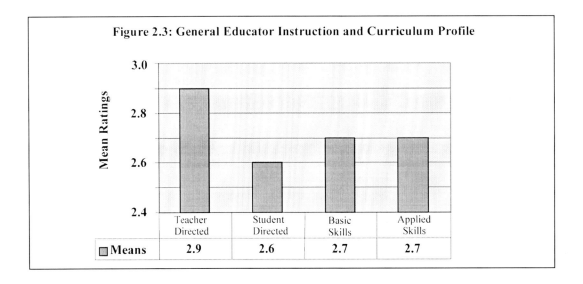

Figure 2.4 presents the instruction and curriculum profiles for the special education teachers from the U.S. It shows that this group's instruction is significantly more teacher- than student-directed ($t_{44} = 9.577$; $p < .000$), and its curriculum to be equally basic and applied skills focused ($t_{44} = .842$; $p < .405$).

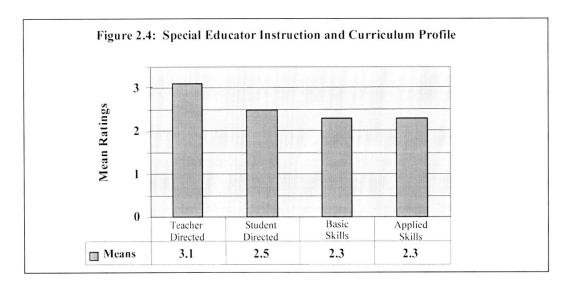

Group Differences. There were significant differences between the three groups as well. Figure 2.5 presents these results. On teacher-directedness, special education teachers rated their teacher-directedness significantly higher than did West Indies special education teachers (F = 5.944, p < .004). On student-directedness, general and special education teachers rated their student-directed instruction significantly higher than did West Indies special education teachers (F = 6.435, p < .002). On curricular emphasis, special education teachers rated their basic skills emphasis significantly lower than did West Indies teachers (F = 9.203, p < .000). And special education teachers rated their applied skills emphasis significantly lower than did general education teachers (F = 4.351, p < .041) or than did West Indies teachers (F = 4.351, p < .040).

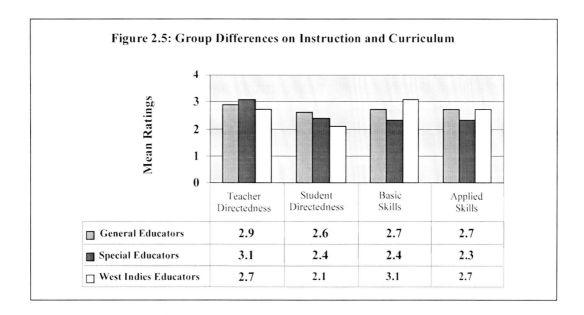

Figure 2.5: Group Differences on Instruction and Curriculum

	Teacher Directedness	Student Directedness	Basic Skills	Applied Skills
General Educators	2.9	2.6	2.7	2.7
Special Educators	3.1	2.4	2.4	2.3
West Indies Educators	2.7	2.1	3.1	2.7

Comparing Your Baseline with the Sample's Baseline

In this section you can compare your instruction and curriculum ratings with ratings for the three groups, using the chart in Figure 2.6 for the instructional comparison, and the chart in Figure 2.7 for the curriculum comparison. To conduct the first comparison, take the average ratings for the two instructional-directedness scales in Table 2.2 and plot them in your instruction space in Figure 2.6. Then make a direct comparison with the other profiles. Is your teacher-directedness like that of the other groups in that it is also higher than for student-directedness? If so, your approach is similar to theirs, and perhaps closer to a direct instruction model then a self-instruction model of teaching.

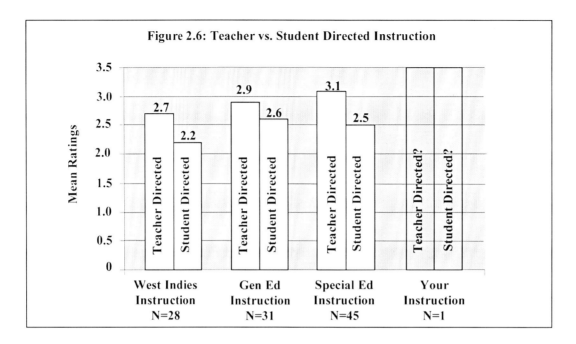

Next, compare your curricular emphasis profile with the group profiles in Figure 2.7. To do this, get the average ratings from Table 2.3 for your basic and applied curriculum emphasis and plot those scores in your curriculum space in Figure 2.7. Then compare them with the profiles of other groups. Are they similar in that

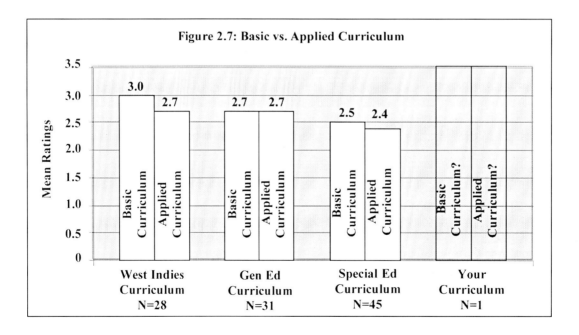

basic and applied skills are similar? If so, then your curriculum, like theirs, does not emphasize the use of new knowledge, skills and behavior in applied situations.

Step 4: The Effects of Changing Your Pedagogy

Now that you have completed your assessment, you can decide whether to shift some control to students by teaching them to use strategies described in upcoming chapters. We predict that if you shift some of that control, your instruction and curriculum profiles will also shift from teacher-directedness to student-directedness and the focus of your curriculum will also shift from basic to applied knowledge and skills. In other words, as illustrated in the Figures 2.8 and 2.9,

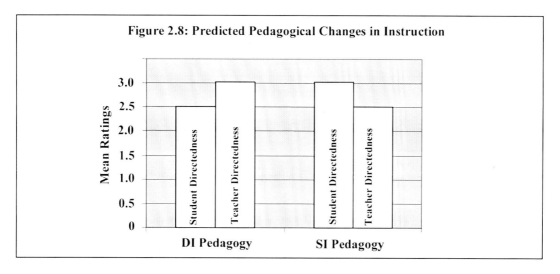

Figure 2.8: Predicted Pedagogical Changes in Instruction

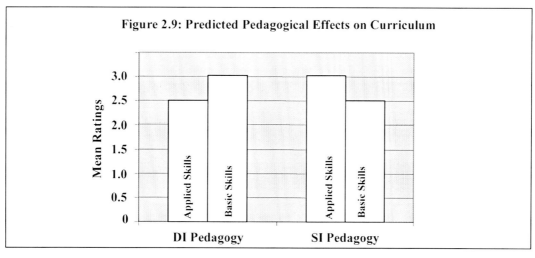

Figure 2.9: Predicted Pedagogical Effects on Curriculum

your instruction and curriculum will look less like direct instruction (DI in the figures) and more like a self-instruction (SI in the figures).

Of course, a change like this will also mean that your students have taken control of the teaching-learning functions you once controlled, for example, by identifying their own needs, interests, and abilities, by setting learning goals to meet those needs and satisfy those interests, by developing plans to meet their goals, by acting on their plans, by evaluating their progress, or by adjusting what they learn and how they learn it based on their self-evaluations.

On the other hand, if you continue to control these functions, the adjustments and learning of your students will continue to be, as Ellis (1986) described, "predetermined by . . . [you] without considering . . . [their] goals, [with] little opportunity . . . [for them] to participate in the decision-making process regarding their education, [and with] little opportunity . . . [for them] to verbally state what is being learned and why." You will, as Mithaug et al. (1988) have indicated, continue to control the "entire teaching learning environment, from setting classroom and student expectations for performance and determining what tasks the student will perform to the allocation of time for each task, prescribing how it is to be performed correcting work, providing immediate feedback, and then directing the student to the next step in the curriculum" (p. 27).

And your instruction and curriculum will continue to match that of the special education teachers in the test sample, who offered significantly fewer *opportunities* for students to control their instructional environments even than did general education teachers. Indeed, when U.S. general and special education teachers were compared, general educators rated none of the instructional opportunity items significantly higher for teacher- than for student-directedness, whereas special educators rated 5 of the 6 opportunity items significantly higher for teacher control. This *excluded* opportunities for students to (a) discover what they like, what they want, and what they can do to satisfy their interests and needs; (b) set goals for what they needed and wanted to learn; (c) construct their own plans to meet those goals; (d) follow through on plans for students to meet learning goals; and (e) adjust their plans frequently and repeatedly in order to improve their results.

Our Plan for Changing Your Pedagogy

We wrote this book to change this approach to teaching students with disabilities. Our plan to achieve this goal is presented in Table 2.4. The first column presents the baseline phase, which we attempted to establish in the first two chapters of the book. Chapter 1 explained the dominance of teacher-directedness and the rationale for student-directedness, and this Chapter 2 provided data on the likely baseline for teachers like you who tend to be teacher-directed throughout the

Table 2.4: Using Self-Instruction Pedagogy to Shift from Teacher Directedness to Student Directedness					
Chapters 1 & 2 **My Current Baseline** *Teacher-Directness*	Chapter 3 Step 1 Teaching Self-Control	Chapter 4 Step 2 Teaching Self-Regulation	Chapter 5 Step 3 Promoting Self-Determined Learning	Chapter 6 Step 4 Promoting Self-Determined IEPs and ITPs	Chapters 7 & 8 **My Expected Baseline** *Student-Directedness*
I learn what my students like so I can make decisions based on their preferences. I learn what students can do so that I can make decisions based on their abilities.	I identify my students; needs, interests, abilities	I identify my students' needs, interests, & abilities	**Student** Identified needs, interests, abilities	**Student** identified needs, interests, abilities for IEPs and Transitions	My students learn what they like so they can make choices based on that knowledge My students learn what they can do so they can make choices based on their abilities.
I set goals for students based on what they need or want and what they are able to do to satisfy those needs and wants.	I set goals to meet students' needs and interests based on their abilities.	**My students** set goals to meet their needs and interests based on their abilities	**My students** set goals to meet their needs and interests based on their abilities	**My students** set goals to meet their needs and interests based on their abilities in their IEPs and ITPs.	My students learn to set goals based on what they need or want and what they are able to do to satisfy their needs and wants.
I make plans for how students will meet learning and behavior goals.	I make plans to meet those goals	**My students** make plans to meet their goals	**My students** make plans to meet their goals	**My students** make plans to meet their IEPs and Transition goals	My students make their own plans to meet their goals.
I monitor students' results by comparing them with their goals in order to determine whether my plans are working for them.	**My students** monitor their actions to follow plans	**My students** monitor their actions to follow their plans	**My students** monitor their actions to follow their plans	**My students** monitor their actions to follow their IEP and Transition plans	My students monitor their results by comparing them with goals in order to determine whether their plans are working.
I use my evaluations of student results to adjust their goals, plans, and actions so that they will improve next time.	**My students evaluate** the results of their actions	**My students evaluate** the results of actions on their plans	**My students evaluate** the results of actions on their plans	**My students evaluate** the results of actions on their IEP and Transition plans.	My students use their evaluations of results to adjust their plans to improve next time.
I learn about my students by adjusting to results repeatedly until I know what decisions and actions produce the results I want for them.	**My students** adjust their actions and plans to improve their results	**My students** adjust their actions and plans to improve their results	**My students** adjust their actions and plans to improve their results	**My students** adjust their actions and plans to improve their progress on IEP and Transition goals	My students learn by adjusting to their results until they know what choices and actions produce the results they want.

teaching-learning process. The first column represents this expected baseline by listing items from the *Instruction and Curriculum Scale for Self-Determined Learning* that reflect the teacher-directed model of instruction.

The second component of our plan introduces the meta-adjustment strategy for students to learn (Chapters 3–6) and the self-instruction pedagogy for you to teach that strategy. Our expectation is that if you incorporate this approach in your teaching, your student-directedness will increase, and your students will be empowered to learn how to learn. Chapter 3 introduces the first three components of that strategy: self-monitoring, self-evaluation, and self-reinforcement. Chapter 4 introduces the fourth component – the expectation-results match strategy. Chapter 5 applies that meta-adjustment strategy to three-part problem solving so students can engage in discovery learning. And Chapter 6 describes instructional materials in the form of pictorial displays, cue cards, and instructional forms that help students use the meta-adjustment strategy to control the development of their IEPs and ITPs.

The final chapters of the book cover the third phase of our plan, which is represented by the last column of the table. Chapter 7 describes results of studies indicating that when teachers are unaware of the limits of teacher-directedness (Chapter 1), of their tendency to over-control student learning (Chapter 2), and of how to shift control to students (Chapters 3–6), they persist with too much teacher-directedness when they teach. Chapter 8 describes the change from this baseline that is likely when teachers like you learn about their teacher-directedness and about the meta-adjustment strategy students must learn to become self-determined learners. The items in the columns represent the shift toward student-directedness we expect once you finish the book.

REFERENCES

Bickel, W. E., & Bickel, D. D. (1986). Effective schools, classrooms, and instruction: Implications for special education. *Exceptional Children, 53*(6), 489–500.

Ellis, E. S. (1986). The role of motivation and pedagogy on the gneralization of cognitive strategy training. *Journal of Learning Disabilities, 19*(2), 66–70.

Guess, D., Benson, H. A., & Siegel-Causey, E. (1985). Concepts and issues related to choice-making and autonomy among persons with severe disabilities. *The Journal of The Association of Persons With Severe Handicaps,10,* 79–86.

Mithaug, D. E., Agran, M., Martin, J. E., & Rusch, F. R. (1988). *Why special education graduates fail: How to teach them to succeed.* Colorado Springs, CO: Ascent Publications.

Chapter 3

HOW STUDENTS DEVELOP LEARNER CONTROL

Martin Agran

Step 1 Teaching Self-Control	Step 2 Teaching Self-Regulation	Step 3 Promoting Self-Determined Learning	Step 4 Promoting Self-Determined IEPs and ITPs
I identify my students' needs, interests, abilities	I identify my students' needs, interests, & abilities	Student Identified needs, interests, abilities	Student identified needs, interests, abilities for IEPs and Transitions
I set goals to meet students' needs and interests based on their abilities	My students set goals to meet their needs and interests based on their abilities	My students set goals to meet their needs and interests based on their abilities	My students set goals to meet their needs and interests based on their abilities in their IEPs and ITPs
I make plans to meet those goals	My students make plans to meet their goals	My students make plans to meet their goals	My students make plans to meet their IEPs and Transition goals
My students monitor their actions to follow plans	My students monitor their actions to follow their plans	My students monitor their actions to follow their plans	My students monitor their actions to follow their IEP and Transition plans
My students evaluate the results of their actions	My students evaluate the results of actions on their plans	My students evaluate the results of actions on their plans	My students evaluate the results of actions on their IEP and Transition plans
My students adjust their actions and plans to improve their results	My students adjust their actions and plans to improve their results	My students adjust their actions and plans to improve their results	My students adjust their actions and plans to improve their progress on IEP and Transition goals

This is the first step in our pedagogical shift from teacher to student control. As indicated in the table above, it focuses on teaching the self-control strategies that are necessary for students to master the meta-adjustment strategy described in Chapter 4, the discovery learning strategy described in Chapter 5, and the

45

self-determination strategies for IEP and ITP development described in Chapter 6. Indeed, when students learn these self-determined learning strategies, they can direct their expectations, choices, actions, and results toward the satisfaction of their own needs and interests. Hence, they will know how to learn when pursuing their goals.

The chapter begins by identifying a significant obstacle to achieving this outcome for students with disabilities, which is the discrepancy between what teachers know about self-determination and self-control and what they do about it when they teach. It seems that although most teachers are aware of the importance of self-determination, few teach the strategies that promote it in their students. Instead, they teach in ways that promote the opposite, which is passive engagement in tasks and dependence on teachers for learning. The first step toward eliminating this problem is to teach students to use self-monitoring, self-evaluation, and self-reinforcement strategies when they learn. This chapter describes how to do this for students with a full range of disabilities.

The Gap Between Beliefs and Practice

There is an interesting paradox in the relationship between what teachers believe about students' self-determination and how they teach. Agran, Snow, and Swaner (1999) found, for example, that close to 80 percent of the educators in their survey believed that promoting self-determination was a high priority, whereas only half acted on that belief by including it in their students' IEPs. Moreover, of the multiple self-control strategies needed for self-determination, teachers usually taught but one of them. For example, 75 percent of survey respondents reported that they taught students a self-reinforcement strategy, but only 52 percent taught the equally important self-monitoring strategy. Also, only 46 percent of the respondents taught the self-instructions needed to regulate effective use of any of these strategies. Finally, most teachers believed that students with severe disabilities were incapable of benefiting from such instruction.

These findings have been reported in other studies, as well. For example, Wehmeyer, Agran, and Hughes (2000) found in their national survey of teachers of secondary-age students with mental retardation that teacher perceptions of the value of self-determination were similar. Sixty percent of the 1,219 respondents indicated they were familiar with the term "self-determination," and the majority indicated they believed promoting it would be "somewhat helpful" for success at school and "very helpful" for success after school. And when comparing teachers of students with mental retardation who received limited supports with teachers of students with mental retardation who received extensive or pervasive supports, there were other significant differences. Teachers of students with more severe disabilities were significantly less likely to rate student-directed learning as important, and, consequently, were less likely to provide the instruction needed to promote it. And when ranking reasons for these beliefs, they indicated that their students would not benefit from that type of instruction.

In all, it appears that despite the substantial attention self-determination has received from researchers in the field, very little has reached the classroom. So, as findings of positive effects have increased, translation of results into practice has not, which is regrettable given the importance of motivating and sustaining self-determined learning in all students with disabilities.

Passive Engagement

In our view, the consequences of failing to teach essential self-control strategies are learning passivity and risk avoidance among students who don't adjust well to new challenges. Indeed, students in special education tend to exhibit this inability more than their peers (Mithaug, Campeau, & Wolman, 2003; Mithaug & Mithaug, 2003), and their teachers allow these deficiencies to persist by regulating their adjustments for them. Of course, this is standard practice in a profession that trains teachers to regulate all the cues and consequences of learning. We call this teacher-directed learning because teachers, not students, direct and control everything. It is based on two beliefs derived from operant learning theory: (a) that all behavior is a function of externally controlled antecedent and consequent events, and (b) that teacher manipulation of those events produces the learning needed for school achievement.

The pedagogy derived from these beliefs is called direct instruction because it prescribes teacher manipulation of the following factors affecting student learning – setting goals, developing plans, evaluating progress, and adjusting to results (Agran, 1997). Indeed, when teachers use this pedagogy to regulate student behavior, the quality and quantity of student responding comes under control of teacher-directed cues and consequences (Greer & McDonough, 1999). Consequently, when they teach, students learn, and when they do not, students do not learn.

This is the self-regulation problem that never gets resolved in special education. Students learn when their teachers are present and in control and avoid learning when free of that control (Agran & Hughes, 1998; Mithaug, Martin, & Agran, 1987; Mithaug, Mithaug, Agran, Martin, & Wehmeyer, 2003; Sands & Wehmeyer, 1996; Wehmeyer, 1992; Wehmeyer & Sands, 1998). Then they are as disengaged, passive, and risk averse as ever. Eisenberger, Conti-D'Antonio, and Bertrando (2000) describe this persistent problem as follows:

Students with learning disabilities may not approach tasks with a plan of action nor be able to estimate accurately how much time a task will require. Some of these students may exhibit disorganized thinking and have problems in planning, organizing, and controlling their lives in academic and social settings. Their school performance, when compared with their ability, may be poor. This issue may be evidenced on report cards that are rife with Ds and Fs. The work that they do may be incomplete or of poor quality. They may attribute their lack of work to personal feelings, request adult intervention and "help" before making an attempt, or avoid tasks completely by treating teachers and other adults as enemies to fight. They often have no strategies for comprehending, retrieving, or using information. They may have a tendency to complete only work that is effortless and openly complain if work requires effort. They behave as though they have no influence over how they live their lives. These are students who have not developed self-efficacy, the belief that they have the abilities needed to produce quality work through sustained effort. Because these students approach difficult tasks without self-efficacy, they make very poor use of their capabilities. (pp. 3–4)

The Self-Control Strategies

The alternative to this instructional model is to maximize participation of students in the learning process and to teach them to make the educationally relevant decisions that will enhance their involvement in learning (Agran, King-Sears, Wehmeyer, & Copeland, 2003). To achieve this outcome, the value of instructing students on how to use student-directed learning strategies, alternatively referred to as self-regulated learning strategies, has been advanced. These strategies involve teaching students to modify and regulate their own behavior (Agran, 1997). Such strategies enable students to become active participants in their own learning. Indeed, to advance the participation of students with disabilities into general education, Fisher, Sax, and Jorgensen (1998) suggest that students need to be taught to become self-directed learners. To do so, they need to learn strategies that will allow them to problem solve; retrieve, process, and synthesize information; and manage their own behavior – in other words, self-regulate. These are skills ostensibly lacking in the traditional special education model.

Self-regulation strategies have demonstrated educational efficacy across a wide age range of learning and adaptive skills and students with a variety of disabilities, and have been well-validated and supported in the literature (see Agran, 1997; Agran & Wehmeyer, 1999; King-Sears & Carpenter, 1997; Wehmeyer, Agran, & Hughes, 1998). Among the strategies that have been extensively investigated are *self-monitoring*, *self-evaluation*, and *self-reinforcement*. These strategies aim to teach students how to monitor their performance, identify solutions to present or future problems, reinforce successful performance, and evaluate and adjust their responding. Wehmeyer (1998) included these three strategies as critical to the development of self-determination.

Self-monitoring and *self-recording* involve teaching students to observe whether they have performed a desired behavior. These procedures have been shown to improve the motivation and performance of students with disabilities (Agran, 1998; Wehmeyer et al., 1998). For example, McCarl, Svobodny, and Beare (1991) found that teaching three students with intellectual disabilities to record progress on classroom assignments improved on-task behavior for all students and increased productivity for two of the three. Agran, Sinclair, Alper, Cavin, Wehmeyer, and Hughes (2005) taught students with intellectual disabilities to monitor their own behavior so as to increase their direction-following skills. Kapadia and Fantuzzo (1988) used self-monitoring procedures to increase attention to academic tasks for students with developmental disabilities and behavior problems. Lovett and Haring (1989) demonstrated that self-recording activities enabled adults with intellectual disabilities to improve task completion of daily living activities. Last, Chiron and Gerken (1983) reported that students with intellectual disabilities, who charted their progress on school reading activities, achieved improvements in their reading levels.

Self-evaluation involves teaching the student to compare his or her performance, based on self-monitored records, to a desired goal, standard, or outcome. Schunk (1981) reported that students who verbalized cognitive strategies related to evaluating their study and work skills increased their math achievement scores. Brownell, Colletti, Ersner-Hershfield, Hershfield, and Wilson (1977) indicated that students who determined their performance standards demonstrated increased time on-task when compared with students operating under externally imposed standards.

Last, *self-reinforcement* involves teaching students to select and administer consequences to themselves (e.g., verbally telling themselves they did a good job). Self-reinforcement allows students to provide themselves with reinforcers that are accessible and immediate. Lagomarcino and Rusch (1989) used a combination of self-reinforcement and self-monitoring procedures to improve the work performance of a student with mental retardation in a community setting. Moore, Agran, and Fodor-Davis (1989) used a combination of student-directed activities, including self-instructions, goal setting, and self-reinforcement, to improve the production rate of workers with mental retardation. Self-reinforcement has also been used to improve academic performance (Stevenson & Fantuzzo, 1984), work productivity (Moore et al., 1989) and leisure/recreational skills (Coleman & Whitman, 1984).

In a review of state educational standards across diverse core skills areas, Wehmeyer (2003) reported that all students are expected to learn and apply goal setting, self-monitoring, decision making, and self-evaluation strategies; in other words, self-regulation strategies. Indeed, as mentioned previously, these tool skills provide the problem solving and organizational skills that Fisher et al. (1998) suggest are crucial for students to achieve successful educational outcomes in general education. However, as mentioned previously, few students are learning to employ these skills. The following section describes the key self-regulation strategies cited above.

Self-Monitoring

It is widely accepted that learning to monitor one's behavior is the key or prerequisite to self-regulation (Kanfer, 1970). Students who have learned to monitor their own behavior are in a better position to identify a discrepancy between an actual or existing performance level and a future or desired level. Self-monitoring involves a student's observation of his or her own behavior and recording whether the behavior had occurred or not. The strategy requires that a student understand and successfully implement two activities: (1) discriminate that the desired or goal behavior was or was not performed, and (2) accurately record the occurrence on a monitoring card or recording device. A variety of recording forms can be used to meet the needs of the specific student and the target behavior (e.g., monitoring form, abacus). Essentially any discrete behavior (i.e., a response with a distinguishable beginning and end) can be self-monitored.

Target behaviors may include any behavior the student would like to increase or decrease. For example, Gilberts, Agran, Hughes, and Wehmeyer (2001) taught five middle school students with severe intellectual disabilities, served in a variety of general education classrooms, to monitor a set of classroom "survival" skills. These skills included being in class and in seat when the bell rings, having appropriate materials, greeting the teacher and other students, asking and answering questions, sitting up straight and looking at teacher when addressed, acknowledging teacher and student comments, and using a planner. Positive changes were reported for all students, and the behaviors maintained at 100 percent for all students. Agran, Blanchard, Wehmeyer, and Hughes (2001) taught six secondary-level students with varying disabilities several classroom study and organizational skills (e.g., recording and completing assignments, using a day planner). The students were instructed to place a tally mark on a card after each time they performed the target behavior. Dramatic improvements were reported for all students.

Self-monitoring usually focuses on tasks, behaviors, or processes a student already performs. It is the most basic form of student-directed learning, and involves having a student respond to simple self-prompts or questions about what he or she has done. These may include the following:

- Am I on-task right now? Yes or No.
- Did I complete a problem? If so, I put a checkmark on my self-monitoring form.
- Am I sharing? If so, I take a token.
- Did I finish the task? If so, I put a marble in the jar.
- Was my behavior good? If good, I circle the smiley face.
- Am I organized for this class? Do I have my pencil, paper, and book? If so, I need to check each off on my organization worksheet.
- Did I bring homework today and put it where it belongs? After I do this, I need to check off on my index card that it is completed and turned in.

Students' self-monitoring should be evident in any setting, but it is especially critical in inclusive settings. Agran and Alper (2000) surveyed a sample of general and special educators, and they indicted that self-regulation/student-directed learning is one of the most important skill areas needed for successful inclusion. If students with disabilities are not using self-monitoring (or other self-regulation strategies for that matter), other people (such as general education teachers, special education teachers, or paraprofessionals) may be doing things for students that they should be learning how to do for themselves.

When to Use Self-Monitoring

Self-monitoring is an appropriate student-directed learning strategy to use after a student has learned to perform a task or behavior and the focus is on consistent and correct performance. In such a situation, the instructional focus then shifts to fluency or maintenance of the skill. Teachers can either target a category of behaviors (e.g., on-task behaviors) or a specific behavior within a category (e.g., beginning work on time). Several researchers focus on targeting "pivotal behaviors" or behaviors that are most likely to have a "ripple" or "reactivity" effect; that is, when a student with a disability can use, for example, self-monitoring to increase one behavior, there may be a desirable carry-over effect on other untargeted behaviors (Ferretti, Cavalier, Murphy, & Murphy, 1993; Koegel, Koegel, Harrower, & Carter, 1999). For example, monitoring time on-task by a student with a disability may result in (a) increased on-task behavior, (b) increased productivity of work completed, (c) increased positive teacher attention, and (d) improved grades due to increased productivity. Teachers may want to target behaviors for a student to self-monitor that may affect other behaviors in that response class.

Three general rules guide teachers when to use self-monitoring instruction with students. These include the following:

1. Students can perform skills with teacher or peer direction, and the students' next step is to perform the skill independently and proficiently. Self-monitoring promotes independence and proficiency, and in many areas it is a logical next step for instruction.
2. The student, parents, and/or school personnel agree that the targeted skill is important enough to devote self-monitoring instructional time. In this respect, all stakeholders need to understand the ultimate benefits of teaching students to self-monitor. It can well enhance motivation and independence to new levels.
3. Target a skill the student can use across different settings. When self-monitoring is successfully used to increase, for example, on-task behavior in one setting, there are many other settings in school and at home where increased on-task behavior benefits the student.

Common methods of self-recording include paper and pencil, the use of golf counters, grocery store counters, or wrist counters (Agran, 1997). Most often, paper and a pencil are all that are required to use the strategy. Needless to say, because of individual student's needs, monitoring cards may include different pictorial, verbal, numeral, or visual cues; also, color cues may be used. Finding the appropriate recording procedure may take some time. However, as long as the target behavior is easily discriminated by the student, instruction generally takes relatively little time.

A question often asked by teachers when they are considering using self-monitoring is how honest or accurate the student will be with self-monitoring. Interestingly, students who may not be accurate or honest in monitoring their behaviors can still exhibit desirable behavior changes (Reinecke, Newman, & Meinberg, 1999). Indeed, there is research to suggest that self-monitoring will produce a desired effect even if the student's recordings are inaccurate. This is because the action of self-monitoring produces a reactive effect in which the student attends more to his or her behavior and, by doing so, supplies stimuli to cue the response (Smith & Nelson, 1997). Consequently, the self-monitoring procedure will produce a desired effect without any other intervention (Agran & Martin, 1987; Wehmeyer et al. 1998). Nevertheless, it is helpful to build into the self-monitoring process occasional teacher checks for accuracy; these external checks may occur less frequently as the student becomes more proficient with self-monitoring.

Teaching Self-Monitoring

Self-monitoring is a simple activity to teach to students with disabilities. As mentioned previously, it requires that students can discriminate that the behavior has occurred and record its occurrence in some manner. Table 3.1 lists an instructional sequence. First, the behavior is identified, and the benefits of self-monitoring are discussed. Following, opportunities to practice discriminating the behavior are provided. Next, instruction is provided on using the monitoring card or recording device. Last, guided practice in self-monitoring and using the recording device across a variety of situations is provided.

Table 3.1: Teaching Self-Monitoring

1. Identify target behavior.

2. Develop a self-monitoring recording procedure.

3. Determine mastery criteria for correct self-monitoring.

4. Provide rationale to student.

5. Teach student how to self-monitor behavior.

6. Provide practice and feedback as needed.

7. Assess maintenance and generalization.

8. Intermittently monitor student's performance and use of procedure.

Peer Tutors and Self-Monitoring

Peer tutors can be invaluable instructors for self-monitoring. For example, middle school youngsters with severe disabilities who were participating in a variety of general education settings (with modified curriculum goals) were trained by their typical peers to monitor their performance of appropriate classroom skills (Gilberts et al. 2001). Based on the routines within the general education settings, a checklist listing the target behaviors, corresponding pictures, and a "yes" and "no" response block was developed. Typical peers trained and monitored the performance of their peers with severe disabilities. The students could record at any time during the class period whether or not they had performed each of the targeted behaviors. All students' classroom participation increased during the training period and was maintained after training.

With appropriate feedback, peers can be taught to systematically teach other students how to self-monitor. The advantage of using peer tutors is that it may be far more motivating for students with disabilities to receive instruction from a valued peer rather than a teacher.

Discriminative Properties of Self-Monitoring

Self-monitoring produces behavior change because it may serve as a discriminative stimulus to the student and, thus, cue the desired response. Self-monitoring allows the student to recognize that the specific target behavior has occurred, and to remind the student of present and future contingencies that exist in the environment (i.e., "If I perform this response, this will happen.") The target behavior is more likely to occur when this information is available to the student. As Mithaug (1993) suggested, the more often students have the opportunity to monitor their behavior, the more competent they will be and the more likely they will appreciate the value and utility of self-monitoring.

Self-Evaluation

Self-evaluation involves the comparison of the behavior monitored to the student's desired goal. That is, did the frequency of occurrence of the target or desired behavior match the goal set by either the teacher or the student? It is a critical self-regulation skill because it keeps the student very much aware of whether she or he is meeting a desired goal, and may potentially serve as a reinforcing event (Agran & Hughes, 1997). Self-evaluation extends self-monitoring methods from a "yes" or "no" or two-dimensional response format to a judgment and potential reward. There is some degree of assessment involved in self-monitoring when students determine whether they did or did not (i.e., the "yes" or "no" responses generally required for self-monitoring) perform a desired skill or behavior (or set of behaviors). However, self-evaluation systems require more judgment on the student's part regarding the quality of his or her performance, not just whether or not he or she performed a behavior.

When to Use Self-Evaluation

Self-evaluation provides the student with a standard to assess his or her behavior (Agran, 1997). If the standard is met, the strategy assumes a reinforcing property and promotes the likelihood of the behavior occurring in the future. If the standard is not met, the comparison may serve a corrective function by alerting the student to the apparent discrepancy between the desired performance level and the observed performance level. Of critical importance is the fact that the student provides him- or herself with the feedback and is not dependent on a teacher or other individual. For example, in a study conducted by Agran, Blanchard, and Wehmeyer (2000), a student was taught to give herself the correct amount of insulin at lunchtime. Information was collected from the student, her mother, and doctor to develop a task analysis that guided her through the process. The decision to teach the student to self-evaluate was based on the medical implications of making an error. The goal was for the student to become 100 percent proficient in following the procedures outlined since anything less than that could have life-threatening consequences. The strategy proved to be successful. In this application the student was literally given control over her own health and well-being.

In another application, three adolescents with developmental disabilities participating in general education programs were taught to evaluate their classroom behavior relative to goals they had initially set for themselves (Wehmeyer, Yeager, Bolding, Agran, & Hughes, 2003). The target behaviors included: improving listening skills, not touching other students, increasing on-task behavior, decreasing inappropriate verbalizations, and decreasing disruptive behavior. The students compared their self-monitored recordings to those of a second observer to determine if they met the self-selected goal. Improvements in behavior were reported for all students.

Last, Hoff and DuPaul (1998) taught students with attention deficit and oppositional defiant disorders to self-evaluate their compliance with classroom rules. Initially, the teacher rated the students' compliance behaviors, then the students were instructed to use the same rating system so that they could self-evaluate themselves every five minutes. The rating system consisted of a five-point Likert-type scale in which 1=poor performance and 5=excellent performance. The students' disruptive behaviors during math, recess, and social studies decreased, and compliance with rules increased and was maintained even when the teacher was not present. The students reported that they liked the self-evaluation procedure.

The advantages of self-evaluation are obvious. Needless to say, teachers in inclusive settings spend considerable time providing feedback to students with disabilities about the quality of work products, the appropriateness of their behaviors, or how well tasks are completed. When students learn how to self-evaluate their work or behavior, teachers can shift their attention to other responsibilities. Moreover, students are not dependent on teachers to judge how well they are doing – they learn how to self-evaluate their behaviors and make changes toward improvements. The gains in doing this are well-supported in the self-regulation literature (see Mithaug, Mithaug, Agran, Martin, & Wehmeyer, 2003).

Self-evaluation can be taught independently or as part of a total self-regulation package, which typically would also involve goal setting, self-monitoring, and self-reinforcement. Also, and most importantly, it serves as a critical step in any problem-solving model (Wehmeyer et al., 1998). Prior to determining if an action was successful and reinforcement was warranted, the student must evaluate (or compare) the self-monitored records to the goal standard (either self or teacher-determined). Once such an evaluation is conducted, the student is able to earn desired reinforcers or correct or adjust his or her behavior so that the goal can be achieved. Inherent in the self-regulation process is the role of the student in evaluating his or her progress in meeting goals and then with this information to make a data-based decision on what needs to be done next. The obvious advantage of self-evaluation is that it permits the student to engage in an evaluative activity that traditionally has only been done by teachers.

Typically, self-evaluation involves teaching students to evaluate their performance relative to a verbal or numerical rating system, typically a Likert-type scale. For example, on a scale of 1 to 3, the student may evaluate her performance to determine the rating she would give herself based on the quality of her performance. For example, the following evaluative options: "Is your work very good, OK, or needs improvement?" could correspond to numerical ratings of 1, 2, or 3. For students with significant disabilities, who may have difficulty understanding numerical ratings, pictures may be used (e.g., a continuum of facial expressions with the best performance depicted with a smiley face). The challenge for teachers is to develop a rating system that reveals clear distinctions among numbers or verbal descriptions.

Combining Procedures

Self-evaluation can be combined with other procedures to promote efficacy. Graphs can also be used with self-evaluation as a visual means of illustrating the gains in a student's performance. Grossi and Heward (1998) taught adults with mild mental retardation to self-evaluate their performance on job tasks by using a graphic display. The graph was divided into sections that depicted each participant's current performance level of job completion and targeted performance for the competitive standard. The graph sections near the standard were shaded to depict the desired improvement area. The participants self-monitored and then graphed their performance to evaluate how well they were moving toward accomplishing tasks at the desired quantity (i.e., number of tasks completed well) and duration (i.e., tasks completed within a certain amount of time). If the participants' performances were in the shaded area, they were reaching the targeted standard. If they were not in the shaded area, they needed to work faster or better. Participants in this study also used the graph to set goals for themselves – another factor that promotes self-directed learning (see Chapters 4 and 5).

Middle school students with learning disabilities in general education settings learned how to both self-monitor their behaviors during class and then self-evaluate their classroom behavior at the end of class to increase their on-task behaviors (Dalton, Martella, & Marchand-Martella, 1999). The students used the classroom clock as their cueing system to monitor their work performance (Are you working?) every five minutes. Also, they used a checklist noting specific classroom tasks (e.g., Did you get your homework done?), which also required a "yes" or "no" response. The checklist contained a series of questions for selected classroom behaviors required at the beginning of class (Did you get started on time?), during class (Did you self-monitor to stay on-task?), and at the end of class (Did you follow the teacher's directions?). After completing the checklist throughout each class session, the students evaluated their behavior. The intervention was responsible for increasing the student's on-task behaviors, as well as producing an increase in teachers' ratings of the students' classroom behavior.

Teaching Self-Evaluation

Generally, the same procedure used to teach self-monitoring is used to teach self-evaluation (see Table 3.2). However, an additional step is added: the student is taught to monitor and record the occurrence of the target behavior and then to discriminate whether the frequency of occurrence of the target behavior as reflected in the recordings met was higher or lower than the goal set (specified criterion). As with self-monitoring, this is done via the presentation of examples and non-examples. The student is asked to discriminate whether the recordings match the goal. In terms of the teaching sequence, the student is reinforced first for self-monitoring, then for self-evaluation, followed by self-monitoring and self-evaluation. It is recommended that both the student and teacher assess progress in goal attainment. To ensure that the consequence or next action is contingent on the quality of the student's performance, it is important that the accuracy of the student's self-evaluations is routinely monitored. Comparing the student's self-evaluation to an external evaluation made by the teacher or a designated observer provides a useful standard. After the student gains proficiency in self-evaluation, the number of external reviews can be systematically reduced and, ultimately, removed.

Table 3.2: Teaching Self-Evaluation

---

1. Identify target behavior.

2. Develop a self-evaluation procedure.

3. Determine mastery criteria for correct self-evaluation.

4. Provide rationale for student.

5. Teach student how to self-evaluate behavior.

6. Provide guided practice and feedback as needed.

7. Assess student performance in role-play, then natural situations.

8. Intermittently monitor student's performance and use of procedure.

Self-Reinforcement

Self-reinforcement represents a major component of most conceptualizations of self-regulation or self-determination. Indeed, it is an integral component of any conceptualization of self-regulation. There is evidence to suggest that self-reinforcement is as effective, if not more effective, than teacher-delivered reinforcement. Since the aim of self-regulation is to promote students' independence and control over their learning and development, self-reinforcement represents an important strategy to enhance learning.

Bandura and Perloff (1973) indicated that humans routinely compare themselves to self-prescribed standards and subsequently administer either self-rewarding or self-punishing consequences. Skinner (1953) explained in early research on self-control that when discussing the capacity of individuals to control or direct their own behavior, two responses are involved. The first refers to what he called a controlling response, which affects the probability that the controlled response will occur, and the latter is the target or desired behavior. Self-reinforcement clearly serves the function of a controlling response and increases the likelihood the target behavior will occur again in the future.

Self-reinforcement involves a procedure in which students are taught to reinforce themselves immediately after a desired behavior has occurred (Wehmeyer et al., 1998). Students are always present to administer their own consequences or feedback, so the possibility of lost reinforcement is greatly minimized. Also, students may have difficulty acquiring desired outcomes because the available consequences are too delayed, too small, or not achievable. Self-reinforcement essentially solves this potential problem in providing an opportunity for the student to reinforce him- or herself (Malott, 1984). Traditionally, teachers have always been in control of the consequences in a learning situation. Self-reinforcement shifts that control over to the student.

Two activities are involved in self-reinforcement: discrimination and delivery. A student must discriminate that the target behavior has occurred before he or she can reinforce him- or herself. In this sense, self-reinforcement is functionally linked to self-monitoring. Similar to self-monitoring, self-reinforcement has stimulus properties that may cue appropriate responding.

As with self-monitoring and self-evaluation, self-reinforcement is not acquired automatically for most students. It is safe to say that many individuals, with or without disabilities, are not experienced in overtly reinforcing themselves. However, there are ample illustrations in the research literature that demonstrate that students with varying support needs can be taught systematically to reinforce themselves. For example, Lagomarcino and Rusch (1989) taught a student with profound mental retardation to reinforce himself by placing a coin into an empty slot in a board after completing a work task. The intervention increased the student's productivity.

Teaching Self-Reinforcement

Once a student can accurately self-evaluate his or her performance, self-reinforcement instruction can be easily introduced (Agran et al., 2003). When teaching students to reinforce themselves, the following sequence is recommended (see Table 3.3). First, the target behavior is identified by the student and the teacher. Second, a criterion or desired level of performance is established. Third, a meaningful reinforcer is identified by the student. Reinforcers may include self-generated verbal statements, tally marks or tokens that can be redeemed for other reinforcers, or tangible reinforcers (e.g., edibles, objects). Next, as described previously for self-monitoring and self-evaluation, the student is taught to discriminate the behavior, record its occurrence, and compare the frequency of his or her self-monitored records to the goal standard. Next, a judgment is made if the goal standard has been met. If so, the student is taught to deliver the reinforcer to him- or herself (Note: It is recommended that the student has free access to the reinforcer. If not, the reinforcer remains under the teacher's control and thus mitigates against self-regulation or the student's achievement of self-determined learning outcomes).

As mentioned previously, the learning experiences of most students with disabilities have been largely, as well as principally, controlled by others (Agran, 1998). Accordingly, students assumed, at best, a passive role in which they have responded to the cues and consequences of teachers or paraprofessionals but had little or no active involvement in the determination, delivery, or evaluation of their educational experiences. Consequently, although providing opportunities to students to evaluate and reinforce their own behavior may at first appear to be very appealing to students, students may initially perceive opportunities to evaluate and reinforce their own behavior as very daunting or beyond their capacity. As with self-monitoring or self-evaluation, concentrated efforts must be made to ensure that self-regulatory experiences produce positive outcomes. That is, behaviors need to be selected that students can easily perform, monitor, and evaluate, and that occur frequently enough so that students can reinforce themselves.

Table 3.3: Teaching Self-Reinforcement

1. Identify target behavior.

2. Establish desired criterion for target behavior.

3. Obtain input from student on desired reinforcer.

4. Determine self-evaluation and self-reinforcement procedures.

5. Provide practice in identifying the target behavior and using the self-evaluation procedure.

6. Teach students to use self-reinforcement procedure.

7. Provide practice and feedback as needed.

8. Intermittently monitor student's performance and use of procedure.

Student-Directed Learning and Inclusion

The student-directed learning strategies discussed in this chapter enable students to regulate their own behavior, independent of external control, and allow them to become active participants in their own learning, a valued outcome of the school reform movement.

There is a growing body of research literature that suggests that student-directed learning strategies may greatly enhance a student's participation in general education. Hughes et al. (2002) investigated the effects of goal setting and self-monitoring instruction on the conversational skills (i.e., initiating conversations) of five high school students with extensive support needs (e.g., severe mental retardation, autistic-like behavior). The students indicated that they wanted to increase the amount of time they spend "hanging out" with their general education peers. They were taught to refer to an illustrated communication book in which they would verbalize a question pictured in the book, then point to that picture as a self-monitored response. Prior to instruction, the students performed the target behavior at low frequency levels (i.e., 0%), and the number of conversational topics per session ranged from 0.3 to 2.4. After recurring instruction, their performance increased dramatically, ranging from approximately 60 percent to 100 percent. Further, the number of conversational topics increased to a range of from 10.6 to 26.7 during training and a range of from 16.0 to 27.5 during maintenance. Gilberts et al. (2001) taught five middle school students with severe disabilities to self-monitor a set of classroom survival skills in their general education classrooms (e.g., Spanish, Reading, History). Target behaviors included greeting teachers and students, using a day planner, and asking and answering questions, among others. All students increased their performance levels of all target behaviors, and they reported that the instruction received made them feel a part of their classes and increased their classroom participation. Copeland, Hughes, Wehmeyer, Agran, and Fowler (2002) taught four high school students with mental retardation a set of self-regulation strategies (i.e., goal setting, self-monitoring, goal evaluation) to increase their performance of specified study skills (e.g., responding to worksheets, reading comprehension). These students were enrolled in general education cosmetology classes. The self-determination instruction produced immediate effects, increasing all of the students' report card grades to satisfactory levels. Agran et al. (2001) taught six secondary-level students with varying disabilities to use several student-directed learning strategies (i.e., goal setting, self-monitoring, problem solving) to modify selected academic, study, and social skills (e.g., scheduling time to complete assignments, completing assignments, initiating conversation with peers). All students increased their performance levels from 0–20 percent to 100 percent. Additionally, all indicated that they felt more confident and "good" about their achievements. Last, Agran, Sinclair, et al. (2005) taught six adolescents with mild to moderate disabilities to self-monitor their instruction-following skills in their content classes. Rapid gains were achieved by all. Both the student's special and general educators indicated that the students appeared to be more conscientious about their behavior. They needed less teacher-directed supervision, and tasks were completed more often. We suggest that the studies cited above represent convincing illustrations of the positive effects of self-regulation and student-directed learning strategies.

In all, student-directed learning or self-regulation strategies serve as powerful tools to enhance the participation of students with disabilities in general education. Moreover, given the current interest in self-determination, it is essential that teachers know how to teach their students these skills. Given the challenges of the general curriculum for students with severe learning needs, it is imperative that we teach them strategies that can greatly aid their competence and independent performance. Student-directed strategies represent the basic skills that will allow students to have access to the general curriculum and, ultimately, control over their own learning.

SUMMARY

In this chapter we suggested that the utilization of self-regulation strategies – specifically, self-monitoring, self-evaluation, and self-reinforcement – enable students to be active participants in the learning process and allow them to regulate their own behavior. Additionally, we have suggested that the traditional, teacher-directed special education model has denied students the opportunity to promote their own learning.

We also proposed that the self-regulation strategies discussed represent strategies that allow students to problem solve and engage in student-directed learning. There is an emerging body of research literature extolling the value of self-regulation and student-directed learning strategies in enhancing the quality of educational experiences for students with disabilities in general education, and this chapter seeks to advance this thesis.

REFERENCES

Agran, M. (1997). *Student-directed learning: Teaching self-determination skills.* Pacific Grove, CA: Brooks/Cole.

Agran, M. (1998). Student directed learning. In M. Wehmeyer & D. J. Sands (Eds.), *Making it happen: Student involvement in educational planning* (pp. 355–377). Baltimore: Paul H. Brookes.

Agran, M., & Alper, S. (2000). Curriculum and instruction in general education: Implications for severe delivery and teacher preparation. *Journal of The Association for Persons with Severe Handicaps, 25,* 167–174.

Agran, M., Blanchard, C., & Wehmeyer, M. (2000). Promoting transition goals and self-determination through student self-directed learning: The self-determined learning model of instruction. *Education and Training in Mental Retardation and Developmental Disabilities, 35,* 351–364.

Agran, M., Blanchard, C., Wehmeyer, M., & Hughes, C. (2001). Teaching students to self-regulate their behavior: The differential effects of students vs. teacher-delivered reinforcement. *Research in Developmental Disabilities, 22,* 319–332.

Agran, M., & Hughes, C. (1997). Problem solving. In M. Agran (Eds.), *Student-directed learning: Teaching self-determination skills* (pp. 171–198). Pacific Grove, CA: Brookes-Cole.

Agran, M., & Hughes, C. (1998). Introduction to the special issue of self-determination. *Journal of The Association for Persons with Severe Handicaps, 23*, 1–4.

Agran, M., King-Sears, M. E., Wehmeyer, M. L., & Copeland, S. R. (2003). *Teachers' guide to inclusive practices: Student-directed learning.* Baltimore: Paul H. Brookes.

Agran, M., & Martin, J. E. (1987). Applying a technology of self-control in community environments for mentally retarded individuals. In M. Hersen, R. M. Eisler, & P. M. Miller (Eds.), *Progress in behavior modification* (pp. 108–151). Beverly Hills: Sage.

Agran, M., Sinclair, T., Alper, C., Cavin, M., Wehmeyer, M., & Hughes, C. (2005). Using self-monitoring to increase following-directions skills of students with moderate to severe disabilities in general education. *Education and Training in Developmental Disabilities.*

Agran, M., Snow, K., & Swaner, J. (1999). Teacher perceptions of self-determination: Benefits, characteristics, strategies. *Education and Training in Mental Retardation and Developmental Disabilities, 34*(3), 293–301.

Agran, M., & Wehmeyer, M. (1999). *Innovations: Teaching problem solving to students with mental retardation.* Washington, D.C.: American Association on Mental Retardation.

Bandura, A., & Perloff, B. (1973). Relative efficacy of self-monitored and externally imposed reinforcement systems. In M. R. Goldfried & M. Merbaum (Eds.), *Behavior change through self-control* (pp. 152–161). New York: Holt, Reinhart, and Winston.

Brownell, K. D., Colletti, G., Ersner-Hershfield, R., Hershfield, S. M., & Wilson, G. T. (1977). Self-control in school children: Stringency and leniency in self-determined and externally imposed performance standards. *Behavior Therapy, 8*, 442–455.

Chiron, R., & Gerken, K. (1983). The effects of a self-monitoring technique on the locus of control orientation of educable mentally retarded children. *School Psychology Review, 3*, 87–92.

Coleman, R. S., & Whitman, T. L. (1984). Developing, generalizing, and maintaining physical fitness in mentally retarded adults: Toward a self-directed program. *Analysis and Intervention in Developmental Disabilities, 4*, 109–127.

Copeland, S. R., Hughes, C., Agran, M., Wehmeyer, M. L., & Fowler, S. E. (2002). An intervention package to support high school students with mental retardation in general education classrooms. *American Journal on Mental Retardation, 107*, 32–45.

Dalton, T., Martella, R., & Marchand-Martella, N. (1999). The effects of a self-management program in reducing off-task behavior. *Journal of Behavioral Education, 9*, 157–176.

Eisenberger, J., Conti-D'Antonio, M., & Bertrando, R. (2000). *Self-efficacy: Raising the bar for students with learning needs.* Larchmont, NY: Eye on Education.

Ferretti, R. P., Cavalier, A. R., Murphy, M. J., & Murphy, R. (1993). The self management of skills by persons with mental retardation. *Research in Developmental Disabilities, 14*, 184–205.

Fisher, D., Sax, C., & Jorgensen, C. (1998). Philosophical foundations of inclusive, restructuring schools. In C. Jorgensen (Ed.), *Restructuring high schools for all students* (pp. 29–47). Baltimore: Paul H. Brookes.

Greer, R. D., & McDonough, S. H. (1999). Is the learn unit a fundamental measure of pedagogy? *Behavior Analyst, 1*, 5–16.

Gilberts, G. H., Agran, M., Hughes, C., & Wehmeyer, M. (2001). The effects of peer delivered self-monitoring strategies on the participation of students with severe disabilities in general education classrooms. *Journal of The Association for Persons with Severe Handicaps, 26*, 25–36.

Grossi, T. A., & Heward, W. L. (1998). Using self-evaluation to improve the work productivity of trainees in a community-based training program. *Education and Training in Mental Retardation and Development Disabilities, 33*, 248–263.

Hoff, K. E., & DuPaul, G. J. (1998). Reducing disruptive behavior in general education classrooms: The use of self-management strategies. *School Psychology Review, 27*, 290–303.

Hughes, C., Copeland, S. R., Wehmeyer, M. L., Agran, M., Cai, X., & Hwang, B. (2002). Increasing social interaction between general education high school students and their peers with mental retardation, *Journal of Developmental and Physical Disabilities, 14*, 387–402.

Kanfer, F. H. (1970). Self-regulation: Research, issues, and speculations. In C. Neuringer & J. L. Michael (Eds.). *Behavior modification in clinical psychology,* (pp. 178–220). New York: Appleton-Century-Crofts.

Kapadia, S., & Fantuzzo, J. W. (1988). Training children with developmental disabilities and severe behavior problems to use self-management procedures to sustain attention to preacademic/academic tasks. *Education and Training in Mental Retardation, 23,* 59–69.

King-Sears, M. E., & Carpenter, S. L. (1997). *Teaching self-management to elementary students with developmental disabilities.* Washington, D.C.: American Association on Mental Retardation.

Koegel, L. K., Koegel, R. L., Harrower, J. K., & Carter, C. M. (1999). Pivotal response intervention I: Overview of approach. *The Journal of The Association for Persons with Severe Handicaps, 24,* 174–185.

Lagomarcino, T. R., & Rusch, F. R. (1989). Utilizing self-management procedures to teach independent performance. *Education and Training in Mental Retardation, 24,* 297–305.

Lovett, D. L., & Haring, K. A. (1989). The effects of self-management training on the daily living of adults with mental retardation. *Education and Training in Mental Retardation, 24,* 306–307.

Malott, R. C. (1984). Rule-governed behavior, self-management, and the developmentally disabled. *Analysis and Intervention in Developmental Disabilities, 4,* 199–209.

McCarl, J. J., Svobodny, L, & Beare, P. L. (1991). Self-recording in a classroom for students with mild to moderate mental handicaps: Effects on productivity and on-task behavior. *Education and Training in Mental Retardation, 26,* 79–88.

Mithaug, D. E. (1993). *Self-Regulation theory: How optimal adjustment maximizes gain.* Westport, Conn: Praeger.

Mithaug, D. E., Campeau, & Wolman, J. M. (2003). Assessing self-determination prospects among students with and without disabilities. In D. E. Mithaug, D. K. Mithaug, M. Agran, J. E. Martin, & M. L. Wehmeyer (Eds.). *Self-determined learning theory: Construction, prediction and evaluation,* (pp. 61–76). Mahwah, N.J.: Lawrence Erlbaum.

Mithaug, D. E., Martin, J. E., & Agran, M. (1987). Adaptability instruction: The goal of transitional programming. *Exceptional Children, 53,* 500–505.

Mithaug, D. E., & Mithaug, D. K. (2003). Assessing adjustment gains by students in general and special education In D. E. Mithaug, D. K. Mithaug, M. Agran, J. E. Martin, & M. L. Wehmeyer (Eds.). *Self-determined learning theory: Construction, prediction and evaluation,* (pp. 121–137). Mahwah, N.J.: Lawrence Erlbaum.

Mithaug, D. E., Mithaug, D. K., Agran M., Martin, J. E., & Wehmeyer, M. L. (2003). *Self-determined learning theory: Construction, verification, and evaluation.* Mahwah, NJ: Lawrence Erlbaum.

Moore, S. C., Agran, M., & Fodor-Davis, J. (1989). Using self-management strategies to increase the production rates of workers with severe handicaps. *Education and Training in Mental Retardation, 24,* 324–332.

Reinecke, D. R., Newman, B., & Meinberg, D. L. (1999). Self-management of sharing in three pre-schoolers with autism. *Education and Training in Mental Retardation and Developmental Disabilities, 34,* 312–317.

Sands, D. J., & Wehmeyer, M. L. (1996). *Self-determination across the life span: Independence and choice for people with disabilities.* Baltimore, MD: Paul H. Brookes.

Schunk, D. H. (1981). Modeling and attributional effects on children's achievement: A self-efficacy analysis. *Journal of Educational Psychology, 73,* 93–105.

Skinner, B. F. (1953). Science and human behavior. New York: Free Press.

Smith, D. J., & Nelson, J. R. (1997). Goal setting, self-monitoring, and self-evaluation for students with disabilities. In M. Agran, (Ed.), *Student-directed learning: Teaching self-determination skills* (pp. 80–110). Pacific Grove, CA: Brooks/Cole.

Stevenson, H. C., & Fantuzzo, J. W. (1984). Application of the "generalization map" to a self-control intervention with school-aged children. *Journal of Applied Behavior Analysis, 17,* 203–212.

Wehmeyer, M. (2003). Accessing the general curriculum: The effects of student-directed learning strategies. Paper presented at the 2003 TASH Conference, Chicago, IL.

Wehmeyer, M. (1998). Self-determination and individuals with significant disabilities: Examining meanings and misinterpretations. *Journal of The Association for Persons with Severe Handicaps, 23,* 5–16.

Wehmeyer, M. L. (2002). *Providing access to the general curriculum: Teaching students with mental retardation.* Baltimore, MD: Paul H. Brookes.

Wehmeyer, M. L. (1992). Self-determination and the education of students with mental retardation. *Education and Training in Mental Retardation, 27*, 302–314.

Wehmeyer, M. L., Agran, M., & Hughes, C. (2000). A national survey of teachers' promotion of self-determination and student-directed learning. *The Journal of Special Education, 34*(2), 58–68.

Wehmeyer, M. L., Agran, M., & Hughes, C. (1998). *Teaching self-determination to students with disabilities: Basic skills for successful transition.* Baltimore, MD: Paul H. Brookes.

Wehmeyer, M. L., Lattin, D., & Agran, M. (2001). Promoting access to the general curriculum for students with mental retardation: A decision-making model. *Education and Training in Mental Retardation and Developmental Disabilities, 36*, 329–344.

Wehmeyer, M. L., & Sands, D. J. (1998). *Making it happen: Student involvement in education planning, decision making, and instruction.* Baltimore, MD: Paul H. Brookes.

Wehmeyer, M. L., Yeager, D., Bolding, N., Agran, M., & Hughes, C. (2003). The effects of self-regulation strategies on goal attainment for students with developmental disabilities in general education. *Journal of Physical and Developmental Disabilities, 15*, 79–91.

Chapter 4

HOW STUDENTS ADJUST TO
LEARNER CONTROL

Deirdre K. Mithaug

Step 1 Teaching Self-Control	**Step 2** **Teaching** **Self-Regulation**	Step 3 Promoting Self-Determined Learning	Step 4 Promoting Self-Determined IEPs and ITPs
I identify my students' needs, interests, abilities	I identify my students' needs, interests, & abilities	Student Identified needs, interests, abilities	Student identified needs, interests, abilities for IEPs and Transitions
I set goals to meet students' needs and interests based on their abilities	**My students** set goals to meet their needs and interests based on their abilities **Goal-setting strategy**	My students set goals to meet their needs and interests based on their abilities	**My students** set goals to meet their needs and interests based on their abilities in their IEPs and ITPs
I make plans to meet those goals	**My students** make plans to meet their goals **Self-planning strategy**	My students make plans to meet their goals	My students make plans to meet their IEPs and Transition goals
My students monitor their actions to follow plans: Self-monitoring strategy	**My students** monitor their actions to follow their plans **Self-monitoring strategy**	My students monitor their actions to follow their plans	My students monitor their actions to follow their IEP and Transition plans
My students evaluate the results of their actions Self-evaluation strategy	**My students evaluate** the results of actions on their plans **Self-evaluation strategy**	My students evaluate the results of actions on their plans	My students evaluate the results of actions on their IEP and Transition plans
My students adjust their actions and plans to improve their results Self-reinforcement strategy	**My students** adjust their actions and plans to improve their results **Self-adjustment strategy**	My students adjust their actions and plans to improve their results	My students adjust their actions and plans to improve their progress on IEP and Transition goals

The next step in this shift of instructional control involves teaching the five strategies that help students regulate their responses to any learning challenge. As indicated in the table above, three of these strategies – self-monitoring, self-evaluation, and self-adjustment – were introduced in the previous chapter and the two remaining strategies – goal setting and self-planning will be introduced in this chapter, which shows how *goal-setting strategies* help students regulate the setting of expectations for what they can get from a new situation; how *self-planning strategies* help them regulate their choices on *how* to produce those results; how *self-monitoring strategies* help students match their responses to their choices; how *self-evaluation strategies* help students identify matches between their *results* and *expectations*, and finally how *self-adjustment strategies* help students change their expectations, choices, and actions repeatedly until they get results that match their expectations. Indeed, when students use these five strategies in concert they learn how to meet goals in a manner that is similar to how people who succeed in business, industry, science, and the arts meet theirs. Consequently, they learn from those goal-directed adjustments, too (Agran, 1997; Garfield, 1986; Hill, 1960; Martin, Mithaug, Husch, Frazier, & Huber Marshall, 2003; Martin, Mithaug, Oliphint, Husch, & Frazier, 2002; Martin, Mithaug, Cox, Peterson, Van Dycke, & Cash, M. E., 2003; Mithaug, D. E., 1991, 1993, 1996a,1996b, 1998, 2003; Mithaug, D. K., 1998, 2002; Mithaug, & Mithaug, 2003a, 2003b, 2003c, 2003d, Mithaug, Martin, & Agran, 1987; Mithaug, Martin, Agran, & Rusch, 1988; Mithaug, Martin, Husch, Rusch, & Agran, 1988; Mithaug, Mithaug, Agran, Martin, & Wehmeyer, 2003; Mithaug, Wehmeyer, Agran, Martin, & Palmer, 1998; Robbins, 1987).

The instructional approach that makes this type of self-determined learning possible for students with disabilities is based on early studies suggesting that choice opportunities *and* self-regulation are necessary for autonomous learning and performance in school and beyond (Mithaug, Mithaug, Agran, Martin, & Wehmeyer, 2003). This chapter reviews some of those studies in order to highlight their importance in establishing autonomous learning and performance and in promoting their generalization across subjects, behaviors, settings, and time.

Choice Opportunities and Self-Regulation

As you know by now the central goal of self-instruction pedagogy is to improve the self-regulation of students with learning and behavior problems. Indeed, for decades scholars and researchers have commented on its importance for a full range of students experiencing difficulties learning on their own. Whitman (1990), for example, suggested that students with severe cognitive disabilities fail to develop this capability because they lack the "complex response system that enables individuals to examine their environments and their repertories of responses for coping with those environments, to make plans (decisions) about how to act, to evaluate the desirability of the outcomes of their actions, and to revise their plans as necessary" (p. 373). Zimmerman (1990) made a similar claim about underachievers without disabilities who also lack that ability to "select, organize, and create advantageous learning environments for themselves and plan and control the form and amount of their own instruction" (p. 13).

Self-instruction pedagogy is singularly suited to dealing with these challenges because it prescribes instruction that provides the just-right choice opportunities that provoke the self-regulated adjustments required for autonomous learning (Mithaug, 1991, 1993, 1996a, 1996b, Mithaug, Mithaug, Agran, Martin, & Wehmeyer, 2003). Indeed, all learners benefit from this instructional approach because of its focus on helping students regulate their learning in non-instructed situations. It teaches strategies that help learners regulate their adjustments so they can produce the results they want.

There is substantial research indicating how this is possible for all students, including those in the most difficult of learning-to-learn situations, as Chapter 1 reported. Mithaug and Hanawalt, (1978) and Mithaug and Mar (1980) showed, for example, that just-right choice opportunities were effective in provoking non-verbal young adults with severe to profound cognitive disabilities to adjust their work assignments in accordance with their interests rather than the interests of their teachers. Dunlap, DePerzel, Clarke, Wilson, Write, White and Gomez (1994) showed that students with behavior problems improved their on-task work and productivity when given opportunities to choose their work assignments. Miller and Kelley (1994) showed that children improved their homework assignments when they were given opportunities to choose their goals; and Olympia, Sheridan, Jenson, and Andrews (1994) showed that sixth grade students improved their schoolwork assignments when given opportunities to choose their performance expectations and self-regulation strategies to regulate those adjustments. Other studies have reported similar results when choice opportunities and self-regulation strategies were in effect (Copeland & Hughes, 2002; Grossi & Heward, 1998; Sulzer-Azaroff, Pollack, Hamad, & Howley, 1998).

There is also evidence indicating that use of five self-regulation strategies produces a powerful generalized, adaptive effect across subjects, tasks, settings, and time – the holy grail of effective instruction. Stevenson and Fantuzzo (1984, 1986) reported such effects in studies of underachieving students who learned to use a self-regulation card to control their use of the five strategies. In that research, students used a card to choose their work assignments using goal setting and self-planning strategies, to monitor their responses to those plans using a self-recording strategy, to evaluate their results using a self-evaluation strategy, and to correct their work and choose reinforcers using a self-adjustment strategy. The effects of this approach to strategy use was stunning in that significant generalizations occurred across all possible combinations of subjects, tasks, settings, and times.

Our explanation for these unprecedented adaptive effects is straightforward. Use of the card helps students deal with choice demands that inevitably arise in non-instructed situations. For example, the goal-setting strategy of the card helps students deal with the choice uncertainty of knowing what or how much to expect from a new situation. The self-planning strategy of the card helps them deal with the choice uncertainty of knowing how best to meet their expectations. The self-recording strategy of the card helps them deal with the choice uncertainty of knowing how to act on their circumstances. The self-evaluation strategy of the card helps them deal with the choice uncertainty of knowing how to react to their results. And the self-adjustment strategy of the card helps them deal with the choice uncertainty of knowing what to do when their results did not match their expectations.

In addition, card use itself is motivating because the act of choosing is often self-reinforcing (Deci & Ryan, 1985), which explains perhaps why generalization occurs so readily when card use is in effect. On the one hand, the self-regulation enabled through use of the card allows learners to make effective choices and on the other hand the act of making those choices when using the card is self-reinforcing. In other words, the two essential conditions for autonomous learning – choice opportunities *and* self-regulation – are present when students use a self-regulation card.

This suggests that when either of these two conditions – choice opportunities or self-regulation strategy use – is absent, autonomous adjustment and learning are less likely. There is evidence of this, too, in that when students are taught to use the five strategies in ways that enhance choice making, they are more likely to engage in autonomous work than when they are taught in ways that minimize choice. This was reported in a study investigating the effects of choice opportunities and self-regulation strategy use among young children with severe and multiple disabilities (Mithaug, 1998; 2002; Mithaug & Mithaug, 2003b,c). In this multiple baseline across subjects study, choice opportunity effects were compared during teacher and student-directed instruction. The participants were 5–7 year old students with speech/language impairments, pervasive developmental disorders, attention deficits and hyperactivity, autism, and developmental delays.

During the teacher-directed instructional condition that minimized choice-making opportunities, the teacher instructed students individually on strategy use by *making choices for students.* For example, when she instructed them to choose subjects to be worked and to record the number of worksheets to be completed during work periods, she demonstrated both choice making by choosing the subjects to be worked and recording by writing the number of assignments to be completed. Next, when students worked those tasks she showed them how to record their completed work by making a mark on the card and she showed them how to evaluate their results by circling a "yes" on the card when the subjects and tasks worked matched the subjects and assignments assigned. Then she showed them how to reinforce themselves for recorded yeses by giving them a prize from the prize box for the yeses received on the card. Last, she showed students how to adjust by recording a different set of subjects to be worked and a different number of worksheets to be completed for next work cycle.

During the student-directed instructional condition that maximized choice opportunities, the teacher instructed students individually to make choices using the strategy card. For the goal-setting and self-planning strategy components of the card, she instructed students to choose the subjects they wanted to work and the number of worksheets they planned to complete for each subject. During the 20-minute work period that followed, she instructed students to record the number of worksheets they completed for each subject and to evaluate their work by circling a "yes" when the worksheets they completed matched the number they assigned themselves for each subject, or by circling a "no" when they did not match. Next, she instructed them to choose a prize from the reward box when they had yeses in their evaluations. Last, she instructed students to complete the next work cycle by completing another self-regulation card just as they completed the first one, this time adjusting (changing) their selection of goals and/or their choice of plans (number of assignments to be completed for each subject) if they wanted.

The effects of these two instructional approaches were assessed in 30-minute autonomous work sessions that followed instruction. During these periods students worked alone at workstations, where they were free to use their self-regulation cards to regulate their work on worksheets provided in folders at their desks. The instructor provided no instructions, prompts, or rewards.

Figure 4.1 presents the self-regulated work that occurred during autonomous work sessions. As indicated in the figure, self-regulated performance was significantly higher during the work sessions that followed student-directed instruction than during the work sessions that followed teacher-directed instruction. In other words, students used the five self-regulation strategies – goal setting, self-planning, self-monitoring, self-evaluation, and self-adjustment – more frequently after they had experienced the choice opportunities provided by student-directed instruction. They also completed more worksheets during those sessions, as Figure 4.2 indicates.

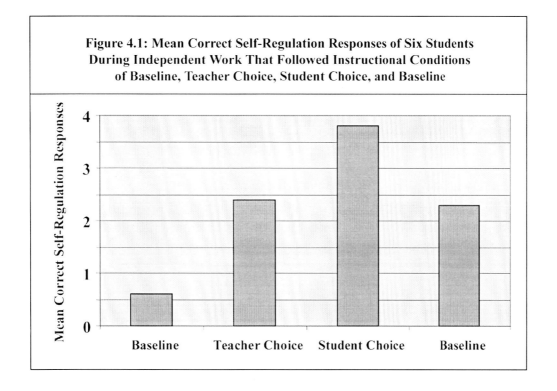

Figure 4.1: Mean Correct Self-Regulation Responses of Six Students During Independent Work That Followed Instructional Conditions of Baseline, Teacher Choice, Student Choice, and Baseline

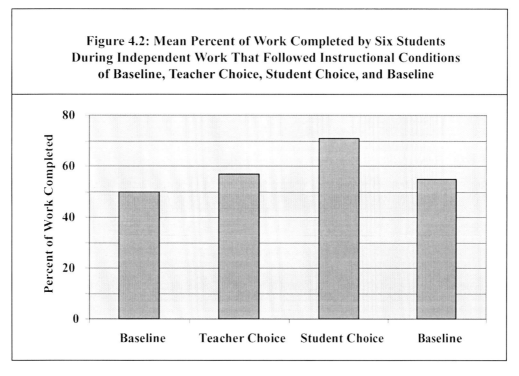

Figure 4.2: Mean Percent of Work Completed by Six Students During Independent Work That Followed Instructional Conditions of Baseline, Teacher Choice, Student Choice, and Baseline

These findings were replicated in a second experiment that included four of the students from the first experiment. Here, instructional interventions were administered in a reversal design that included a multiple baseline across two student pairs who experienced alternate sequences of teacher-and student-choice instruction. The first group of two received a reversal sequence that included a baseline, teacher-directed instruction, student-directed instruction, and a return to baseline, and the second group of two received a staggered reversal sequence that included a baseline, student-directed instruction, teacher-directed instruction, and a return to baseline. Figures 4.3 and 4.4 present these results, which are similar in that students were more engaged and productive during autonomous work that followed student-directed instruction which maximized choice than during the sessions following teacher-directed instruction which minimized choice.

In both experiments, these young children with severe disabilities used a strategy card to regulate their schoolwork during autonomous work periods of sitting alone at their workstations, opening folders for various subject topics, reviewing worksheets assignments, making choices about what and how much to do, and then regulating their behavior by working assignments, recording completed

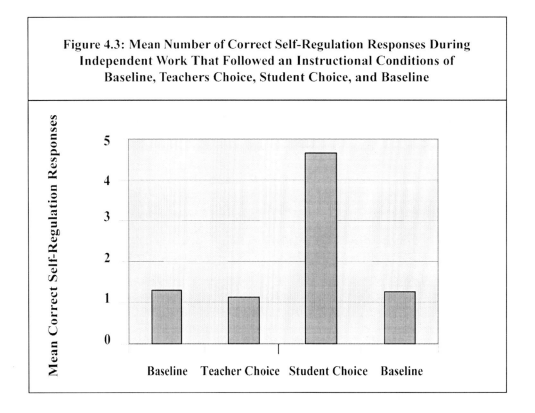

Figure 4.3: Mean Number of Correct Self-Regulation Responses During Independent Work That Followed an Instructional Conditions of Baseline, Teachers Choice, Student Choice, and Baseline

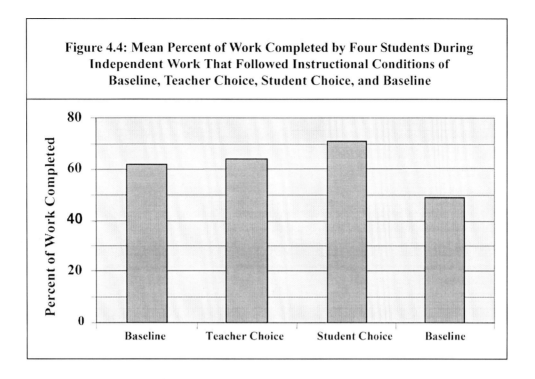

Figure 4.4: Mean Percent of Work Completed by Four Students During Independent Work That Followed Instructional Conditions of Baseline, Teacher Choice, Student Choice, and Baseline

work, and evaluating their results to determine whether the work they completed *matched* the goals they set and the plans they made. Moreover, their engagement during these work adjustment cycles persisted as they repeatedly regulated adjustments to their own goals and results (Mithaug, 2002).

Teaching Self-Regulation

The pedagogy responsible for these autonomous performance effects was self-instruction, which covers a wide range of methods that help learners adjust and learn from their adjustments. There are two types of strategies covered by the pedagogy, one that focuses on the generic self-regulation described here, and the other that focuses on specific subject matter strategies that help learners improve their word recognition, reading comprehension, word problem skills, study skills, note taking, test taking and other academic skills. Both types of strategy instruction – self-regulated adjustments and subject-matter adjustments – help learners direct and control their learning. They help learners self-instruct.

This chapter focuses on the first-order strategies all learners must master to become autonomous learners – goal setting, planning, monitoring, evaluating, and adjusting. It is important to start here when attempting to build autonomous learning capabilities because once students have mastered these five self-regulation strategies, they can use them to regulate use of second order, subject matter strategies to master the varied content of a curriculum.

When teaching these strategies, it is also helpful to consider three methods of support for use of these first-order strategies. For example, mnemonic supports are appropriate for students who only need a reminder of the strategy to use when regulating their learning. The self-talk support approach is appropriate for students who need more than that. It consists of verbal phrases that identify the strategy to use and when. The permanent product support method provides a combination of reminders and direction and works with nearly all students. This chapter reviews each and uses the latter to illustrate how to teach the five strategies. The next section describes the classroom adjustments that you may want to consider if your students are to have the opportunities they need to practice the five self-regulation strategies on their own.

Autonomous Learning Center

One way to ensure students have sufficient opportunities to develop their capacity for autonomous learning is to establish a location in your classroom where they can engage in repeated episodes of self-regulation while using the five strategies. Ideally, this will be a quiet area where they can come and go throughout the day to work autonomously. Of course, it will need to be stocked with materials that students can work on independently. That way their work will be autonomous, meaning it will free them of your direction and encouragement. Also any rules for the area should be posted to remind students of the behavior that is appropriate while working in the center. It is also a good idea to schedule times each day for various independent work projects. For example, you might want to schedule five to 30-minute blocks daily in the morning and afternoon for different purposes. In the studies reported above, autonomous work was scheduled during 20-minute periods in the morning and the afternoon. During morning sessions students worked academic subjects using their self-regulation cards and during afternoon sessions, they worked on other tasks of their choice, like coloring and reading. During both sessions they raised their hands when they had questions or needed help.

Instructional Levels

As indicated above, there are three methods of support to consider when teaching the five self-regulation strategies: the memory approach, the self-talk approach, and the permanent product approach. A brief description of each follows. Identify one that best matches your student's capabilities and then think about it as we discuss how to teach the five strategies in the sections that follow.

MNEMONIC SUPPORTS. This type of strategy support is effective with a wide range of students. There are three types of these memory enhancement techniques: the organization and association method, the visualization or mental imagery method, and rehearsal method (Bos & Vaughn, 1991). The organization and association method arranges or associates information in ways that make it easier to remember. Hetzroni and Shavit (2002), for example, associated picture cues with letters to enhance their recall in children with mental retardation. For self-regulation training this might involve associating each strategy with a letter that forms an acronym (Bos & Vaughn, 1991). Table 4.1 illustrates. Here the strategies are associated with the letters of an acronym: **G-P-A** standing for goals, plans, and actions, and **E-R-A** standing for evaluate, reward, and adjust. To learn these associations, students could sort strategies into the categories represented by their letter in the acronym.

Table 4.1: Example of Mnemonic Cues for Self-Regulation
Goals to meet
Plans to meet goals
Actions monitored to meet plans
Evaluations of results
Rewards for results that match goals and plans
Adjustments in next goals and plans

In visualization, students increase their memory of important information by creating a mental picture of the essential feature of the content. For example, students might visualize actions associated with each of the strategies, with one action associated with setting goals, another for planning actions, and so on. When rehearsing the technique, students would be instructed to say the strategies aloud or to visualize them in their heads repeatedly until they felt confident they could remember them. Mastropieri and Scruggs (1998) and Mastropieri, Sweda, and Scruggs (2000) found that using devices like peg words, key words, and letter strategies improved the memory of students with learning disabilities.

SELF-TALK SUPPORTS. Self-talk phrases are also useful in reminding students what to do and when. This requires that you teach students to utter some key statements that remind them what to do or what not to do (O'Leary & Dubey, 1979). This is often used and generally effective for improving math skills, reading comprehension, instruction following, and work skills. It is also helpful in the maintenance and generalization of learning (Agran, 1997; Agran & Martella, 1991; Hughes, 1991).

To instruct students to use self-talk to control their use of the strategies, model the statement that represents a strategy while the student is using it to complete a task and then ask her to do the same. Of course, the student must be able to implement the strategy before this will work. Remember, self-talk does not teach students to do something they have not yet learned or mastered. It only reminds them when or how to do it after they have the behavior or skill. Given this, it is a good idea to give students practice time using a strategy before introducing self-talk to control its application. Once students know the essential self-talk phrases to utter when implementing a corresponding strategy, provide them with opportunities to use the two together while working on their own. This will indicate whether the self-talk phases are effective controls of strategy use (Zirpoli & Melloy, 1997). Table 4.2 illustrates a sequence of self-talk questions that correspond to the self-regulation cycle of choosing, working, evaluating, adjusting. You can use these phrases when modeling the use of self-talk to regulate independent work.

Table 4.2: Use of Self-Talk to Promote Self-Regulation Strategy Use	
Self-Talk For Self-regulation	**Corresponding Self-Regulation**
What is my goal today?	Student sets goals
What do I need to do to meet my goal today?	Student makes plans to meet goals
What did I do today?	Student monitors actions on plans
Did I meet my goal today?	Student compares results with plans and goals
How many rewards for met goals did I get?	Student self-rewards for matches between results, plans, and goals
How many goals will I set next time?	Student adjusts goals and repeats the sequence

SELF-REGULATION CARD. The self-regulation card with its written or pictorial cues works particularly well for nearly all students, as indicated earlier in studies with underachieving students (Stevenson & Fantuzzo, 1984; 1986) and students with severe disabilities (Mithaug, 1998). The card provides clear cues about what to do and when. In a sense, the card is like the daily list you use to remember what to do throughout the day. The self-regulation card reminds students to set goals for subjects they will engage, to specify what they will accomplish for each, to write down what they accomplished, to evaluate their accomplishments, and to set new goals based on those evaluations.

The card is effective because it presents the strategies in a clear and unambiguous format. One section of the card provides cues for setting goals, another provides cues for making plans to reach those goals, a third section provides written cues for monitoring the completion of those plans, a fourth section provides written cues for evaluating results, a fifth section provides cues for delivering rewards and completed work that matched work that was planned for each goal, and a sixth section provides cues for adjusting goals for the next cycle. The card design presents four of the strategies in a left to right order, the subject matter to be worked in a top to bottom order, and the last strategy to be used at the bottom of the card. When students learn to complete the card, they know when and how to (a) set goals for what they will accomplish, (b) make plans for meeting those goals, (c) monitor their actions on their plans, (d) evaluate their results, and (e) adjust by rewarding themselves for met goals and setting new goals based on those outcomes. In other words, they will know how to regulate their adjustments to get the results they want.

Teaching Tips

This section presents some tips for teaching the strategies in the sequence that they appear on the self-regulation card. For example, the first step teaches goal setting by having students complete that column of the card, the second step teaches self-planning by having them complete that column of the card, and so on. The last step teaches them to adjust. They add up the goals they met to determine how many reward points they earned and based on that they decide how many goals they will meet on their next card.

STEP 1: GOAL SETTING. To teach goal setting present the goal-setting column by itself as indicated in Table 4.3. Ask students to choose the topics (subjects) they want to work by circling a yes or no in the column for each subject listed. In the sample card in the Table 4.4, the student chose to work on reading, math, and writing goals by circling "yes" for those options. She indicated that she did not choose to work on science, social studies, or other activities goals by circling "no" for those options. After choosing subject goals, instruct students to use the card to guide their activities during the autonomous work session. When the session ends, review the subjects worked by asking students whether they worked on their goals. Point to each subject on the card and ask students whether it was a goal and whether they worked on it. Only provide praise for matches between goals chosen and subjects actually worked, as the purpose is to teach students to work *only* those subjects they chose for goals. Provide corrections for mismatches, which would include work on subjects not selected as goals or non-work on subjects selected as goals. When students consistently match their goals with their work, they understand that setting a goal means that they intend to work on activities related to that goal.

Table 4.3 Step 1: Teaching Goal Setting on Self-Regulation Card
Is My Goal Reading? **Yes**/No
Is My Goal Math? **Yes**/No
Is My Goal Science? Yes/**No**
Is My Goal Social Studies? Yes/**No**
Is My Goal Writing? **Yes**/No
Is My Goal Other Activity? Yes/**No**

Table 4.4 Step 2: Student Self-Plans on Self-Regulation Card	
Is My Goal Reading? **Yes**/No	What Will I Do in Reading? **Read 1 chapter in book**
Is My Goal Math? **Yes**/No	What Will I Do in Math? **Complete a math worksheet**
Is My Goal Science? Yes/**No**	What Will I Do in Science? **Nothing**
Is My Goal Social Studies? Yes/**No**	What Will I Do in Social Studies? **Nothing**
Is My Goal Writing? **Yes**/No	What Will I Do in Writing? **Write a Journal entry**
Is My Goal Other Activity? Yes/**No**	What Will I Do in Other Activity? **Nothing**

STEP 2: SELF-PLANNING. To learn self-planning, students indicate what they expect to accomplish in a second column that follows the goal column. In the first row of the sample chart in Table 4.4 for example, the student chose to read one chapter in the second column in order to meet the reading goal selected in the first column. In the second row, she chose to complete one math worksheet in the second column in order to meet the math goal selected in the first column. In the third row, she indicated she would do nothing in science in the second column because she did not choose that goal in the first column. In the fourth row, she also indicated she would do nothing in social studies in column 2 because she did not choose that goal in column 1. In the fifth row, she indicated she would write a journal entry in column 2 because she chose a writing goal in column 1. And in the last row, she indicated she would do nothing in column 2 for other activities because she did not choose that goal in column 1.

After completing these two steps (two columns), review the entries with the student, this time focusing on the match between goals and plans. Do they match? In this example, the student indicated in column 1 that she would work on math, reading, and writing goals but not on science, social studies, or other activity goals. In column 2 , she entered work activities for reading, math, and writing goals, and "nothing" for science, social studies, and other activity that did not have goals. In other words, she wrote a plan that matched her goals. So she received praise for all those matches. Conduct the same review after your students have entered their plans, providing praise for matches and corrections for mismatches. Repeat the activity of writing plans for different combinations of goals set until students consistently write plans that match their goals.

STEP 3: SELF-MONITORING. Add the third column to the card to teach self-monitoring, as indicated in Table 4.5. In this card, students indicate in column 3 the work they actually completed for each goal. In the first row of the chart in the table, for example, the student indicated in column 3 that she read Chapter 1 in a book for her reading goal in column 1. In the second row, she indicated in column 3 that she did nothing for the math goal in column 1. In the third row,

Table 4.5 **Step 3: Student Self-Monitors on Self-Regulation Card**		
Is My Goal Reading? **Yes**/No	**What Will I Do in Reading?** Read 1 chapter in book	**What Did I Do In Reading?** Chapter 1 in book
Is My Goal Math? **Yes**/No	**What Will I Do in Math?** Complete a math worksheet	**What Did I Do In Math?** Nothing
Is My Goal Science? Yes/**No**	**What Will I Do in Science?** **Nothing**	**What Did I Do In Science?** Science Worksheets
Is My Goal Social Studies? Yes/**No**	**What Will I Do in Social Studies?** **Nothing**	**What Did I Do In Social Studies?** **Nothing**
Is My Goal Writing? **Yes**/No	**What Will I Do in Writing?** Write a Journal entry	**What Did I Do in Writing?** Journal entry
Is My Goal Other Activity? Yes/**No**	**What Will I Do in Other Activity?** Nothing	**What Did I Do In Other Activity?** Nothing

she indicated in column 3 that she completed science worksheets for her science goal in column 1. In the fourth row, she indicated in column 3 that she did nothing in social studies, for which she had no goal in column 1. In the fifth row, she indicated in column 3 that she wrote a journal entry for her writing goal in column 1. And in the last row, she indicated in column 3 that she did nothing for the other activity goal, for which she had no goal in column 1.

To get students to complete this component of the card, request that they record the work they complete in the third column of the card immediately after they finish it. This will require that they pay attention to the card as they work so they can record what they did or did not do on their card. Again, when the period ends, review the self-record column with students by requesting them to show you the work they completed in that column. Remember, the goal for this instruction step is *accurate* self-monitoring and not compliance to the plan. That comes later.

STEP 4: SELF-EVALUATING. Once students accurately record their work during autonomous work periods, they are ready to evaluate what they recorded using the fourth column in the card, as illustrated in Table 4.6, which answers the question "Did I Meet My Goal?" To get this answer, students compare what they recorded in column 3 with their plan in column 2 and their goal in column 1. When all three match, they answer, "yes" that they met their goal. When any of the three columns do not match, they answer "no" they did not meet their goal. It is important to acknowledge both answers with approval because the goal is to teach accurate evaluations. Consequently, if the goal or plan is not met, a "no" response is as commendable as a "yes" given that both are based on matches. In this step you want to praise students for accuracy (correct yeses and correct noes) rather that for success – only correct yeses.

Provide instruction on this column immediately after students finish an autonomous work session and have entered their responses in the first three columns of the card. Then point to column 4 of the card and ask whether the work they completed in column 3 matched their plan in column 2 and their goal in column goal 1. Next, point to the goal, plan, and the result and ask whether the three match, and if they did (or did not) whether they met their goal. If the three match, instruct them to write (or circle) a "yes" in that row. If there is no match, instruct them to write (or circle) a "no" for that row's evaluation. Repeat these instructions for each subject on the card, always emphasizing the match between what was accomplished in column 3 with what was expected and planned in columns 1 and 2. Provide praise for correctly entered yeses and correctly entered noes.

Table 4.6 illustrates this component of the self-regulation card. In the first row, the student wrote a "yes" in column 4 indicating that the work recorded in column 3 matched her goal and plan in columns 1 and 2. In the second row, she wrote a

			Table 4.6 Step 4: Student Self-Evaluates On Self-Regulation Card			

Is My Goal Reading?	**What Will I Do in Reading?**	**What Did I Do In Reading?**	**Did I Match (Meet) My Goal?**	
Yes	Read 1 chapter in book	Chapter 1 in book	**YES**	No
Is My Goal Math?	**What Will I Do in Math?**	**What Did I Do In Math?**	**Did I Match (Meet) My Goal?**	
Yes	Complete a math worksheet	Nothing	Yes	**NO**
Is My Goal Science?	**What Will I Do in Science?**	**What Did I Do In Science?**	**Did I Match (Meet) My Goal?**	
No	Nothing	Science Worksheets	Yes	**NO**
Is My Goal Social Studies?	**What Will I Do in Social Studies?**	**What Did I Do In Social Studies?**	**Did I Match (Meet) My Goal?**	
No	Nothing	Nothing	**YES**	No
Is My Goal Writing?	**What Will I Do in Writing?**	**What Did I Do in Writing?**	**Did I Match (Meet) My Goal?**	
Yes	Write a Journal entry	Journal entry	**YES**	No
Is My Goal Other Activity?	**What Will I Do in Other Activity?**	**What Did I Do In Other Activity?**	**Did I Match (Meet) My Goal?**	
No	Nothing	Nothing	**YES**	No

"no" in column 4 indicating that the work recorded in column 3 did not match her goal and plan in columns 1 and 2. In the third row, she also wrote a "no" in column 4 indicating that her completed science work in column 3 did not match her goal or plan for science in columns 1 and 2 because she completed worked she did not intend to work. Therefore, she did not meet that goal. In the fourth row, she wrote a "yes" in column 4 indicating that her doing nothing in social studies matched her goal and plan to do nothing in social studies. In the fifth row, she wrote a "yes" in column 4 indicating that her journal entry completed in column 3 matched her goal and plan for writing in columns 1 and 3. And in the last row, she wrote a "yes" in column 4 indicating that her doing nothing in column 4 matched her goal and plan to do nothing in the other activity for columns 1 and 2.

As you can see from this evaluation, the student was 100 percent accurate in her evaluations because she entered yeses for completed work that matched goals and plans and noes for work or for non-work that did not match her goals and plans. At the same time she was only 67 percent successful in meeting her goals and plans, in that she only entered yeses for four of her six goals. We will focus this last component of self-regulation in the next step.

STEP 5: SELF-ADJUSTING. The goal of this step is to teach students to increase their yeses because the more of them that they have in their evaluations, the closer they are to knowing how to self-regulate accurately; the more often they do what they say they will do, which is the goal of this instruction. You can motivate accurate self-regulation by providing incentives for yeses, which is a reward contingency for matching goals, plans, and results. Table 4.7 illustrates how to set this up. Using a form like this, ask students to count the number of yeses they record in column 4 of the card and then to write that number in the row space below the self-evaluation column. Then inform them that they will earn a reward point for each "yes" they accurately record. Next, ask them how many points they earned from the yeses they just recorded, and then ask them to indicate in the last row the number of yeses (and points) they expect to earn on their next card.

Conclude by having students repeat several regulation cycles using a new self-regulation card each time. This gives them repeated opportunities to adjust their goal setting and self-planning of each cycle until they begin regulating their work accurately – until they figure out what adjustments are necessary to do exactly what they say they will do each time – to get yeses. Figure 4.5 illustrates how students should line their cards together functionally so they learn to adjust by using one card to decide what to do on the next card. In the figure, the self-regulation occurs when they complete the card, but the adjustment occurs when they finish work on one card and start work on the next one. As indicated in the figure, each change from one card to the next is an opportunity for students to adjust and learn from the adjustment. This is how self-regulated adjustments occur naturally, too. We try something out (set goals, make plans, take actions). We find out what works (self-monitor and self-evaluate) and then decide whether to do the same thing or something different the next time (new card). By repeating the process frequently, we learn from our adjustments and move successively closer to our goal.

Finally, it is worth considering why there is no additional reinforcement during this type of instruction. The main reason is that the matching contingency is sufficient to produce the accurate self-regulation we are seeking. Not only does it optimally motivate students to adjust in order to do what they say they will do,

Table 4.7 Step 5: Student Self-Reinforces and Self-Adjusts On Self-Regulation Card			

Is My Goal Reading?	**What Will I Do in Reading?**	**What Did I Do In Reading?**	**Did I Match (Meet) My Goal?**
Yes	Read 1 chapter in book	Chapter 1 in book	**YES** No
Is My Goal Math?	**What Will I Do in Math?**	**What Did I Do In Math?**	**Did I Match (Meet) My Goal?**
Yes	Complete a math worksheet	Nothing	Yes **NO**
Is My Goal Science?	**What Will I Do in Science?**	**What Did I Do In Science?**	**Did I Match (Meet) My Goal?**
No	Nothing	Science Worksheets	Yes **NO**
Is My Goal Social Studies?	**What Will I Do in Social Studies?**	**What Did I Do In Social Studies?**	**Did I Match (Meet) My Goal?**
No	Nothing	Nothing	**YES** No
Is My Goal Writing?	**What Will I Do in Writing?**	**What Did I Do in Writing?**	**Did I Match (Meet) My Goal?**
Yes	Write a Journal entry	Journal entry	**YES** No
Is My Goal Other Activity?	**What Will I Do in Other Activity?**	**What Did I Do In Other Activity?**	**Did I Match (Meet) My Goal?**
No	Nothing	Nothing	**YES** No
		Number of Goals Met (Matches)?	**4**
		Number of Met Goals (Matches) Next Time?	**5**

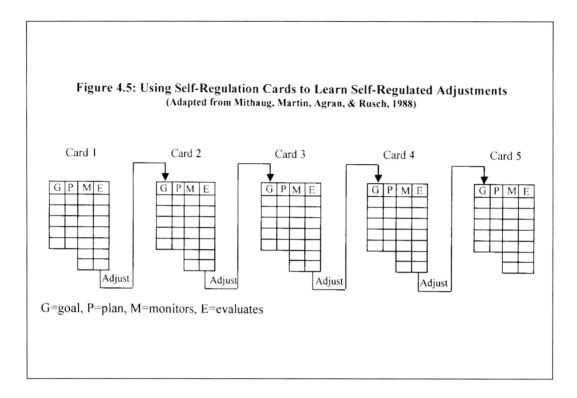

Figure 4.5: Using Self-Regulation Cards to Learn Self-Regulated Adjustments
(Adapted from Mithaug, Martin, Agran, & Rusch, 1988)

G=goal, P=plan, M=monitors, E=evaluates

but it also eliminates the need for praising hard (or fast) work, which only serves to motivate them to work for you rather than for themselves. We want to avoid these types of incentives, especially if our goal is to build intrinsically motivated learners. If you permit the match contingency to encourage student control of the adjustment process, you may be surprised at the levels of learning, performance, and generalization that result.

CONCLUSION

This chapter described three important factors to consider when teaching students to regulate their learning: the use of an appropriate support system for strategy use, the establishment of autonomous work periods, and the teaching of the five self-regulation strategies. If you consider these factors when teaching students to regulate their work, you will have an empowering impact on your students' ability to adjust and learn on their own.

The first factor, the level of strategy support, is important because students vary in their ability to remember when and how to use strategies that help them adjust effectively to new circumstances. For example, some students benefit from using mnemonic devices to remember what to do. Others benefit from using self-talk phrases to remember the strategies of adjustment. But most students benefit from the physical reminders provided by a self-regulation card, especially students who cannot read but who respond well to the pictorial cues indicating the strategies to use and when.

The second factor, the autonomous work center, is essential to teaching self-regulation because it provides the just-right opportunities students need in order to learn how to adjust repeatedly to their own attempts at completing work they say they will do. Indeed, this is a very different opportunity from the ones that are provided during teacher-directed instruction. Under these circumstances students learn to adjust too, but they learn to adjust to the teacher's cues and consequences rather than to their cues and consequences (as provided by a self-regulation card).

The third factor, systematic teaching of the five self-regulation strategies, is, of course, the capstone of self-instruction pedagogy in that it gives students the means to regulate their adjustments to any challenge they may face when they are on their own. The sample self-regulation cards described in this chapter illustrate how students can learn to compare their goals and plans with their behaviors and results in order to determine whether they accomplished what they set out to do, and if not, what to do next time.

If you consider these factors when developing various programs of instruction, you will discover your students are more engaged when working on their own, more intrinsically motivated to improve, and more able to generalize what and how they learn from your classroom to other classrooms and environments. In other words, you will discover that your students can adjust and learn in a manner similar to how other self-determined students adjust and learn.

REFERENCES

Agran, M. (1997). *Student-directed learning: Teaching self-determination skills.* Pacific Grove, CA: Brooks/Cole Publishing Company.

Agran, M., & Martella, R. (1991). Teaching self-instructional skills to persons with mental retardation: A descriptive and experimental analysis. In M. Hersen, R. M. Eisler, and P. M. Miller (Eds.), *Progress in behavior modification* (pp. 36–55). Newbury Park, CA: Sage.

Bos, C.S., & Vaughn, S. (1991). *Strategies for teaching students with learning and behavior problems.* Needham Heights, MA: Allyn and Bacon.

Copeland, S. R., & Hughes, C. (2002). Effects of goal setting on task performance of persons with mental retardation. *Education and Training in Mental Retardation and Developmental disabilities, 37*(1), 40–54.

Deci, E. L., & Ryan, D. M. (1985). *Intrinsic motivation in human behavior.* New York: Plenum.

Dunlap, G., DePerczel, M., Clarke, S., Wilson, D., Wright, S., White, R., & Gomez, A. (1994). Choice making to promote adaptive behavior for students with emotional and behavioral challenges. *Journal of Applied Behavior Analysis, 27*(3), 505–518.

Garfield, C. A. (1986). *Peak performers: The new heroes of American business.* New York: Avon.

Grossi, T.A., & Heward, W. L. (1998). Using self-evaluation to improve the work productivity of trainees in a community-based restaurant training program. *Education and Training in Mental Retardation and Developmental Disabilities, 33*(3), 248–63.

Hetzroni, O. E., & Shavit, P. (2002). Comparison of two instructional strategies for acquiring form and sound of Hebrew letters by students with mild mental retardation. *Education and Training in Mental Retardation and Developmental Disabilities, 37*(3), 273–282.

Hill, N. H. (1960). *Think and grow rich.* New York: Ballantine Books.

Hughes, C. (1991). Independent performance among individuals with mental retardation: Promoting generalization through self-instruction. In M. Hersen, R.M. Eisler, and P. M. Miller (Eds.), *Progress in Behavior Modification, 27,* 7–35. Newbury Park, CA: Sage.

Martin, J. E., Mithaug, D. E., Cox, P., Peterson, L. Y., Van Dycke, J. L., & Cash, M. E. (2003). Increasing self-determination: Teaching students to plan, work, evaluate, and adjust. *Exceptional Children, 69*(4), 431–446.

Martin, J. E., Mithaug, D. E., Husch, J. V., Frazier, E. S., & Marshall, L. (2003). The effects of optimal opportunities and adjustments during job searches by adults with severe disabilities. In D. E. Mithaug, D. K. Mithaug, M. Agran, J. E. Martin, & M. Wehmeyer (Eds.), *Self-determined learning theory: Construction, verification, and evaluation* (pp. 188–205). Mahwah, NJ: Lawrence Erlbaum.

Martin, J. E., Mithaug, D. E., Oliphint, J. H., Husch, J. V., & Frazier, E. S. (2002). *Self-directed employment: A handbook for transition teachers and employment specialists.* Baltimore, MD: Paul H. Brookes.

Mastropieri, M. A., & Scruggs, T. E. (1998). Enhancing school success with mnemonic strategies. *Intervention in School and Clinic, 33*(4), 201–208.

Mastropieri, M. A., Sweda, J., & Scruggs, T. E. (2000). Putting mnemonic strategies to work in an inclusive classroom. *Learning Disabilities Research and Practice, 15*(2), 69–74.

Miller, D. L., & Kelley, M. L. (1994). The use of goal setting and contingency contracting for improving children's homework performance. *Journal of Applied Behavior Analysis, 27*(1), 73–84.

Mithaug, D. E. (1991). *Self-determined kids: Raising successful and satisfied children.* Lexington, MA: Lexington Books.

Mithaug, D. E. (1993). *Self-regulation theory: How optimal adjustment maximizes gain.* Westport, CT: Praeger.

Mithaug, D. E. (1996a). *Equal opportunity theory.* Thousand Oaks, CA: Sage Publications.

Mithaug, D. E. (1996b). The optimal prospects principle: A theoretical basis for rethinking instructional practices for self-determination. In D. J. Sands & M. L. Wehmeyer (Eds.), *Self-determination across the life span: Independence and choice for people with disabilities* (pp. 147–165). Baltimore: Paul H. Brookes Publishing Co.

Mithaug, D. E. (2000). *Learning to theorize: A four-step strategy.* Thousand Oaks, CA: Sage Publications.

Mithaug, D. E. (2003). Evaluating the credibility and worth of self-determination theory. In Wehmeyer, M. L., Abery, B. H., Mithaug, D. E., & Stancliffe, R. J. (Eds.). *Theory in self-determination: Foundations for education practice* (pp. 154–173). Springfield, IL: Charles C Thomas.

Mithaug, D. E., & Hanawalt, D. A. (1978). The validation of procedures to assess prevocational task preferences in retarded adults. *Journal of Applied Behavior Analysis, 11,* 153–162.

Mithaug, D. E., & Mar, D. K. (1980). The relation between choosing and working prevocational tasks in two severely retarded young adults. *Journal of Applied Behavior Analysis, 13,* 177–182.

Mithaug, D. E., & Mithaug, D. K. (2003a). Assessing self-determination prospects among students with and without disabilities. In D. E. Mithaug, D. K. Mithaug, M. Agran, J. E. Martin, & M. L. Wehmeyer (Eds.) *Self-determined learning theory: Construction, prediction, and evaluation* (pp. 61–76). Mahwah, N.J.: Lawrence Erlbaum.

Mithaug, D. E., Martin, J. E., & Agran, M. (1987). Adaptability instruction: The goal of transitional programming. *Exceptional Children, 53,* 500–505.

Mithaug, D. E., Martin, J. E., Agran, M. & Rusch, F. R. (1988). *Why special education graduates fail: How to teach them to succeed.* Colorado Springs, CO: Ascent Publications.

Mithaug, D. E., Martin, M. E., Husch, J. V., Rusch, F. R., & Agran, M. (1988). *When will persons in supported employment need less support?* Colorado Springs, CO: Ascent Publications.

Mithaug, D. E., Mithaug, D. K., Agran, M., Martin, J. E., & Wehmeyer, M. L. (2003). *Self-determined learning theory: Construction, prediction, and evaluation.* Mahwah, N.J.: Lawrence Erlbaum.

Mithaug, D. E., Wehmeyer, M. L., Agran, J., Martin, J., & Palmer, S. (1998). The self-determined learning model of instruction: Engaging students to solve their learning problems. In M. Wehmeyer & D. J. Sands (Eds.), *Making it happen: Student involvement in educational planning, decision-making, and instruction* (pp. 299–328). Baltimore, MD: Paul Brooks Publishing Co.

Mithaug, D. K. (1998). *The generalization effects of choice contingencies on the self-regulated work behavior of young children with behavior problems.* Unpublished doctoral dissertation. Teachers College, Columbia University, New York.

Mithaug, D. K. (2002). "Yes" means success: Teaching children with multiple disabilities to self-regulate during independent work. *TEACHING Exceptional Children, 35*(1), 22–27.

Mithaug, D. K., & Mithaug, D. E. (2003b). Effects of teacher-directed versus student-directed instruction on self-management of young children with disabilities. *Journal of Applied Behavior Analysis, 36*(1), 133–136.

Mithaug, D. K., & Mithaug, D. E. (2003c). The effects of choice opportunities and self-regulation on the self-engagement and learning of young children with disabilities. In D. E. Mithaug, D. K. Mithaug, M. Agran, J. E. Martin, & M. L. Wehmeyer (Eds.) *Self-determined learning theory: Construction, prediction, and evaluation* (pp. 141–157). Mahwah, N.J.: Lawrence Erlbaum.

Mithaug, D. K., & Mithaug, D. E. (2003d). The effects of choice opportunities on the engagement of prospective teachers in student-determined learning. In D. E. Mithaug, D. K. Mithaug, M. Agran, J. E. Martin, & M. L. Wehmeyer (Eds.) *Self-determined learning theory: Construction, prediction, and evaluation* (pp. 206–250). Mahwah, N.J.: Lawrence Erlbaum.

O'Leary, S.G., & Dubey, D.R. (1979). Applications of self-control procedures by children: A review. *Journal of applied Behavior Analysis, 12,* 449–465.

Olympia, D. E., Sheridan, S. M., Jenson, W. R., & Andrews, D. (1994). Using student managed interventions to increase homework completion and accuracy. *Journal of Applied Behavior Analysis, 27*(1), 85–99.

Robbins, A. (1987). *Unlimited power.* New York: Ballantine Books.

Stevenson, H.C., & Fantuzzo, J.W. (1984). Application of the "generalization map" to a self-control intervention with school-aged children. *Journal of Applied Behavior Analysis, 17,* 203–212.

Stevenson, H.C., & Fantuzzo, J.W. (1986). The generality of social validity of a competency-based self-control training intervention for underachieving students. *Journal of Applied Behavior Analysis, 19,* 269–276.

Sulzer-Azaroff, B., Pollack, M.J., Hamad, C., & Howley, T. (1998). Promoting widespread, durable service quality via interlocking contingencies. *Research In Developmental Disabilities, 19*(1), 39–61.

Whitman, T. L. (1990). Development of self-regulation in persons with mental retardation. *American Journal on Mental Retardation, 94*(4), 373–376.

Zimmerman, B. J. (1990). Self-regulated leaning and academic achievement: An overview. *Educational Psychologist, 25*(1), 3–17.

Zirpoli, T. J. & Melloy, K. J. (1997). *Behavior management: Applications for teachers and parents.* N.J.: Prentice-Hall, Inc.

Chapter 5

HOW STUDENTS DIRECT THEIR LEARNING

MICHAEL L. WEHMEYER

Step 1 Teaching Self-Control	Step 2 Teaching Self-Regulation	**Step 3 Promoting Self-Determined Learning**	Step 4 Promoting Self-Determined IEPs and ITPs
I identify my students' needs, interests, abilities	I identify my students' needs, interests, & abilities	**My Students identify their needs, interests, abilities**	Student identified needs, interests, abilities for IEPs and Transitions
I set goals to meet students' needs and interests based on their abilities	My students set goals to meet their needs and interests based on their abilities Goal-setting strategy	**My students set goals to meet their needs and interests based on their abilities**	My students set goals to meet their needs and interests based on their abilities in their IEPs and ITPs
I make plans to meet those goals	My students make plans to meet their goals: Self-planning strategy	**My students make plans to meet their goals**	My students make plans to meet their IEPs and Transition goals
My students monitor their actions to follow plans: Self-monitoring strategy	My students monitor their actions to follow their plans Self-monitoring strategy	**My students monitor their actions to follow their plans**	My students monitor their actions to follow their IEP and Transition plans
My students evaluate the results of their actions Self-evaluation strategy	My students evaluate the results of actions on their plans Self-evaluation strategy	**My students evaluate the results of actions on their plans**	My students evaluate the results of actions on their IEP and Transition plans
My students adjust their actions and plans to improve their results Self-reinforcement strategy	My students adjust their actions and plans to improve their results Self-adjustment strategy	**My students adjust their actions and plans to improve their results**	My students adjust their actions and plans to improve their progress on IEP and Transition goals

As indicated in the table above, this chapter completes the shift in instructional control that allows students to direct *and* regulate their adjustments in order to learn. The previous two chapters showed how students increase their control of learning by using five self-management strategies to regulate their adjustments. This chapter shows how they gain complete control by using three problem-solving strategies to discover *what* as well as *how* they learn.

Student-Directed Learning

The purpose of this next step then is to fully empower students to direct their learning, which involves more than allowing them to regulate their adjustments to the subject matter you prescribe and list on a self-regulation card. The instructional aim here is to teach students to solve three interrelated problems of discovery: (a) figuring out what they want to know, (b) figuring out how to get that information, and (c) figuring out how to adjust effectively to the results of their searches. When students use three strategies to solve everyday discovery problems, they know how to direct *and* regulate their learning.

The *Self-Determined Learning Model of Instruction* offers guidelines for implementing this final shift in instructional control. It is based on the view that success in life requires more than adjustment to existing circumstances. It also requires altering circumstances to make them more favorable for desirable pursuits. Accounts of famous people overcoming formidable obstacles to get what they need and want attest to the necessity of this approach to adjustment, which is amply evident among people who are successful and self-determined.

Indeed, people who are self-determined act in ways that reveal their actions and behaviors to be *"self"* caused (autonomous determinism) as opposed to *"other"* caused (heteronomous determinism). The adjective *"causal"* refers to the underlying interaction between *cause* and *effect* that represents this type of pursuit; and the term *"agent"* reflects the authority of the actor initiating those changes, which explains why self-determined people are said to be *causal agents* in their lives. They act with authority to make something happen in their lives, and as they cause those things to happen, they move closer to their outcomes. This is different from changing something in response to an event or circumstance. When people are causal agents they adjust in order to produce the result they want, as Bandura (1997) explains below.

> Most human behavior, of course, is determined by many interacting factors, and so people are contributors to, rather than the sole determiners of, what happens to them. In evaluating the role of intentionality in human agency, one must distinguish between the personal production of action for an intended outcome, and the effects that carrying out that course of action actually produce. Agency refers to acts done intentionally. (Bandura, 1997, p. 3)

This link between causal agency and student-directed learning is important because it clarifies the function of directedness during learning for all students, including those with severe disabilities. It suggests, for example, that directedness does not require independence in performing every step of a task. But it does require causal agency. Students must be in control of the choices that affect their goals and their plans to meet them.

The *Self-Determined Learning Model of Instruction* identifies the skills and supports that empower students to make these choices so they can achieve the goals that will satisfy their self-determined needs and interests. Napoleon Hill was the first to describe the problem-solving strategies that serve this purpose. In his 1938 best-selling book titled *Think and Grow Rich*, Hill identified a five-step problem-solving strategy he claimed all successful people use to get what they need and want in life. That five-step sequence was (1) to identify a definite goal to be obtained, (2) to develop sufficient power to attain your goal, (3) to perfect a practical plan for attaining your goal, (4) to accumulate specialized knowledge necessary for the attainment of your goal, and (5) to persist in carrying out your plan (Mithaug, 1991, 57). These steps can be restated as six questions any child or adult can ask in order to achieve goal-directed problem solving (Mithaug, 1991).

1. What do I need and want?
2. What goal will satisfy my needs and wants?
3. What plan will reach that goal?
4. What actions will complete my plan?
5. What results did I get?
6. What do I need to do next time?

What we have learned from this reconstruction of Hill's formula is that there is a sequence of thoughts and actions that causal agents follow in order to produce the results they seek. This causal sequence is a means-ends chain that moves the actor from where she is – her actual state of affairs of not having what she wants – to where she wants to be – her goal state of affairs. The method for getting from the one state of affairs to the other is self-regulated problem solving to reduce the difference between actual and desired circumstances. The *Self-Determined Learning Model of Instruction* provides key questions to guide students' problem solving in the construction of those means-ends pathways between actual and desired state circumstances.

This suggests, of course, that self-directed learning is more than solving a single problem in order to find a correct answer. It is solving a series of interrelated problems that lead to a goal state condition. Hence, it requires many problem-solving episodes over time. The strategy we recommend to teach this type of problem solving is captured in three sets of questions students answer when they: (1) construct goals to meet their needs to know, (2) construct plans of action to meet their goals, and (3) adjust their actions and plans to reduce or eliminate their need to know. Indeed, when students engage in strategic, recursive problem solving, they become self-determined learners (Agran, Blanchard, Hughes, & Wehmeyer, 2002; Agran, Blanchard, & Wehmeyer, 2000; Agran, King-Sears, Wehmeyer, & Copeland, 2003).

The Self-Determined Learning Model of Instruction

Joyce and Weil (1980) defined a model of teaching as "a plan or pattern that can be used to shape curriculums (long-term courses of study), to design instructional materials, and to guide instruction in the classroom and other settings" (p. 1). Such models are derived from theories of human behavior, learning, or cognition, and teachers use them to guide the teaching of various types of learners. The *Self-Determined Learning Model of Instruction* is such a model. It is based on the principles of self-determined learning theory (Mithaug, Mithaug, Agran, Martin, & Wehmeyer, 2003) and is designed to meet the instructional needs of students with disabilities. Indeed, the model makes discovery learning possible for students that many have claimed are incapable of experiencing (Gersten & Dimino, 1993; Lewis & Doorlag, 2003). It does this by provoking students to determine for themselves what they *want* to learn.

The three phases of the model illustrated in Figures 5.1–5.3 pose questions for students to answer as they discover what they want to know. For example, Figure 5.1 presents the first phase, which poses the question "What is my goal?" Figure 5.2 presents the second phase, which poses the question "What is my plan?" Figure 5.3 presents the third phase, which poses the question "What have I learned?" Figure 5.4 illustrates the recursive problem-solving process represented by the search for answers to these questions.

Students regulate their problem solving by finding answers to questions in each of these phases, which means that in this context, problems are simply knowledge domains, tasks activities, or situations that students want to know about. They are gaps or differences between what students currently know and what they don't know about those domains. Hence, they are similar to Bransford and Stein's (1984) problem condition, which exists "when there is a discrepancy between an initial state and a goal state and there is no ready-made solution for the problem solver" (p. 7). The questions in phase 1 are intended to provoke a sequence of thinking and acting in students that will systematically reduce that distance between what they know and what they want to know. In other words, the questions provoke the same recursive problem solving in Figure 5.4 that is in John Dewey's discovery learning, the scientific method, Newell and Simon's General Problem Solver, and in constructive theorizing (Mithaug, 2000).

Figure 5.1: Instructional Phase 1 of Self-Determined Learning Model of Instruction

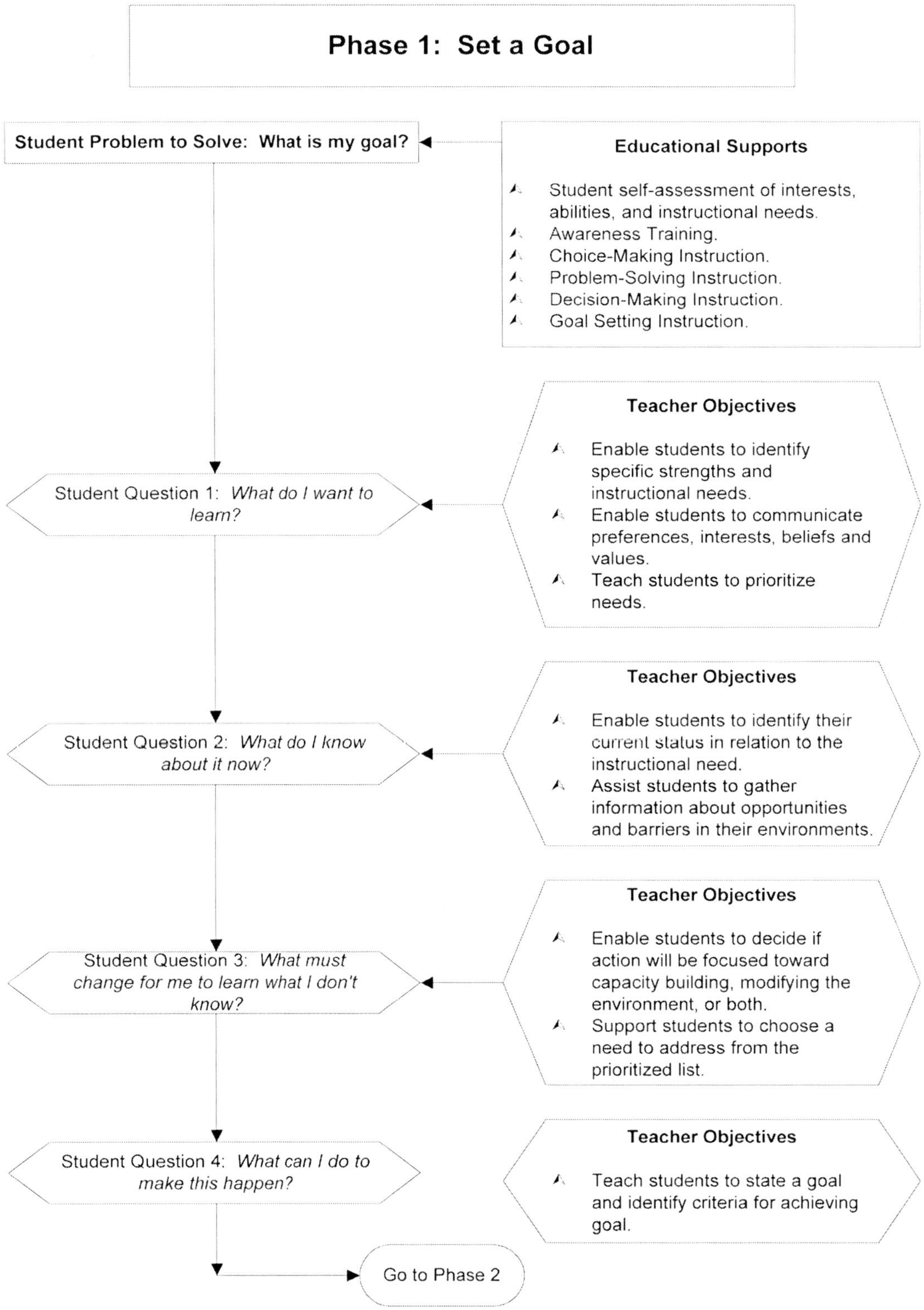

Phase 1: Set a Goal

Student Problem to Solve: What is my goal?

Educational Supports

- Student self-assessment of interests, abilities, and instructional needs.
- Awareness Training.
- Choice-Making Instruction.
- Problem-Solving Instruction.
- Decision-Making Instruction.
- Goal Setting Instruction.

Student Question 1: *What do I want to learn?*

Teacher Objectives

- Enable students to identify specific strengths and instructional needs.
- Enable students to communicate preferences, interests, beliefs and values.
- Teach students to prioritize needs.

Student Question 2: *What do I know about it now?*

Teacher Objectives

- Enable students to identify their current status in relation to the instructional need.
- Assist students to gather information about opportunities and barriers in their environments.

Student Question 3: *What must change for me to learn what I don't know?*

Teacher Objectives

- Enable students to decide if action will be focused toward capacity building, modifying the environment, or both.
- Support students to choose a need to address from the prioritized list.

Student Question 4: *What can I do to make this happen?*

Teacher Objectives

- Teach students to state a goal and identify criteria for achieving goal.

Go to Phase 2

Figure 5.2: Instructional Phase 2 of Self-Determined Learning Model of Instruction

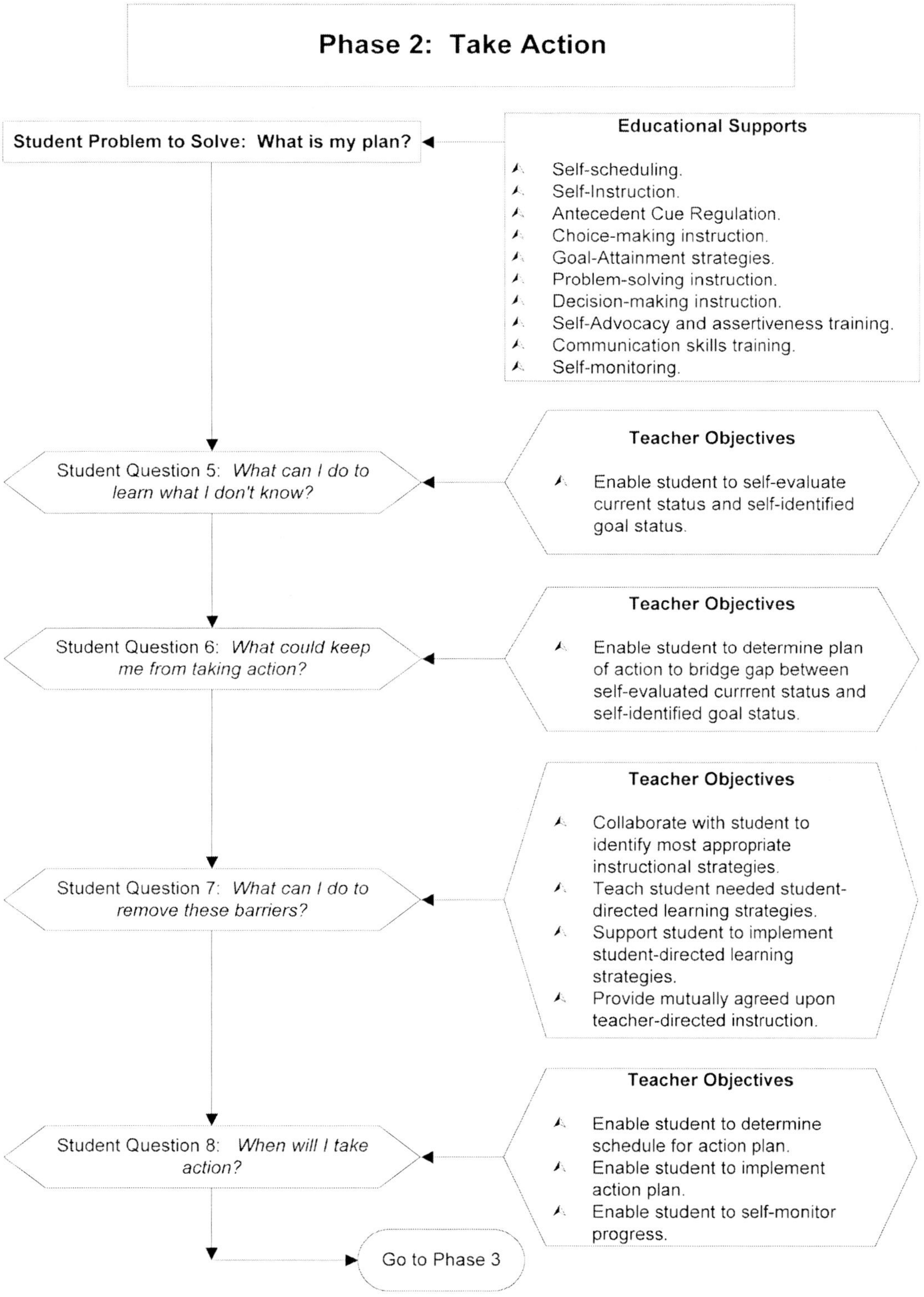

Phase 2: Take Action

Student Problem to Solve: What is my plan?

Educational Supports

- Self-scheduling.
- Self-Instruction.
- Antecedent Cue Regulation.
- Choice-making instruction.
- Goal-Attainment strategies.
- Problem-solving instruction.
- Decision-making instruction.
- Self-Advocacy and assertiveness training.
- Communication skills training.
- Self-monitoring.

Student Question 5: *What can I do to learn what I don't know?*

Teacher Objectives

- Enable student to self-evaluate current status and self-identified goal status.

Student Question 6: *What could keep me from taking action?*

Teacher Objectives

- Enable student to determine plan of action to bridge gap between self-evaluated currrent status and self-identified goal status.

Student Question 7: *What can I do to remove these barriers?*

Teacher Objectives

- Collaborate with student to identify most appropriate instructional strategies.
- Teach student needed student-directed learning strategies.
- Support student to implement student-directed learning strategies.
- Provide mutually agreed upon teacher-directed instruction.

Student Question 8: *When will I take action?*

Teacher Objectives

- Enable student to determine schedule for action plan.
- Enable student to implement action plan.
- Enable student to self-monitor progress.

Go to Phase 3

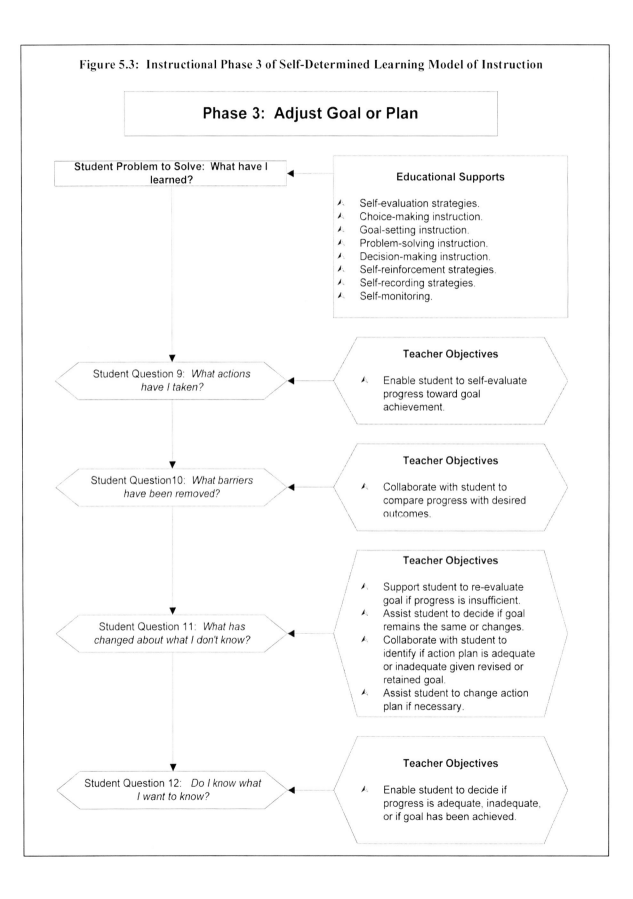

Figure 5.3: Instructional Phase 3 of Self-Determined Learning Model of Instruction

Phase 3: Adjust Goal or Plan

Student Problem to Solve: What have I learned?

Educational Supports

- Self-evaluation strategies.
- Choice-making instruction.
- Goal-setting instruction.
- Problem-solving instruction.
- Decision-making instruction.
- Self-reinforcement strategies.
- Self-recording strategies.
- Self-monitoring.

Student Question 9: *What actions have I taken?*

Teacher Objectives

- Enable student to self-evaluate progress toward goal achievement.

Student Question10: *What barriers have been removed?*

Teacher Objectives

- Collaborate with student to compare progress with desired outcomes.

Student Question 11: *What has changed about what I don't know?*

Teacher Objectives

- Support student to re-evaluate goal if progress is insufficient.
- Assist student to decide if goal remains the same or changes.
- Collaborate with student to identify if action plan is adequate or inadequate given revised or retained goal.
- Assist student to change action plan if necessary.

Student Question 12: *Do I know what I want to know?*

Teacher Objectives

- Enable student to decide if progress is adequate, inadequate, or if goal has been achieved.

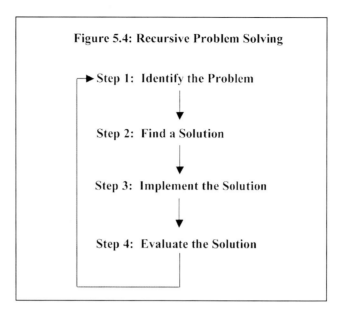

In the model, *Student Questions* are written in the first person voice and in an easy-to-understand format. Most students will be able to respond to all 12 of them as stated. Others may need to have them rephrased or perhaps even paraphrased. Feel free to adjust the questions as necessary as the aim is to get students engaged in the type of problem solving indicated in Figure 5.4. Once students learn to ask themselves the questions on their own, they are self-instructing to discover what they don't know. The focus, then, is to get them to use the questions in a self-instructional format and then to search for answers by engaging in recursive problem solving. Students who cannot verbalize the questions will need additional supports. Again, adjust your teaching to those needs perhaps by providing picture cards or other permanent cue reminders of the questions in need of answers.

Each of the *Student Questions* is linked to a set of *Teacher Objectives* that assist in implementing the model, which, in turn, is facilitated by strategies in the *Educational Supports* section. For example, the first *Student Question*, "What do I want to learn?" and its *Teacher Objectives* identify activities for students to engage to find answers. This might include identifying strengths and weaknesses, preferences, interests, beliefs and values, and prioritizing them on a list. The *Educational Supports* section identifies the strategies that help students find answers, which include, of course, the self-management strategies identified in Chapters 3 and 4 – goal setting, self-planning, self-monitoring, self-evaluation, and self-reinforcement. Finally, keep in mind that it is self-defeating to provide the answers for students in that this would eliminate the incentive to engage in the recursive problem solving that is central to discovery learning. So, avoid solving problems for students. Empower them to problem solve instead.

Implementing the Instructional Model

To introduce this approach, meet with your students to discuss the objectives and activities of the model and describe some of what lies ahead. The following points may help in this initial meeting. First, emphasize that you want to help them learn the knowledge, skills, and behaviors they want to learn. For many, this will be the first time a teacher has had such discussion with them. So be prepared if they are surprised or uncertain as to what you intend to do. Also, the concepts you will be using may be new, too. For example, problem solving to meet goals may be new and confusing especially if they view it negatively. You can introduce this idea simply by explaining that problem solving is figuring out what you want to know and then finding your own answers. Also, if any of your students believe that problems are all "bad" and to be avoided, explain that they just are obstacles to be removed in order to get what you want. Then explain that goals are what you plan to achieve in order to make this happen. Illustrate with goals you have chosen for yourself and then ask them for sample goals they might have for themselves.

Phase 1: Set a Goal

Once you have discussed the process, begin Phase 1 as illustrated in Figure 5.1 by introducing goal setting with four questions. Note that first question, what do I want to learn, is phrased with the term "Want" rather than "Need." This is because asking "What do you need to do?" is likely to provoke an answer that reflects what you want them to learn rather than what they want to learn, which is exactly the opposite of what we are attempting to accomplish here. To keep the focus on *students'* needs and interests try to avoid phrases like "What should you do?" or "What do you need to do?" This may take some time. Also, it helps if you encourage students to identify what they already know or have learned and then based on that determine what more they want to learn. This builds on their strengths rather than weaknesses and leads to more reasonable expectations for what they choose to learn.

Once students can answer the question, "What do I want to learn?" they are ready to answer the second question, "What do I know about it now?" This leads them to consider what exactly they know about the circumstances in question. The intent here is to get them to consider the full extent of their knowledge about the topic, from knowing nothing about it to knowing everything. It also provokes them to identify possible barriers or difficulties in discovering more about the topic.

The third question – "What must change for me to learn what I don't know?" – is intended to provoke students to think about activities that will yield the information they seek. After answering the first two questions, they will be better able to answer this one, which requires them to choose a particular piece of an unknown topic to search out and then to identify actions that will contribute to that search. Here you may want to have students consider several ways of discovering what they want to learn, especially before they attempt to answer the next and last question in this phase.

This question is – "What can I do to make this happen?" It is intended to provoke students to identify criteria for determining when they meet their goal. You can help with this by showing them how actions identified during the previous question help them recognize the end point in their search. It also leads to questions about how to write measurable goals, how to identify steps to reach them, as well as how to choose criteria for measuring progress.

Phase 2: Take Action

After students have identified their learning goal, they are ready to take action to meet it, which begins by developing a plan. Hence, the lead question for this phase is "What is my plan?" Again, they find answers by addressing another set of four questions in another means-end problem-solving sequence. The first question is "What can I do to learn what I don't know?" The second is "What could keep me from taking action?" The third question is "What can I do to remove these barriers?" And the fourth question is "When will I take action?"

The phase begins with students evaluating their current situation against the mastery criteria they identified in Phase 1, which established a basis for judging progress toward the goal. Considering these criteria helps them to think of ways of meeting their goals. Your guidance is critical here because most students have limited experience in developing strategies or plans for getting what they want. Encourage them to step through all of the details of a plan, which would include laying out steps to take to gather information they seek, figuring out how much time it will take to complete each step, and deciding how frequently to check progress to make sure they are on track to meeting their goal.

The list of educational supports listed in Figure 5.2 may help, as will the teacher objectives for each question. To answer the first question, which is number 5 in Figure 5.2, ask students to review their current situation of knowing what to do to meet goal expectations. Then introduce the next question, which is 6 in Figure 5.2, and prompt them to develop plans to remove obstacles to meeting their goals. Next, ask what they can do to remove barriers, which is question

7 in Figure 5.2.

Here, collaborative support is appropriate with you offering possible strategies for dealing with obstacles. Remember to allow students to choose the ones they are most comfortable using. Conclude the phase by introducing the last question, question 8 in Figure 5.2, that asks when actions will be taken to remove obstacles and advance toward goals. Suggest use of a calendar to indicate when actions will be taken and how much time will be spent on each as self-monitoring is critical for successful discovery problem solving. It provides information students need to evaluate what they have accomplished, what remains to be done, as well as what adjustments are needed.

Phase 3: Adjust Goal or Plan

Once students have a plan and have taken action, they are ready for the third and final phase of learning through adjustment, which is finding out what they know and what they have yet to learn. The first two questions in the phase focus on actions taken and barriers removed (questions 9 and 10 in Figure 5.3). Answering them helps students make decisions about the next actions to take. This is the adjustment phase and is responsible for learning. Unfortunately, it is often omitted in instructional models that focus primarily on goal-attainment. Although the goal serves as a powerful incentive for learning and achievement, it does not produce learning on its own. Repeated adjustments to reach the goal are responsible for that.

This means that the objective here is for students to repeat the cycle of goal setting, action taking, and adjusting many, many times so they learn how to learn from their own adjustments to the learning challenge. To promote this level of recursive problem solving (see Figure 5.4), encourage students to evaluate their progress data by comparing it with their goal expectations and based on that to decide what is working in, what is not, and what to change to make things work better.

This self-evaluation process is provoked by final two questions: what has changed about what I don't know and do I know what I want to know (question 11 and 12 in Figure 5.3)? By comparing goal expectation information with information collected from their self-monitoring, students can determine what has changed and then conclude whether those results match their expectations and they have met their goal, whether their results almost match their expectations and they are close to meeting their goal, or whether their results do not match their expectations at all and there is much more to do.

Each of the conclusions produces a different adjustment. If their results match their goal then they have learned what they want to know for that particular pursuit. However, if their goal and results do not match they must adjust (a) by changing their responses to their plan, (b) by changing their plan, or (c) by changing their goal. In other words, they return to previous phases of the model and adjust their goals, plans or actions.

This is the recursive problem solving that builds student capacity to persist in learning from adjustment. It is also the self-regulatory mechanism that allows you to abstain from critiquing and adjusting students' goals, plans, and actions for them. Most students with disabilities never develop this capacity because their teachers make all the needed corrections for them. But in this instructional model, self-adjustment is central to learning through discovery. It is the mechanism students use to discover what they have learned, what remains to be learned, and what they must change to learn what remains.

Your Role in Student-Directed Learning

Your role in this approach to teaching is substantially different from the role you perform when the instructional model emphasizes teacher control of behavior. Here you function as a facilitator and advocate as well as a teacher. You advocate for opportunities for students to self-engage, self-direct, and self-adjust and you facilitate their efforts to control their own learning when they have those opportunities. In many ways it is more difficult than directly controlling what students learn or how they behave. This is because here you must balance between giving students directions on what to do and allowing them to struggle to find answers on their own. Hence, you try to balance your offers of help with your expectations for self-engagement, your use of feedback with your expectations for self-correction, and your ability to simplify with your expectations for independent problem solving.

This is clearly the case when facilitating self-engagement by making difficult-to-understand concepts understandable and when making daunting problems and essential tasks valuable and doable. When performing these behind-the-scenes preparations for students, you are no longer the authoritarian figure with all the answers. You are a resource that students rely on *to help them* find answers.

But, of course, you are still a teacher with expertise in content areas and with insights on how students can access that knowledge. Hence, like any other expert you offer choices for students to consider when they decide how to solve the problem of not having access to that information. At the same time, of course, you are not directly responsible for imparting that knowledge and those skills to students. Instead, you are responsible for helping them gain that knowledge and skills through their own self-regulated efforts.

Finally, you are an advocate in that you support students' goal pursuits and are prepared to speak up for them when opportunities are available that can advance those ends in significant ways. In this sense you are not expected to speak for students so as to protect them from difficulty. Rather, you are expected to speak up for them when their rights to a fair chance or an equal opportunity are at risk as compared with other students who routinely have richer and often more interesting opportunities for self-directed, discovery learning.

Research on the Model

In our experience, these role changes come somewhat naturally when you use this model to guide your teaching, which has been shown to be effective with a wide range of students with disabilities. Wehmeyer, Palmer, Agran, Mithaug, and Martin (2000), for example, conducted a field test of the model with 21 teachers responsible for the instruction of adolescents receiving special education services in two states (Texas and Wisconsin). Each teacher was asked to identify at least one but no more than three students with whom to implement the model, resulting in a total of 40 students with mental retardation, learning disabilities, or emotional or behavioral disorders. Students identified a total of 43 goals they wanted to address (three students chose two goals). Of the 43 goals, 10 focused on acquiring or modifying social skills or knowledge, 13 focused on behavioral issues (compliance with school procedures, controlling behavior in specific circumstances, learning more adaptive behavior) and 20 addressed academic needs.

The efficacy of the model to enable students to achieve educationally valued goals was examined using the Goal Attainment Scaling (GAS) process. The GAS has been used to measure goal attainment and to determine program effectiveness (Kiresuk & Lund, 1976) and has been extended to special education (Carr, 1979). According to Carr (1979), GAS "basically involves establishing goals and specifying a range of outcomes or behaviors that would indicate progress toward achieving those goals" (p. 89). GAS scores were determined by the following sequence. For each goal selected by the student, his or her teacher identified five potential outcomes, ranging from most unfavorable to most favorable. The midpoint on this scale is the expected outcome, that is, what you would consider a satisfactory outcome from the instructional process. These five outcomes were assigned a numerical value, ranging from -2 to $+2$ (midpoint is 0). When instructional activities were completed, the teacher returned to the five potential outcomes and identified the outcome that most closely matched the student's actual achievement and the student received the score associated with that outcome. Using a raw-score conversion key for Goal Attainment Scaling, raw scores were then converted to standardized T-scores (Kiresuk & Lund, 1976) with a mean of 50 and a standard deviation of 10. The transformation of the raw scores to a standardized score allows comparison between goal areas across subjects independent of the particular goal area. When interpreting scores from the GAS, it is important to note that the converted mean T-score value of 50 represents an acceptable outcome, where an "acceptable" outcome means that students learned the goal or skills *to the level expected by the teacher.* Standardized scores of 40 or below indicate that the student did not achieve an acceptable outcome, and scores of 60 and above indicate that the student's progress exceeded expectations. GAS scores for students who worked on more than one goal were calculated by averaging the standardized scores from the two goals. In addition to this indicator of goal attainment, we also collected pre- and post-intervention data regarding student self-determination using *The Arc's Self-Determination Scale* (Wehmeyer, 1996).

The field test indicated that the model was effective in enabling students to attain educationally valued goals. The mean GAS score for the total sample was 49. Twenty-five percent of the standardized GAS scores equaled 50, while 30 percent of the scores were higher than 50, indicating that teachers rated 25 percent of the total number of goals on which students received instruction as having been achieved as expected and rated progress on 30 percent of the total goals as having exceeded expectations. Of the remainder, slightly more than 25 percent of the GAS scores were between 40 and 49, indicating that students made progress on their goal, but did not fully achieve it, and just under 20 percent were rated as the least favorable outcome, essentially indicating no progress on the goal. Additionally, there were significant differences in pre- and post-intervention scores on self-determination and locus of control, in both cases with post-intervention scores more positive than pre-intervention scores. Finally, students showed a general trend toward more effective goal-oriented behavior.

In a separate study, Agran, Blanchard, and Wehmeyer (2000) examined the efficacy of the *Self-Determined Learning Model of Instruction* for students with more significant levels of disability. Nineteen adolescents classified as having severe disabilities under the State of Utah guidelines were involved in instructional activities in which their teachers implemented the model. Unlike the previous study, the research design utilized by these researchers involved a delayed multiple-baseline across three groups design. Students collaborated with their teachers to implement the first phase of the model and, as a result, identified one goal as a target behavior to focus on. Prior to implementing phase 2 of the model, teachers and researchers collected baseline data on student performance of these goals. At staggered intervals subsequent to baseline data collection, teachers implemented the model with students and data collection continued through the end of instructional activities and into a maintenance phase. As was the case with the previous study, Agran and colleagues also collected data about goal attainment using the GAS procedure. At the conclusion of the training period, teachers were asked to report their perceptions of the effects of the model on student performance. Specifically, they were asked to detail the student's progress and changes made by the student.

As before, the model enabled teachers to teach students educationally valued goals. The mean GAS score for the total sample was 60, indicating that, on the average, students exceeded teachers expectations for achievement of their goals. Twenty-one percent of the standardized GAS scores equaled 50, indicating that students attained a satisfactory level of achievement, while 68 percent of the scores were higher than 50, indicating that over two-thirds of the students exceeded expectations of their teachers in relation to goal attainment. Only 10 percent of the students ($\underline{N} = 2$) were rated as the least favorable outcome, essentially indicating no progress on the goal. Thus, in total, 89 percent ($\underline{N} = 17$) of the participants achieved their personal goals at or above the teacher-rated expected outcome levels.

Of the six teachers participating in the study, four completed the social validation forms for 13 students. All forms included feedback regarding the status of guiding students through the three phases of the *Self-Determined Learning Model of Instruction.* All teachers indicated that students appeared to like the process, were willing to work toward their own goals, enjoyed being in charge of their learning, and liked being responsible for their own decisions and actions. One teacher recommended that educators discuss with students the most important skills needed to promote self-determination for successful community employment and adult living. Another suggested that adequate time must be allowed to work with students in the goal-setting process. Of the 19 student participants, 12 provided feedback on their perceptions of the value of the model. All 12 indicated that the model increased their skill proficiency or independence, and five indicated it improved their self-confidence. Last, all said they liked the process. Reasons given included appreciation for the problem-solving process, having the opportunity to talk to their teachers about themselves, making their own choices, and learning new skills based on those decisions. Agran, Blanchard, Wehmeyer and Hughes (2002) also used the *Self-Determined Learning Model of Instruction* as one of several interventions to promote the involvement of students with more significant disabilities in the educational process and obtained similar results.

Finally, we have suggested that the model is applicable for students of all ages as well as students with and without disabilities. Palmer and Wehmeyer (2003) examined the efficacy of the model with elementary age (K–3) students with disabilities. Fourteen teachers from two states (Texas and Kansas) were recruited to implement an early elementary version of the *Self-Determined Learning Model of Instruction* (Palmer & Wehmeyer, 2003) with 50 students, grades K–3 who were identified as having a disability or at risk for such. The mean teacher-rated GAS score was 52.90 (ranging from 30–70) indicating that students achieved goals to an acceptable level. Students also showed gains in knowledge about goal setting and teachers indicated that they found the process effective for teaching their students.

CONCLUSION

This chapter contributes to the pedagogy of self-instruction by showing how the teaching of 12 self-instructional questions fully shifts the control and direction of learning to students. It completes the shift from teacher to student control that began with Chapter 3's showing that student use of three self-management strategies – self-monitoring, self-evaluation, and self-reinforcement – establishes self-control, and with Chapter 4's showing that use of five self-management strategies – goal setting, self-planning, self-monitoring, self-evaluation, and self-reinforcement – establishes self-regulatory control. This chapter completes the shift by showing how use of 12 self-instructional questions establishes problem-solving control over discoveries of how to meet student-identified needs and interests. Indeed, when students learn to ask and answer the 12 discovery questions, they learn to set goals that are consistent with *their* learning needs and interest, they learn to develop plans to meet *their* goals, they learn to take action to implement *their* plans, they learn to evaluate the results of *their own* problem solving, and they learn to adjust their goals, plans, and actions based on *their* evaluations. In other words, they learn to self-instruct in order to discover what they want to learn and how they want to learn it, as summarized in Table 5.1.

The *Self-Determined Learning Model of Instruction* provides an effective way of introducing the self-instructions that promote self-regulated problem solving to learn something new. It identifies key instructional objectives to guide your teaching, key instruction objectives to guide your students' learning, and key educational supports to facilitate learning. The model also underscores important insights into student learning that are often overlooked when attempting to promote discovery learning. They are that (a) students are more likely to discover their needs and interests when they express them as goals to achieve what they want than when they are told by their teachers what they need or like to do, (b) students are more likely to engage in problem solving to meet goals when they have chosen how to achieve them than when they are told what to do to achieve them, and (c) students are more likely to learn through discovery when they are allowed to adjust to their results than when they are told how to adjust to their results. In other words, students are more likely to become independent, au-

---

Table 5.1: The 12 Self-Instructions for Student-Determined Discovery Learning

---

In Order to Set Goals for What I Want to Know,
I ask myself:
1. What do I want to learn?
2. What do I know about it now?
3. What must change for me to learn what I don't know?
4. What can I do to make this happen?
In Order to Take Action to Meet My Goal
I ask myself:
5. What can I do to learn what I don't know?
6. What could keep me from taking action?
7. What can I do to remove these barriers?
8. When will I take action?
In Order to Adjust My Goals and Actions for My Next Discovery,
I ask myself:
9. What actions have I taken?
10. What barriers have been removed?
11. What has changed about what I don't know?
12. Do I know what I want to know?

---

tonomous, self-determined learners when they are supported rather than directed to learn something new. Hopefully, use of this approach to teaching will help you take into account these insights as you shift learning control to students and as they become the self-determined learners they are capable of being.

REFERENCES

Agran, M., Blanchard, C. Hughes, C., & Wehmeyer, M. L. (2002). Increasing the problem-solving skills of students with severe disabilities participating in general education. *Remedial and Special Education, 23,* 279–288.

Agran, M., Blanchard, C., & Wehmeyer, M. L. (2000). Promoting transition goals and self-determination through student-directed learning: The Self-Determined Learning Model of Instruction. *Education and Training in Mental Retardation and Developmental Disabilities, 35,* 351–364.

Agran, M., King-Sears, M, Wehmeyer, M.L., & Copeland, S.R. (2003). *Teachers' guides to inclusive practices: Student-directed learning strategies.* Baltimore: Paul H. Brookes.

Bandura, A.B. (1997). *Self-efficacy: The exercise of control.* New York: W.H. Freeman and Co.

Bransford, J.D., & Stein, B.S. (1984). *The IDEAL problem solver* (2nd ed.). New York: W.H. Freeman.

Carr, R.W., (1979). Goal attainment scaling as a useful tool for evaluating progress in special education. *Exceptional Children, 46,* 88–95.

Gersten, R. & Dimino, J. A. (1993). *Visions and Revisions: A Perspective on Whole Language Controversy.* Remedial and Special Education, 14 (4), 5-13.

Joyce, B., & Weil, M. (1980). *Models of teaching* (2nd ed.). Englewood Cliffs, NJ: Prentice Hall.

Kiresuk, T.J, & Lund, S.H. (1976). Process and measurement using goal attainment scaling. In G.V. Glass (Ed.), *Education Studies Review Manual, Volume 1.* Beverly Hills, CA: Sage.

Lewis, R.B., & Doorlag, D.H. (2003). *Teaching Special Students in General Education Classrooms* (6th Edition). Englewood Cliffs, NJ: Prentice Hall.

Mithaug, D. E. (1991). *Self-determined kids: Raising satisfied and successful children.* Lexington, MA: D.C. Lexington Books.

Mithaug, D. E. (2000). *Learning to theorize: A four-step strategy.* Thousand Oaks, CA: Sage Publications.

Mithaug, D. E., Mithaug, D. K., Agran, M., Martin, J. E., & Wehmeyer, M. L. (2003). *Self-determined learning theory: Construction, verification, and evaluation.* Mahwah, N.J.: Lawrence Erlbaum Associates, Publishers.

Mithaug, D., Wehmeyer, M.L., Agran, M., Martin, J., & Palmer, S., (1998). The self-determined learning model of instruction: Engaging students to solve their learning problems. In M.L. Wehmeyer & D.J. Sands (Eds.), *Making it happen: Student involvement in educational planning, decision-making and instruction* (pp. 299–328). Baltimore: Paul H. Brookes Publishers.

Palmer, S., & Wehmeyer, M.L. (2003). Promoting self-determination in early elementary school: Teaching self-regulated problem-solving and goal setting skills. *Remedial and Special Education, 24,* 115–126.

Wehmeyer, M.L. (1996). A self-report measure of self-determination for adolescents with cognitive disabilities. *Education and Training in Mental Retardation and Developmental Disabilities, 31,* 282–293.

Wehmeyer, M. L., Abery, B., Mithaug, D. E., & Stancliffe, R. J. (2003). *Theory in self-determination: Foundations for educational practice.* Springfield, IL: Charles C Thomas, Publisher, LTD.

Wehmeyer, M.L., Palmer, S., Agran, M., Mithaug, D., & Martin, J. (2000). Promoting causal agency: The Self-Determined Learning Model of Instruction. *Exceptional Children, 66,* 439–453.

Chapter 6

HOW SELF-DETERMINED LEARNING INCREASES AT SCHOOL AND WORK

James E. Martin
Lori Y. Peterson
Chauncey D. Goff

Chapter 3 Step 1: Teaching Self-Control	Chapter 4 Step 2: Teaching Self-Regulation	Chapter 5 Step 3: Teaching Self-Determined Learning	**Chapter 6** **Step 4:** Promoting Self-Determined Transitions
Teacher identifies needs, interests, abilities	Teacher identifies needs, interests, abilities	Student identifies needs, interests, abilities	**Student** identifies needs, interests, abilities for IEPs and Transitions
Teacher sets goals to meet teacher identified needs/interests	Student sets goals to meet teacher identified needs/interests	Student sets goals to meet teacher identified needs/interests	**Student** sets goals to meet needs/interests based on abilities for IEPs and Transitions
Teacher plans to meet goals	Student plans to meet goals	Student plans to meet goals	**Student** makes plans to meet goals for IEPs and Transitions
Student monitors actions to follow plans	Student monitors actions to follow plans	Student monitors actions to follow plans	**Student** monitors actions to follow plans for IEPs and Transitions
Student evaluates results of actions	Student evaluates results of actions and plans	Student evaluates results of actions and plans	**Student** evaluates results of actions and plans for IEPs and Transitions
Student adjusts by self-reinforcing the actions that improve results	Student adjusts by altering plans and actions to get the results that match expectations	Student adjusts by altering plans and actions to get the results that match expectations	**Student** adjusts actions and plans to improve results for IEPs and Transitions

There are many naturally occurring opportunities for students to learn strategies that promote self-determined learning. Take the real-life case of Cody, a vivacious third grader with a significant learning disability who exhibited self-determined learning when given the opportunity to choose what he wanted to learn. This led him to setting goals for learning, developing plans to meet them, self-monitoring, self-evaluating and then adjusting repeatedly until he knew what he wanted to know. His teacher provoked these self-determined learning episodes when she asked him to choose reading assignments that matched his needs, interests, and abilities, as prescribed in the first row of the table above. Cody responded by using her 1-minute timed readings to determine how much he accomplished at the reading. After each one he counted words read correctly and charted results to evaluate his progress. Next, he asked for strategies to help him read faster and understand more. Over time Cody discovered he had made significant gains, which provoked him to set successively higher goals for reading. Then one day, he brought a book to school he asked his parents to buy but that was too difficult to read alone. So he decided to set goals for the number of pages he would read each day and developed a plan to meet them, which included getting help from this teacher who recommended a tutor. He followed through with that suggestion and was soon reading entire books on his own, although at slower rates than he wanted.

Cody generalized these experiences to other areas of his life, too. For example, at a Boy Scout annual sales contest offering a prize for the person selling the most popcorn, Cody announced he would sell $1,000 worth of the product. He followed through the next day with a plan to get to as many houses in his community as possible with his pitch. This involved walking to all homes within a three-mile radius and having his dad drive him to those farther away. He also planned to sell popcorn every evening and weekend. He followed through and met his goal, which won the contest and the prize of meeting a famous basketball player. The local paper published his picture with the star athlete and the next year he entered the contest this time selling $1,500 worth of popcorn. Each year after he sold even more, enjoying meeting goals but never winning again.

Clearly, Cody is unusual in how he adjusts and learns in that other students with disabilities rarely act on plans to meet goals in school or at home. Indeed, most of them enter the middle and secondary years showing little if any determination in their pursuits, which means they leave school lacking the competencies of self-direction and self-correction that are necessary for success in life. There is a reasonable explanation for this, too if you consider students' participation rates at IEP meetings where they are routinely excluded from choosing, deciding, planning, or acting on the educational plans that direct most of their learning in special education (Lehmann, Bassett, & Sands, 1999; Lovitt, Cushing,

& Stump, 1994; Martin, Marshall, & Sale, in press; Martin, Marshall, Wray, Wells, O'Brien, Olvey, & Johnson, 2004; Morningstar, Turnbull, & Turnbull, 1995; Powers, Turner, Matuszewski, Wilson, & Loesch, 1999). There is also the explanation offered some time ago that too much of teacher-directedness during individualized instruction actually reduces students' ability to adjust and learn on their own (Mithaug, Agran, & Martin, 1987). This explains in part why students with disabilities drop out of school twice as often as students without disabilities, why they graduate with standard diplomas 73 percent as often as students without disabilities, and why they find jobs 60 percent as often as students without disabilities (AYPF & CEP, 2002).

The ChoiceMaker Solution

This chapter offers practical solutions to these problems by describing a *Choice-Maker Self-Determination Transition Curriculum* that increases student control over their education programs *and* their school-to-work transitions. This curriculum incorporates the factors affecting self-determined learning that were identified in the self-determined learning model of instruction (Mithaug, Wehmeyer, Agran, Martin, & Palmer, 1998) and explained by the theory of self-determined learning (Mithaug, Mithaug, Agran, Martin, & Wehmeyer, 2003). Consequently, it helps students find answers to the three key learning-to-learn questions: "What do I want to know? What is my plan finding out?" and "Have I learned what I want to know?" The following sections describe the procedures, materials, and assessments used with this approach.

The Materials

The *ChoiceMaker* consists of seven sets of materials and an assessment tool. Each set can be used separately or in combination to increase opportunities for students to control the content and direction of their learning. The assessment is a 54-item curriculum-referenced procedure that measures student progress in the curriculum. It also measures opportunities at school for students to practice and master competencies prescribed by the curriculum. Table 6.1 outlines its scope and sequence, which cover three domains: choosing goals, expressing goals, and taking action. These domains represent the three key dimensions (or activities) of self-determination. These domains were identified and field-tested by a team of curriculum developers who also wrote the lessons for goals and objectives identified in the table. Teachers from middle schools and high schools used them in field tests, and students provided feedback for adjustments and revisions. Various research teams across the country tested the effectiveness of final versions of the curriculum.

Table 6.1: ChoiceMaker Self-Determination Curriculum Matrix									
1. Choosing Goals				2. Expressing Goals		3. Taking Action			
A. Student IEP Understanding	B. Student Interests	C. Student Skills & Limits	D. Student Goals	E. Student Leading IEP Meeting	F. Student Reporting	G. Student Plan	H. Student Action	I. Student Evaluation	J. Student Adjustment
A1. Indicate goal setting purpose & component	B1. Express school interests	C1. Express school skills & limits	D1. Indicate options & choose school goals	E1. Begin meeting & introduce participants	F1. Express interests (from B1-7	G1. Break general goals into specific goals that can be completed now	H1. Record or report performance	I1.Determine if goals are achieved	J1. Adjust goals if necessary
A2. Identify student rights	B2. Express employment interests	C2. Express employment skills & limits	D2. Indicate options & choose employment goals	E2. Review past goals & performance	F2. Express skills & limits (from C1-6)	G2. Establish standard for specific goals	H2. Perform specific goals to standard	I2. Compare performance to standards	J2. Adjust or repeat goal standards
A3. Identify goal setting roles & timelines	B3. Express post-high school education interests	C3. Express post-high school education skills & limits matters,	D3. Indicate options & choose post-high school education goals	E3. Ask questions if don't understand	F3. Express options & goals (from D1-6)	G3. Determine how to get feedback from environment	H3. Obtain feedback on performance	I3. Evaluate feedback	J3. Adjust or repeat method for feedback
	B4. Express personal matters, interests	C4. Express personal matters, skills & limits	D4. Indicate options & choose personal matters, goals	E4. Ask for feedback		G4. Determine motivation to complete specific goals	H4. Motivate self to complete specific goals	I4. Evaluate motivation	J4. Adjust or repeat motivation
	B5. Express housing & daily living interests	C5. Express housing & daily living skills & limits	D5. Indicate options & choose housing & daily living goals	E5. Deal with differences in opinion		G5. Determine strategies for completing specific goals	H5. Use strategies to perform specific goals	I5. Evaluate effectiveness of strategies	J5. Adjust or repeat strategies
	B6. Express community participation interests	C6. Express community participation skills & limits	D6. Indicate options & choose community participation goals	E6. Close meeting by summarizing decisions		G6. Determine support needed to complete specific goals	H6. Obtain support needed	I6. Evaluate support used	J6. Adjust or repeat support
	B7. Express what is most important					G7. Prioritize & schedule to complete specific goals	H7. Follow schedule	I7. Evaluate schedule	J7. Adjust or repeat schedule
						G8. Express belief that goals can be obtained		I8. Evaluate belief	J8. Adjust or repeat belief that goals can be obtained

The Choosing of Goals

The *Choosing Goals* component provides opportunities for students to express their interests and abilities across various personal, educational, and employment domains. It includes: *Choosing Employment Goals* (Marshall, Martin, Maxson, & Jerman, 1997), *Choosing Education Goals* (Martin, Marshall, Hughes, Jerman, & Maxson, 2000), and *Choosing Personal Goals* (Marshall, Martin, Jerman, Hughes, & Maxson, 1999). These programs help students set goals during various transitions in their lives. For example, students who have yet to identify post-school employment goals use one of the programs to identify goals that are consistent with their post-school interests. A video entitled *Choosing Goals to Plan Your Life* (Martin, Marshall, Maxson, & Hallahan, 1997) provides examples of high school students with disabilities setting goals in different domains. After watching the video and completing the lessons, students complete worksheets and choose goals that are consistent with *their* needs and interests. Then they use the worksheets to discuss their plans during transition class, meetings with parents, and IEP meetings. Cross, Cooke, Wood, and Test (1999) found that the program was significant in getting students to participate actively and constructively at meetings.

Education Goals. During the *Choosing Education Goals* program, students set goals for their high school and postsecondary pursuits that are consistent with their interests, abilities, and opportunities. They also develop plans of study for their IEP meetings, as required by the Individuals With Disabilities Education Act (IDEA). Throughout the lessons, they use choice-making procedures to:

- Determine their vocational, income, personal, and educational goals for different stages of their lives.
- Identify school subjects they like.
- Complete a personalized plan of study to be used at their IEP meeting.
- Develop an individualized education performance summary that examines test scores, grades, class ranking, and other indicators (see Figure 6.1).
- Learn postsecondary education terminology and available postsecondary programs that match their interests, skills, and limits.
- Complete study habits, work habits, and academic skills self-assessment (see Figure 6.2).
- Develop an individualized postsecondary education options information table.
- Choose secondary and postsecondary goals to match their interests and abilities.
- Maintain a study habits log.

Peterson, Van Dycke, Borland, Crownover, and Martin (2004) found that when students use this component of the curriculum, they significantly improve their planning capabilities, which is a central goal of the curriculum.

**Figure 6.1: Sample Section of the Educational Performance Summary Form
from the *ChoiceMaker Choosing Education Goals* Program**

Educational Performance Summary

Name: _____ Date: _____

Directions: Meet with your school counselor to complete this form.

School Year	G.P.A.	Class Rank	School Year	G.P.A.	Class Rank
9th			11th		
10th			12th		

Name of test: Type of test: Date of test:

Sub-categories	Stand. score	Percentile	Range		
1. English			below average	average	above average
2. Math			below average	average	above average
3. Science			below average	average	above average
4. Social Studies			below average	average	above average
5. *Other:*			below average	average	above average
6. Overall Score			below average	average	above average

Personal Goals. The *Choosing Personal Goals* lessons help students develop a quality-of-life plan. Because most of the activities in this domain take place in social settings, students discover their interests and abilities by interacting with others in various situations and then evaluating their interactions. First, they determine the types of personal leisure activities they like most using a rating form similar to the one illustrated in Figure 6.3. Then, they compare their ratings with how they actually interact with others during free time. Based on this comparison, they discover for themselves what they like, as indicated by the match or lack thereof between pre- and post-interaction ratings. They repeat this procedure until their claims about what they like are consistent with their behavior in various social situations. In the course of completing this component of the curriculum, students:

- Investigate activities, events, and services that are available at school and in their communities.
- Evaluate interests, skills, and limits associated with these activities and consider alternatives they suggest.
- Act on a preferred activities and evaluate reactions to those outcomes.

Figure 6.2: Sample Section of the School Work Habits and Academic Skills Form from the *ChoiceMaker Choosing Education Goals* Program

School Work Habits and Academic Skills

Student's Name _____ Class _____

Teacher's Name _____ Date _____

Teacher Directions: Below is a list of school work habits and academic skills. Please complete the "Teacher Thinks" column. Choose the response that best describes the work habits and academic skills this student displays in your class. You may also write responses in the "comments" column.

Student Directions: Below is a list of school work habits and academic skills. Please complete the "I Think" column. Choose the response that best describes the work habits and academic skills you display in the class.

Rating Scale		
3 = very good	2 = O.K.	1 = needs improvement

School Work Habits	I Think			Teacher Thinks			Matches		Comments
	3	2	1	3	2	1	Y	N	
1. Attends class regularly									
2. Arrives to class on time									
3. Brings needed materials									
4. Ready when class begins									
5. Turns in completed homework									
6. Does readings before class									

The Assessment

The *ChoiceMaker Assessment* covers the same three components of the curriculum: choosing goals, expressing goals, and taking action. The choosing goals assessment evaluates student abilities to set goals based on their interests and skills in school, employment, and postsecondary domains. The expressing goals assessment evaluates students' leadership capabilities at IEP meetings, and the take action assessment evaluates their goal attainment skills. The full assessment instrument is curriculum-referenced, with its 54 items comparing performance ratings with benchmarks in the curriculum. It also provides progress data on students' self-determined learning. A series of reliability studies in targeted states indicated test-retest consistencies of the instrument in the range of .8 between first and second administrations over a 2-week period.

Using ChoiceMaker for Self-Directed IEPs

The *ChoiceMaker* also prepares students 14-years and older to direct their IEP meetings as required by law (Field, Martin, Miller, Ward, & Wehmeyer, 1998).

Figure 6.3: Sample Form Used to Evaluate Personal Leisure Values in the
ChoiceMaker Choosing Personal Goals

What's Important to Me Worksheet

Name _____ Date _____

Directions: For each item below, color in the sections that represent how important
each item is to you. Number 1 means "not important" to you and
4 means "very important" to you.

	Not Important	Very Important

Family
A sense of belonging, feeling like someone is there for me, acceptance

Pets & Animals
Caring for animals, companionship, or appreciation for wildlife

Friends & Relationships
Companionship, connections to people, or socializing

Religion
Spirituality, belief in higher power, or belonging to religious groups

Caring/Helping Others
A sense of responsibility to other people or doing things that benefit others

Learning
Learning new things, improving my skills, or being challenged

Creativity & the Arts
Participating in creative activities like art, music, or drama, or doing
things in new and unique ways

Recreation
Physical activity or participating in sports

Indeed, studies have shown that students who attend IEP meetings without first receiving instruction like this avoid participating because they don't know what is going on or why they are there, and consequently they think that such meetings are a waste of time (Lehmann, Bassett, & Sands, 1999; Lovitt, Cushing, & Stump, 1994; Martin, Marshall, & Sale, in press; Morningstar, Turnbull, & Turnbull, 1995; Powers, Turner, Matuszewski, Wilson, & Loesch 1999).

Self-Directed IEPs

The Self-Directed IEP program seeks to promote the value of student-directed IEP meetings by providing a sequence of 11 lessons that teach students to be participant-directors of their own meetings. The lessons include the following video, instruction, and worksheet components:

- *Self-Directed IEP in Action* video (7 minutes) (Martin, Marshall, & Hallahan, 1996). This component introduces the main players of the meetings: the student, parents, teachers, and school administrators. It shows students with various disabilities using their meetings to discuss their experiences and interests with other members of the team present.
- *Self-Directed IEP video* (17 minutes) (Martin, Marshall, Maxson, & Hallahan, 1996). This component shows a student explaining to his friend how he directed his IEP meeting. Through a series of flashbacks the student models the steps of the *Self-Directed IEP*, which include:

  1. Beginning the meeting by stating its purpose;
  2. Introducing everyone;
  3. Reviewing past goals and performance;
  4. Asking for feedback from others;
  5. Stating transition goals;
  6. Asking questions;
  7. Dealing with differences of opinion;
  8. Stating supports needed;
  9. Summarizing goals;
  10. Closing the meeting by thanking everyone; and
  11. Working on IEP goals all year.

- *Teacher's Manual.* This publication provides background information, lesson plans, and answer keys to quizzes and activities. The lesson plans provide strategies and activities for teaching the IEP-meeting competencies that include mnemonic strategies, vocabulary-building exercises, role-playing, discussions, readings, and writing responsibilities.
- *Student Workbook.* This publication helps students follow each step of the *Self-Directed IEP* program at meetings. It includes a script for students to follow that covers all the steps needed to direct and control the proceedings.

A study of the effectiveness of this approach with Florida high school students with learning disabilities and mental retardation reported that students who completed this component of the curriculum:

- Attended more IEP meetings;
- Had more parents at IEP meetings;
- Talked more about their interests;
- Shared more of their dreams;
- Talked more about the jobs they wanted after leaving school;
- Felt like they were boss of the IEP meeting; and
- Felt more confident about reaching IEP goals (Sweeney, 1997).

Snyder and Shapiro (1997) and Snyder (2002) similarly found that *Self-Directed IEPs* taught adolescents with emotional and behavior problems the skills needed to direct their own IEP meetings, and Allen, Smith, Test, Flowers, and Wood (2001) reported a functional relationship between mastery of self-direct IEP competencies and participation at meetings. Similar results have been reported using other self-directed methods and materials, as well (Halpern, Herr, Doren, & Wolf 1997; McGahee-Kovac, 1995;).van Reusen, Bos, Schumaker, & Deshler, 1994; Wehmeyer, Lawrence, Kelchner, Palmer, Garner, & Soukup, 2004).

Take Action

After mastering the competencies needed to direct IEP meetings, students must learn to take action to meet the goals they set at those meetings. The *Take Action* program provides this instruction. It includes a 10-minute video that shows students developing action plans to meet their IEP goals (Martin, Marshall, Maxson, & Hallahan, 1999). The competencies targeted here are: (1) setting a standard for goal attainment, (2) identifying a means to get performance feedback, (3) identifying a means of motivating action on plans, (4) identifying strategies that help, (5) seeking needed support, and (6) developing a schedule for implementing the plan. The following lessons summarize these features.

- *Lesson 1* introduces the *Take Action* process. Here students learn the four parts of taking action: planning, acting, evaluating, and adjusting. Next, they complete a quiz to reflect that understanding as illustrated in Figure 6.4. Last, they break their goals into doable action units as illustrated in Figure 6.5.
- *Lesson 2.* This lesson introduces the plan component, which begins with a 10-minute video entitled *Take Action* that demonstrates the construction of plans and the taking of action to enact them. After watching the video, students identify the main components of a plan, which are the standard for knowing when a goal is met, the motivation for taking action, a strategy to use when taking action, and a schedule and timeline for taking action. Next, they complete a series of activities demonstrating mastery of each step. The session ends with students completing a quiz indicating their mastery of these planning competencies. Figure 6.6 presents the self-instructional form students use during this lesson.
- *Lesson 3.* During this lesson, students develop their own plan in a hands-on activity guided by these self-instruction questions: What is my standard? What is my motivation? What is my strategy? What is my schedule? What are my supports? What is my feedback?
- *Lesson 6.* Last, they evaluate results and adjust plans based on evaluations in a recursive process that allows them to control their progress toward goal attainment.

Figure 6.4: Quiz from Lesson 1 of *ChoiceMaker Take Action*

STEPS: Act   Adjust   Plan   Evaluate

1. _____

2. _____

3. _____

4. _____

**Figure 6.5: Initial Goal Breakdown Exercise from the
ChoiceMaker Take Action Instructional Program**

Roland Coaster's
Breaking Down Long-Term Goals

Roland Coaster's Story
Roland wants to spend his birthday with his friends at Joy Rides Amusement Park. He went there with his friend John on John's birthday and it was really fun. The problem is Roland doesn't know how to get there, when it's open, or how much it costs. To go, he'll need to get that information.

Long-Term Goal *What you want to accomplish*

Write your long-term goal in the box below.

Spend my birthday at the amusement park

Short-Term Goals

Smaller goals leading to your long-term goal you can start working on this week

Write your short-term goals in the boxes below.

Is the short-term goal a smaller goal that will lead to your long term goal?   yes   no
Is the short-term goal one you can work on this week?   yes   no

Sequence
Do your short-term goals need to be completed in a certain sequence? If yes, number them in that sequence on the lines below the boxes.

Figure 6.6: Progress Quiz from Lesson 2 of the
***ChoiceMaker Take Action* Instructional Program**

Plan Parts   **Questions I ask myself**

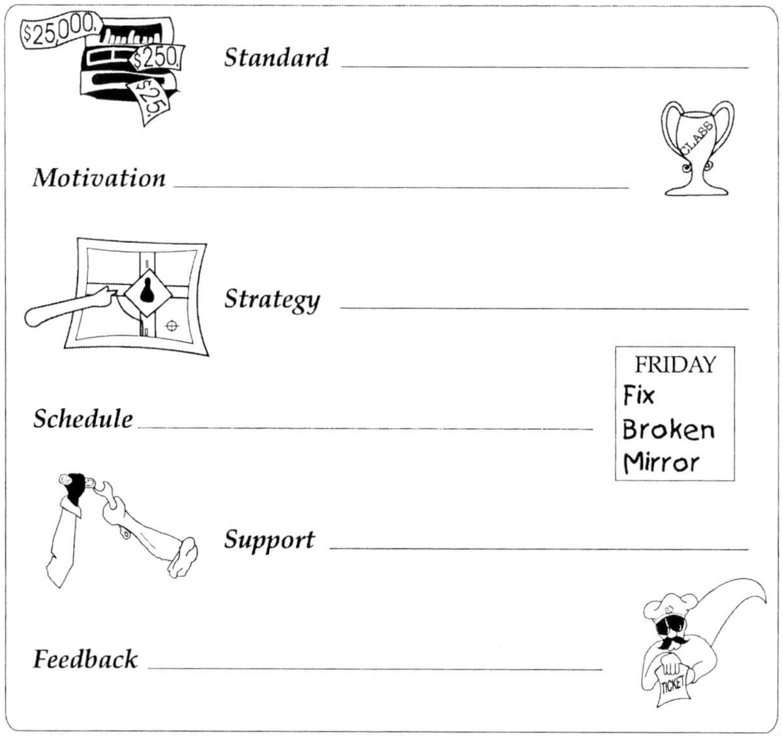

Standard _____

Motivation _____

Strategy _____

FRIDAY
Fix
Broken
Mirror

Schedule _____

Support _____

Feedback _____

German, Martin, Marshall, and Sale (2000) conducted a study on the effectiveness of the *Take Action* component with students with mild to moderate mental retardation and found that after completing the lessons, students made significant gains in their ability to meet their daily goals. During a pre-instruction condition, for example, they met 25 percent or less of their daily goals. After instruction, however, they met between 80 and 100 percent of their goals.

Of course, success like this must occur in as many situations as possible for students to generalize their self-directed learning across settings and time. Indeed, Walden (2002) found in a study of university students with learning disabilities that even though students learned the goal attainment competencies by completing the *Take Action* program, they did not apply these strategies in their pursuits generally, which suggests that mastering self-determination competencies for IEP meetings is probably insufficient for generalized use of strategies in the full range of challenging situations.

Self-Instructions for Self-Directed Employment

Clearly, if students are to be fully competent at controlling the content and direction of their learning, they must use all six self-determined learning strategies routinely across as many tasks and situations as possible. Indeed, when this level of competency is established, students automatically (a) identify their need to learn something new from a situation, (b) identify the outcome that will satisfy that need to know, (c) develop plans and identify strategies to meet that learning goal, (d) self-monitor the use of those strategies, (e) evaluate the outcomes of their plan, and (f) adjust to results and repeat the process until they learn what they want to know. As Martin, Mithaug, Oliphint, Husch, Frazier, and Marshall (2003) reported, workers with severe disabilities who routinely employed these learning-to-learn strategies across various work and task situations during employment pursuits were more likely to get and keep jobs they wanted than were workers who did not.

The Self-Directed Employment Model

Figure 6.7 presents the conceptual basis of this approach to job seeking, which was developed and validated by Mithaug, Martin, and Agran (1987); Mithaug, Martin, Agran, and Rusch, (1988); and Martin, Mithaug, Oliphint, Husch, & Frazier (2002). The approach is based on the argument that if all learning is adjustment as claimed by self-determined learning theory (Mithaug, Mithaug, Agran, Martin, & Wehmeyer, 2003), then learning through adjustment is as functional in the workplace as it is in the classroom. The following curriculum is based on that approach to job seeking. It empowers job seekers to choose, manage, evaluate, and adjust until they find the job they want. It teaches them to use the same self-determination strategies to solve performance problems on the job that were prescribed in previous chapters to solve achievement problems in the classroom. Figure 6.8 shows how this particular problem-solving cycle is guided by self-instructional questions that identify desirable jobs (assessment), get one of them (placement), and then succeed at that job (follow-up).

Assessment. During this phase, job seekers choose jobs they want based on what they like, what is available, and what they can do. They get this information about themselves and about job opportunities by visiting job sites in the community and then comparing their pre-visit ratings with their post-visit ratings for each job. They repeat these before and after ratings until they consistently rate their job site experiences on what they like, what they can do, and what they want.

The form in Figure 6.9 illustrates how this works. Prior to visits, workers circle the job characteristics they "think" they like. After visiting the site, they rate their

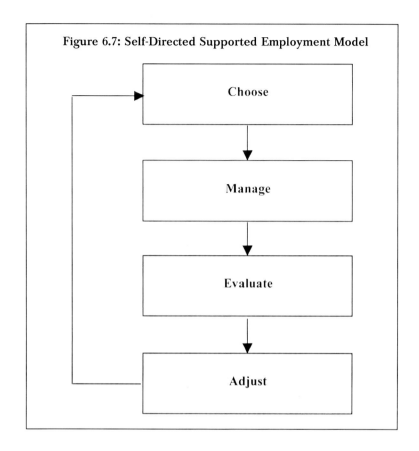

Figure 6.7: Self-Directed Supported Employment Model

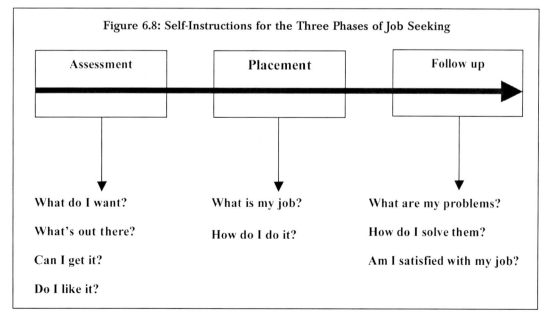

Figure 6.8: Self-Instructions for the Three Phases of Job Seeking

Figure 6.9: Self-Directed Employment's Written Characteristics I Like Assessment
(Martin, Mithaug, Oliphant, et al., 2002, p. 303)

I:B:7:1   **Characteristics I Like versus What Is Here: Form A**   Exploring Choices
Testing Choices

Name: _____   Jobsite: _____   Date: _____

What I like (Before)		★	✓	What is here (After)		(Matches)
Work alone	Work with others			Work alone	Work with others	Yes No
Quiet workplace	Noisy workplace			Quiet workplace	Noisy workplace	Yes No
Part-time	Full-time			Part-time	Full-time	Yes No
Weekdays only	Weekends, too			Weekdays only	Weekends, too	Yes No
Hard job	Easy job			Hard job	Easy job	Yes No
Work inside	Work outside			Work inside	Work outside	Yes No
Few rules	Defined rules			Few rules	Defined rules	Yes No
Work standing up	Work sitting down			Work standing up	Work sitting down	Yes No
Mornings	Evenings			Mornings	Evenings	Yes No
Attractive place	Looks of place do not matter			Attractive place	Looks of place do not matter	Yes No
Detail is important	Detail is not important			Detail is important	Detail is not important	Yes No
Dress up for work	Do not dress up			Dress up for work	Do not dress up	Yes No
Physical work	Thinking work			Physical work	Thinking work	Yes No
Important to work fast	Speed is unimportant			Important to work fast	Speed is unimportant	Yes No
Same tasks every day	Different tasks every day			Same tasks every day	Different tasks every day	Yes No
Work with people	Work with things			Work with people	Work with things	Yes No
Little supervision	A lot of supervision			Little supervision	A lot of supervision	Yes No
Daytime work	Nighttime work			Daytime work	Nighttime work	Yes No
Small business	Large business			Small business	Large business	Yes No
Other:	Other:			Other:	Other:	Yes No
Other:	Other:			Other:	Other:	Yes No

Number of matches:
_____
Available matches:

= ____.____

Characteristics match
x   100

= _____ %

Percentage of characteristics match

100%
Good match
75%
Okay match
50%
Poor match
25%
Not a match
0%

After determining the four top-ranked characteristics and checking them, write "okay" beside each checked item that matches the characteristic circled in the "What is here" column.

Number of okays:
_____
4

x 100   =   _____ %

Percentage of most important characteristics match

preferences again to determine whether anything changed. They repeat this self-rating process several times for each job site until their preference ratings prior to visits match their preference ratings after visits. By repeating this process, they discover what they like. As indicated earlier, Martin, Mithaug, Husch, Frazier, and Marshall (2002) used this approach with more than 750 individuals with severe disabilities and found that those who learned what they liked and wanted through this process of discovery and adjustment were significantly more successful after their job closures than were those who did not.

Placement. Once job seekers get the job they like and want, they usually experience social, personal, and work challenges that interfere with their performance, which require additional problem solving to resolve. Again, adjustment contracts are useful in that workers use them to identify discrepancies between their self-ratings and their supervisor's ratings. For example, when a difference between the two ratings occurs – a supervisor indicates "no" and the worker indicates "yes" on a rating – the worker targets the questionable behavior by setting goals, developing plans, taking action, evaluating results, and then adjusting as needed. Figure 6.10 illustrates a picture-based contract used for this purpose in the supported employment program described by Martin, Mithaug, Oliphint, Husch, and Frazier (2002).

Follow-up. During the follow-up phase, workers learn to adapt and learn from the changes they make on the job. This stage focuses wholly on on-the-job learning, which requires frequent, repeated adjustments over time, again with each adjustment directed and controlled by the same goal setting, planning, acting, evaluating, and adjusting, as before. And again, adjustment contracts help direct this problem-solving process. For example, each morning workers use contracts to set at least one goal to be accomplished for that day. Next, they develop plans to meet it. Then, they direct their work and behavior toward the attainment of their goal. After the shift, they solicit feedback from the supervisor to identify whether they met their goal or whether another round of adjustments is necessary. For example, if they receive a "no" on their supervisor's evaluation of their social behavior due to their talking too much with other workers, they set a goal to talk less often the next day. The next day they focus on that goal, repeating the process of getting supervisor feedback to guide their adjustments for the following day.

To illustrate with actual cases, a 32-year-old former mechanical engineer with traumatic brain injury used improvement contracts like these to help him fill 15 cu. ft. bags with packing material, mark inventory sheets, and then stack bags in designated areas. Prior to use of the contracts he had received negative evaluations from his supervisor for his failure to perform these tasks correctly. The cause of his difficulty was the requirement that he record each completed bag as regular or anti-static and then write its weight in an appropriate column. His plan was to

Figure 6.10: Sample Work Improvement Contract

I:C:12:5	**Work Improvement: Form B**	Testing Choices

Name: _____ Jobsite: _____ Date: _____ Session: _____

Goal	Plan	Evaluation		Great	Match	Next
Follow company rules		I think ☐ / Job coach thinks ☐ Follow company rules	Break company rules ☐ / ☐		Yes No	
Come to work		I think ☐ / Job coach thinks ☐ Come to work	Miss work ☐ / ☐		Yes No	
Come to work on time		I think ☐ / Job coach thinks ☐ Come to work on time	Come to work late ☐ / ☐		Yes No	
Call if you miss work		I think ☐ / Job coach thinks ☐ Call if you miss work	Miss work without calling ☐ / ☐		Yes No	
Work accurately		I think ☐ / Job coach thinks ☐ Work accurately	Make mistakes ☐ / ☐		Yes No	
Pay attention to work		I think ☐ / Job coach thinks ☐ Pay attention to work	Pay little attention ☐ / ☐		Yes No	
Work at the right pace		I think ☐ / Job coach thinks ☐ Work at the right pace	Work too fast or too slow ☐ / ☐		Yes No	
Work safely		I think ☐ / Job coach thinks ☐ Work safely	Work unsafely ☐ / ☐		Yes No	
Take specified breaks		I think ☐ / Job coach thinks ☐ Take specified breaks	Take too many breaks ☐ / ☐		Yes No	
Listen and use feedback		I think ☐ / Job coach thinks ☐ Listen and use feedback	Reject feedback ☐ / ☐		Yes No	

Number of matches: _____ = . _____ x 100 = _____ %
Available matches: Percentage of work matches

Number of positive job coach answers: _____ = . _____ x 100 = _____ %
Available answers: Percentage of positive job coach work answers

Self-Directed Employment: A Handbook for Transition Teachers and Employment Specialists by James Martin et al. © 2002 Paul H. Brookes Publishing Co.

memorize and follow these two self-instructions: "Mark in yellow, Weigh in blue," which corresponded with the color coded columns on the inventory sheet. He used this strategy the following day and as a result improved his performance rating from zero to 82 percent positive, which met his goal.

In another case, a 25-year-old man suffering from traumatic brain injury and learning disabilities was employed as a machinist while attending college. At work, he was responsible for measuring and cutting stock, grinding, de-burring, counting and packaging finished products for shipment, daily cleanup, and other duties. After working two weeks, his supervisor contacted the supported employment staff because his production levels were substandard. Again, use of an improvement contract helped. This one required that he set production goals for the number of pieces he expected to finish each hour, compare his results with his goals, the shop standard, and with his supervisor, and then reset his goals the next period based on those comparisons. Using this strategy, his supervisor's "yes" evaluations increased from 43 to 88 percent.

In yet another actual case example, an 18-year-old worker with an autism diagnosis was employed at a fast-food restaurant maintaining the salad bar. He had difficulty managing his responsibilities so he learned to use a picture-based contract that helped him record daily tasks to be completed in several work, social, and personal domains. At the end of each day, he evaluated his accomplishments using his ratings and those of his supervisor, which allowed him to identify the problem to address with the next day's goals. This resulted in "yes" evaluations from his supervisor increasing from 35 percent to 95 percent.

How Self-Determined Employment Works

The *ChoiceMaker* curriculum uses contracts like these to teach students to control their job-seeking pursuits and adjustments (see B2: express employment interests, C2: express employment skills and limits, and D2: Indicate options and choose employment goals in Table 6.1). These lessons focus on topics usually covered in work-study, on-the-job training, volunteer work, and afterschool jobs, although here the focus is on getting students *to discover for themselves* what they like and can do. Hence, the lessons introduce job characteristics and job duties that students rate on worksheets as: *Job Characteristics I Like,* and *Job Duties I Like, My Work, Social, and Personal Skills.* By rating themselves on these factors repeatedly over time, they discover what they like and can do across many job categories. Then they use that information to develop a vocational profile, which they share with others at IEP meetings. Figure 6.11 illustrates a worksheet students would use to identify the job characteristics *they prefer,* and Figure 6.12 illustrates a worksheet they would use to identify the work strengths and weaknesses *they identified.*

Figure 6.11: *ChoiceMaker* Choosing Employment Goals' Graph of Chosen Job Characteristics

Characteristics	Times I Chose Each Characteristic
1. work alone / lots of people around	
2. quiet workplace / noisy workplace	
3. weekdays only / weekends too	
4. easy job / challenging job	
5. dress up for work / do not dress up / wear uniform	
6. standing up / sitting down / moving around	

Figure 6.12: Self-Determination Contract to Solve On-the-Job Problems

Name: Joe   Date: _____   Site: Grocery Store

Important Skills at This Job	How I Did	Supervisor Thinks	Supervisor, Teacher, or Student Comments	Matches
Work				
1. Work fast	very good 3 / OK 2 / needs improvement 1	very good 3 / OK 2 / needs improvement 1		YES NO
2. Put items in correct place	very good 3 / OK 2 / needs improvement 1	very good 3 / OK 2 / needs improvement 1		YES NO
3. Read labels correctly	very good 3 / OK 2 / needs improvement 1	very good 3 / OK 2 / needs improvement 1		YES NO

Choose and Take Action To Find the Right Job

The *Choose and Take Action* program combines software, classroom lessons, and community experiences to empower students with disabilities to make practical career choices. The video segments illustrate how use of the forms guides students' job choices as well as their adjustments to those choices. The lessons teach students to:

• Choose from a variety of work options;
• Plan whether they want to watch or do the activity;
• Complete plans in the community setting;
• Evaluate what they like and do not like about the setting, activity, and work-site characteristics, as well as how well they work in those settings; and
• Use information gained in the experience to make informed choices.

The Choose and Take Action Cycle

The *Choose and Take Action* cycle consists of several steps. First, students view pairs of randomly presented videos of the employment settings, activities, and job characteristics present in most community jobs (see Figure 6.13). It is based on the method

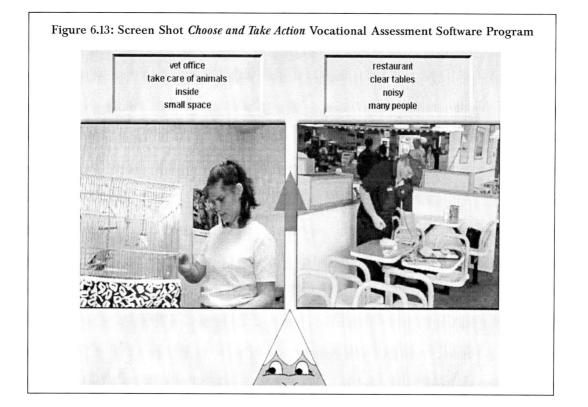

Figure 6.13: Screen Shot *Choose and Take Action* Vocational Assessment Software Program

of paired comparisons (Mithaug, & Hanawalt, 1978; Mithaug & Mar, 1980) that requires all possible combinations of tasks and work conditions to be presented as pair options for choosing only one from each pair. Using video presentations, all possible pair combinations of tasks, jobs, and settings are presented until the surviving option is the one most favored by the student. Based on this choice information, students go to community jobs consistent with their choices in order to directly experience those chosen tasks, work conditions, and co-worker relationships. After these visits, they use the self-rating comparison forms to adjust their preferences and choices.

Throughout, teachers provide guidance so students can complete each step as independently as possible. The 31, 20-second clips of the software cover 14 settings and 15 activities that represent the jobs, entry-level tasks, and work characteristics of most communities. The software also records student choices at each phase of the adjustment cycle, with summary reports indicating choice patterns across employment options. Charts like the one in Figure 6.14 reflect the range of task preferences reported by one student.

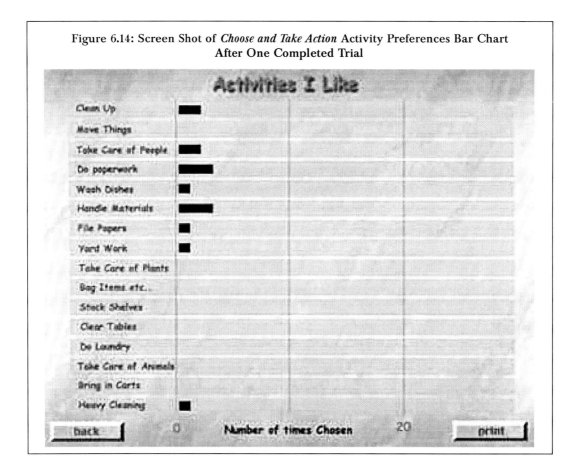

Figure 6.14: Screen Shot of *Choose and Take Action* Activity Preferences Bar Chart After One Completed Trial

CONCLUSION

This chapter addressed some of the credibility and effectiveness challenges that face special education today. The credibility challenge addressed was the insipient failure of the IEP process to involve students more fully in decisions that directly impact their lives, and the effectiveness challenge addressed was the persistent failure of students to succeed after they leave school. Our view is that both challenges can be met if we adopt the view that all learning is adjustment and that teaching students to adjust teaches them to learn "how to learn" in any challenging situation. In this chapter we showed how teaching students to adjust as they learn to direct and control their IEPs could make their educational pursuits more empowering, just as teaching them to adjust to their pursuits of community jobs could make their school-to-work transitions more successful. Indeed, both of these outcomes are within grasp if students master the learning-to-learn strategies that direct and control all of their learning pursuits. This chapter presented a curriculum that showed this to be both a practical and effective approach to enhancing positive outcomes of student-directed IEPs and school-to-work transitions.

REFERENCES

Allen, S. K., Smith, A. C., Test, D. W., Flowers, C., & Wood, W. M. (2001). The effects of *self-directed IEP* on student participation in IEP meetings. *Career Development for Exceptional Individuals, 24*(2), 107–120.

American Youth Policy Forum (AYPF) & Center on Education Policy (CEP). (2002). *Twenty-five years of educating children with disabilities: The good news and the work ahead.* Washington, D.C.: Author.

Cross, T., Cooke, N. L., Wood, W. M., & Test, D. W. (1999). Comparison of the effects of MAPS and Choice-Maker on student self-determination skills. *Education and Training in Mental Retardation and Developmental Disabilities, 34*(4), 499–510.

Field, S. S., Martin, J. E., Miller, R. J., Ward, M., & Wehmeyer, M. L. (1998). *A practical guide for teaching self-determination.* Reston, VA: Council for Exceptional Children.

German, S. L., Martin, J. E., Huber Marshall, L., & Sale, P. (2000). Promoting self-determination: Using *Take Action* to teach goal attainment. *Career Development for Exceptional Individuals, 23*(1), 27–38.

Halpern A.S., Herr, C. M., Doren, B., & Wolf, N. K. (1997). *NEXT S.T.E.P.* Austin, TX: PRO-ED.

Lehmann, J. P., Bassett, D. S., & Sands, D. J. (1999). Students' participation in transition-related actions: A qualitative study. *Remedial and Special Education, 20*, 160–169.

Lovitt, T. C., Cushing, S. S., & Stump, C. S. (1994). High school students rate their IEPs: Low opinions and lack of ownership. *Intervention in School and Clinic, 30*, 34–37.

Marshall, L., Martin, J. E., Jerman, P. A., Hughes, W. M., & Maxson, L. L. (1999). *Choosing personal goals.* Longmont, CO: Sopris West, Inc.

Marshall, L., Martin, J. E., Maxson, L. L., & Jerman, P. A. (1997). *Choosing employment goals.* Longmont, CO: Sopris West, Inc.

Martin, J. E., & Marshall, L. (1996). ChoiceMaker: Infusing self-determnaton instruction into the IEP and transition process. In D. J. Sands, & M. L. Wehmeyer (Eds.), *Self-determination across the life span* (pp. 215–236). Baltimore: Paul H. Brookes.

Martin, J. E., Marshall, L., & DePry, R., L. (2001). Participatory decision-making. In R. W. Flexer, T. J. Simmons, P. Luft & R. M. Baer (Eds.), *Transition planning for secondary students with disabilities* (pp. 304–332). Columbus, OH: Merrill Prentice Hall.

Martin, J. E., Marshall, L., & Sale, R. P. (in press). Student participation in their own IEP meetings: A three-year study. *Exceptional Children.*

Martin, J. E., Marshall, L., Hughes, W. M., Jerman, P. A., & Maxson, L. L. (2000). *Choosing educational goals.* Longmont, CO: Sopris West.

Martin, J. E., Marshall, L., & Hallahan, M. (1996). *Self-directed IEP in action* [instructional video]. Longmont, CO: Sopris West.

Martin, J. E. Marshall, L., Maxson, L. L., & Hallahan, M. (1996). *Self-directed IEP.* Longmont, CO: Sopris West.

Martin, J. E., Marshall, L., Maxson, L. L., & Hallahan, M. (1997). *Choosing goals to plan your life.* Longmont, CO: Sopris West.

Martin, J. E. , Marshall, L., Maxson, L. L., & Hallahan, M. (1999). *Take Action.* Longmont, CO: Sopris West.

Martin, J. E., Mithaug, D. E., Husch, J. V., Frazier, E. S., & Marshall, L. (2003). The effects of optimal opportunities and adjustments during job searches by adults with severe disabilities. In D. E. Mithaug, D. K. Mithaug, M. Agran, J. E. Martin, & M. Wehmeyer (Eds.), *Self-determined learning theory: Construction, verification, and evaluation* (pp. 188–205). Mahwah, NJ: Lawrence Erlbaum.

Martin, J. E., Marshall, L., Wray, D., Wells, L., O'Brien, J., Olvey, G., & Johnson, C. (2004). *Choose and take action: Finding the right job for you.* Longmont, CO: Sopris West.

Martin, J. E., Mithaug, D. E., Oliphint, J. H., Husch, J. V., & Frazier, E. S. (2002). *Self-directed employment: A handbook for transition teachers and employment specialists.* Baltimore, MD: Paul H. Brookes.

McGahee-Kovac, M. (1995). *A student's guide to the IEP.* Washington, D.C.: National Information Center for Children and Youth with Disabilities.

Mithaug, D. E., & Hanawalt, D. A. (1978). The validation of procedures to assess prevocational tasks preferences in three severely retarded young adults. *Journal of Applied Behavior Analysis, 11*, 153–162.

Mithaug, D. E., & Mar, D. K. (1980). The relation between choosing and working prevocational tasks in two severely retarded young adults. *Journal of Applied Behavior Analysis, 13*, 177–182.

Mithaug, D. E., Martin, J. E., & Agran, M. (1987). Adaptability instruction: The goal of transitional programming. *Exceptional Children, 53*(6), 500–505.

Mithaug, D. E., Martin, J. E., James V. Husch, Agran, M., & Rusch, F. R. (1988). *When will persons in supported employment need less support?* Colorado Springs, CO: Ascent Publications.

Mithaug, D. E., Mithaug, D. K., Agran, M., Martin, J. E. , & Wehmeyer, M. L. (2003). The credibility and worth of self-determined learning theory. In D. E. Mithaug, D. K. Mithaug, M. Agran, J. E. Martin, & M. L. Wehmeyer (Eds.), *Self-determined learning theory: Construction, verification, and evaluation* (pp. 223–245). Mahwah, NJ: Lawrence Erlbaum Associates.

Mithaug, D. E., Wehmeyer, M. L., Agran, M., Martin, J. E., & Palmer, S. (1998). Self-determined learning model of instruction: Engaging students to solve their learning problems. In M. Wehmeyer & D. J. Sands (Eds.), *Making it happen: Student involvement in educational planning, decision-making, and instruction* (pp. 299–328). Baltimore, MD: Paul H. Brookes.

Morningstar, M. E., Turnbull, A. P., & Turnbull, H. R. III. (1995). What do students with disabilities tell us about the importance of family involvement in the transition from school to adult life? *Exceptional Children, 62*, 249–260.

Peterson, L. Y., Van Dycke, J. L., Crownover, C., Roberson, R. L., Borland, B. J., & Martin, J. E. (2004). *Teaching students with learning disabilities to complete plans of study.* Manuscript submitted for publication.

Powers, L. E., Turner, A., Matuszewski, J., Wilson, R., & Loesch, C. (1999). A qualitative analysis of student involvement in transition planning. *The Journal for Vocational Special Needs Education, 21*(3), 18–26.

Snyder, E. P. (2002). Teaching students with combined behavioral disorders and mental retardation to lead their own IEP meetings. *Behavioral Disorders, 27*(4), 340–357.

Snyder, E. P., & Shapiro, E. (1997). Teaching students with emotional/behavioral disorders the skills to participate in the development of their own IEPs. *Behavioral Disorders, 22*(4), 246–259.

Sweeney, M. A. (1997). *The effects of self-determination training on student involvement in the IEP process.* Florida State University, Tallahassee.

Van Reusen, A. K., Bos, Candace S., Schumaker, J. B., & Deshler, D. D. (1994). *Self-advocacy strategy for education and transition.* Lawrence, KS: Edge Enterprises.

Walden, R. J. (2002). *Teaching a goal attainment process to university students with learning disabilities.* Unpublished doctoral dissertation, University of Oklahoma, Norman.

Wehmeyer, M., Lawrence, M., Kelchner, K., Palmer, S., Garner, N., & Soukup, J. (2004). *Whose future is it anyway? A student-directed transition planning program.* Lawrence, KS: Beach Center on Disability.

Chapter 7

WHY TEACHERS ARE RELUCTANT TO CHOOSE CHOICE

DEIRDRE K. MITHAUG

One of the central arguments of this book has been that improving the capacity of students to adjust to new learning challenges requires a different teaching approach than that offered by direct instruction. Indeed, it requires instruction that helps students regulate their adjustments to any circumstance they may face in or outside the classroom. It requires instruction that helps them adjust to those self-selected challenges that are beyond the direct control of teachers. The previous chapters described several approaches to build this capability in students. In Chapter 3, Agran described three self-management strategies students can learn to improve their control of the adjustments they must make to various classroom demands. In Chapter 4, I described a self-regulation strategy students can learn that will help them regulate their expectations, choices, actions, and results during autonomous work situations. In Chapter 5, Wehmeyer described a self-regulated problem-solving strategy students can use during the discovery process that typifies self-determined learning, and in Chapter 6, Martin explained how these strategies help young adults with disabilities direct and control the development of their own Individualized Education and Transition Plans.

This chapter takes a different turn in that it focuses on the appeal of this instructional approach to preservice teachers taking a practicum course to complete requirements for certification in special education. The chapter describes several studies that assess whether beginning teachers are likely to choose a self-instructional approach when given that opportunity during their practicum work with students enrolled in the public schools.

This question was originally addressed in a study conducted with 31 preservice teachers who experienced four choice conditions during their practicum work (Mithaug & Mithaug, 2003). These conditions included (a) a baseline when teachers were free to choose from ten goal options presented on a self-regulation card that they then used to regulate their teaching during practicum for that day (see Figure 7.1), (b) a professor-choice condition with the practicum professor selecting two goals from the card for the teachers to meet in addition to the goals they chose, (c) a teacher-choice condition with teachers alone choosing the number and type of goals to meet on the card and (d) a student-choice condition with teachers required to choose the tenth goal option in addition to their own goal choices. The tenth goal option required them to provide their students with a self-regulation card similar to theirs that allowed students to choose their own goals and then to regulate work to meet them (see Figure 7.2). During all but the baseline condition, the professor gave points when the goals that teachers selected on their self-regulation card (Figure 7.1) matched the goals they met during the practicum sessions that followed. Also, throughout the study teachers were free to choose goal #10 option at any time, which would require that they allow their students to use a similar self-regulation card (Figure 7.2) to choose goals for their self-regulated work during the practicum.

The results were surprising in that the functional similarity between the self-regulation cards the teachers used and the self-regulation card the students were to use had no apparent effect on the choice opportunities they received because none of these teachers chose Goal #10, which allowed students to choose their goals during practicum. Only when the professor required the Goal #10 option in the final student-choice condition did students have that opportunity to choose their goals and to regulate work to meet them.

One explanation for this surprising result was that the adjustments required of teachers during the choice condition were considerably more demanding than what was required of them when they chose goals for their practicum students. This was evident in the optimality of their adjustments in that during the student choice condition the optimality of their adjustments was significantly higher than during the teacher choice condition. In other words, teachers selected significantly more goals, worked more goals, and met more goals when students made choices and used their self-regulation cards than when teachers made those choices. This suggests another explanation for teacher preferences for controlling all choices, namely that they reduced the unpredictability associated with allowing their students to choose goals to be met. Indeed, preparing for this ambiguity may have demanded more preparation for the subject matter material required if students made choices about what to learn. In other words, the teacher-choice condition may have made it easier for teachers to plan for their practicum sessions than when students were allowed to make choices.

It is also possible that the professor condition requiring work on the goals she

---

Figure 7.1: Sample Teacher Self-Planner/Evaluator

Teacher: _____

Date: _____

A. Goal Choices: (Circle)

1. Letter/Number Recognition and Identification
2. Sight-Word Vocabulary
3. Reading Comprehension
4. Spelling
5. Math
6. Handwriting/Literacy
7. Extra Curricular Activities (Games, Art, Puzzles)
8. Appropriate Classroom Behavior (On-task, Compliant, In-seat)
9. Data Collection
10. Child Behavior Contract

B. Goals Met: (Place a check mark next to each goal listed down below that was met)

1 __ 2 __ 3 __ 4 __ 5 __   6 __   7 __   8 __   9 __   10 __

Others? _____

C. How many goals were met in all? (Add up how many *matches* you have between goals chosen under "A.", and goals completed under "B." and write it down here)

Total = _____

---

selected diminished teachers' motivation to offer choice opportunities to students. After all, the limiting of options by that requirement may have reminded participants of what the professor wanted rather than what their students may have wanted. The reward contingency may have had a similar distracting effect if teachers also believed they had a better chance of earning points by choosing goals they knew they could meet rather than Goal #10 that allowed students to choose goals that may have been difficult to meet.

Figure 7.2: Sample Student Self-Record Card **(Adapted from Mithaug, 2002)**				
Name: _____ Date: _____				

Subjects	Assignments Number to Do?	Completed Work: Number Done?	Goal Met: Do They Match?
Science Reading Math Social Studies Writing	1. _____	1. _____	1. YES NO
	2. _____	2 _____	2. YES NO
	3. _____	3. _____	3. YES NO
	4. _____	4. _____	4. YES NO
	5. _____	5. _____	5. YES NO
Number of "Yes" Responses Circled?			_____
Prize Earned?			_____

Effects of Teacher and Student Choice on Practicum Work

With this in mind, a second study was conducted to determine whether the reluctance of teachers to provide their students goal choices would be present in the absence of the professor-choice and goal reward conditions.

Participants and Setting

The study was part of a special education course in a teacher education program at a university in a midwestern state. The course had a practicum component that required preservice teachers to work with K–4th grade elementary students at a local school. The teachers worked one-on-one with assigned practicum students in a tutoring space adjacent the classroom. One group worked with tutees during 30-minute morning sessions and the second group worked with tutees during 30-minute afternoon sessions.

The 39 participants were undergraduate special education majors enrolled in two sections of the same special education practicum course offered the previous semester. They included one male and 38 females. Group 1 consisted of 21 participants and Group 2 consisted of 18 participants. They included 11 juniors, 25 seniors, and 3 graduate students. Their grade point averages ranged from 2.4 to 4.0.

Materials

All materials in the study were similar to those used in the Mithaug and Mithaug (2003), except that three goals were added to the teacher-choice regulation cards. The goal menu on the cards now included these 13 options: (1) letter/number recognition and definition, (2) sight-word vocabulary (3) reading comprehension (4) spelling (5) math (6) handwriting (7) extracurricular activities (8) on-task behavior (9) compliant behavior (10) in-seat behavior (11) social/emotional behavior (12) data collection and (13) student-choice regulation card.

Goal Indicators

Teacher goal indicators included the number of teacher goals set, the number of goals worked and the number of goals met across 13 goal options during practicum. Student goal indicators also included goals set, goals worked, and goals met during practicum.

Design

Table 7.1 presents the study design, a reversal across group comparison on number of goals set, goals worked, and goals met by teachers and practicum students. Following three days of a baseline of the professor's presenting information about use of the contracts, the two groups of teachers experienced five days of teacher-choice, five days of teacher-choice combined with student-choice, and five days of teacher-choice again.

During baseline, the professor provided three days of lectures on use of choice contracting to improve student performance. This occurred during regularly scheduled lecture periods in a classroom at the university. To illustrate the choice

	Baseline	**Condition I**	**Condition II**	**Condition I**
	Baseline 3 Days of Lecture	*Teacher- Choice Contracting*	*Teacher and Student-Choice Contracting*	*Teacher-Choice Contracting*
Group 1 N=21 **Group 2** N = 18	Teacher and Student Choice Contracts Available w/ no contingency to complete them	Teacher and Student Choice Contracts Available w/ no contingency to complete them	Teacher and Student Choice Contracts Available with contingency to complete Goal #13, Student Contract.	Teacher and Student Choice Contracts Available w/ no contingency to complete them

Table 7.1: Reversal Across Groups Design

contract approach, the professor handed out teacher-choice contracts teachers would use in subsequent conditions. She showed them how to use them to select their practicum goals, record their goal work, and indicate whether they met their goals. The professor also handed out a student-choice contract for use in the practicum, Goal #13 on their contracts. During this baseline, there was no requirement for teachers to use either contract during the practicum tutoring sessions that followed. Nor was there any explanation for why student-choice contracts were desirable for use with students or why they should choose Goal #13 for their students.

During the teacher choice condition, the professor handed out teacher-choice contracts to each teacher at the end of the class session and required them to return the contracts at the end of their 50-minute tutoring sessions. There were no instructions or requirements on goals to set or work during the practicum sessions that followed.

During the Teacher- Plus Student-Choice Contracting condition, the professor circled Goal #13 on the teacher-choice contracts for participants from both groups. To complete this goal, teachers could use the sample student-choice contract provided in their binder of materials, or their own version of that student-choice contract. Teachers were also free to choose any of the remaining 12 goal options from the card. As in the previous condition, teachers were required to return their choice-contracts to the professor at the end of each practicum session. During the final teacher-choice condition, the professor discontinued circling Goal #13 option on the teacher-choice contracts.

Reliability. The practicum professor collected reliability data by recording the goals teachers chose for work during a practicum and the goals that the professor observed the teacher working that day. She conducted checks on ten sessions for each teacher. For Group 1, the average agreement between her observations and teacher reports of work on goals was 94 percent. For Group 2, the average agreement was 97 percent.

Results

Figure 7.3 charts data on goals chosen and worked by the two groups of teachers across the four conditions. The mean goals worked for Group 1 for each condition were 1.9 for baseline, 2.8 for the first teacher-choice condition, 4.1 for the teacher-choice and student-choice requirement condition, and 3.3 goals for the final teacher-choice condition. The mean goals worked for Group 2 were 1.9 for baseline, 2.8 for the first teacher-choice condition, 4.0 for the teacher-choice with student-choice requirement condition, and 3.8 goals for the final teacher-choice condition.

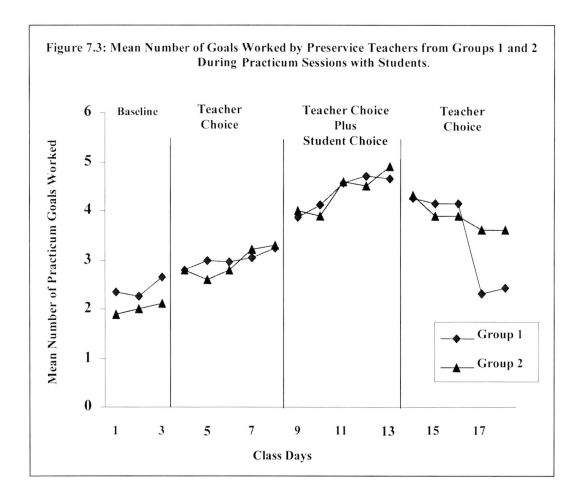

Figure 7.3: Mean Number of Goals Worked by Preservice Teachers from Groups 1 and 2 During Practicum Sessions with Students.

Although there were no significant group differences in goals chosen or worked, there were significant differences between conditions. Goals worked during teacher-choice conditions were significantly higher than goals worked during baselines $(p < .05)$; goals worked during the combination of teacher-choice and student-choice condition were significantly higher than goals worked during the preceding teacher-choice condition. For Group 2 only, goals worked during the final teacher-choice condition were significantly lower than goals worked during the preceding combined teacher-choice with student-choice condition $(p < .05)$.

The mean number of goals chosen and worked by practicum students tutored by Group 1 teachers were as follows: 0.0 for baseline, 0.0 for teacher-choice, 4.1 for the teacher choice-student choice requirement condition, and .6 for the final teacher-choice condition. The mean number of goals worked for practicum students tutored by Group 2 teachers were as follows: 0.0 for baseline, 0.0 for teacher-choice, 2.7 for the teacher choice-student choice requirement condition, and 0.3 for the final teacher-choice condition. Again, there were no significant group differences, although there were significant between condition differences. Goals worked were significantly higher during the combination teacher and student-choice condition $(p < .05)$.

The top charts in Figures 7.4 and 7.5 provide data on the average number of goals met across all conditions for the two groups. For Group 1 in Figure 7.4 the average accuracy rate – the percent match between goals set and goals worked – increased across the four conditions. For Group 2 in Figure 7.5, however, the averages increased during the first three conditions and then decreased slightly in the fourth condition. The bottom charts present the averages for goals set and goals worked for the two groups. In both figures the averages were higher during the combined teacher and student-choice condition than during baseline or the teacher-choice conditions.

Discussion

The results of this study are consistent with those reported by Mithaug and Mithaug (2003) in that none of the teachers chose the student goal choice option even though that option would have given practicum students the same opportunity to regulate their goal choices that teachers experienced with their practicum supervisor. Apparently, being taught in a self-directed manner does not translate into teaching in a self-directed manner at least in these studies. Nor, did teachers choose Goal option #13 in the final teacher-choice condition after they had been required to do so by their professor. Hence, it seems that neither the experience of choosing their own goals nor the experience of providing that opportunity to practicum students was sufficient to provoke them to offer choice opportunities to students when they were free to do so in that last condition of the study.

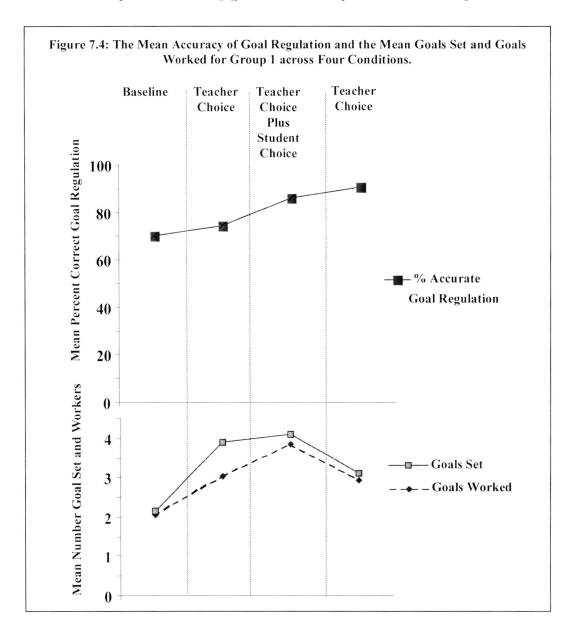

Figure 7.4: The Mean Accuracy of Goal Regulation and the Mean Goals Set and Goals Worked for Group 1 across Four Conditions.

The data in Figures 7.3–7.5 offer a plausible explanation for this apparent avoidance of student-choice option, which is that it required more work. Figure 7.3 shows, for example, that the number of goals worked increased dramatically in condition 3 when the student-choice was required and then decreased precipitously when it was discontinued in the last condition. The charts show how these differences were expressed for each group. The top charts of Figures 7.4 and 7.5 show, for example, that the efficiency of Group 1's goal work, as measured by

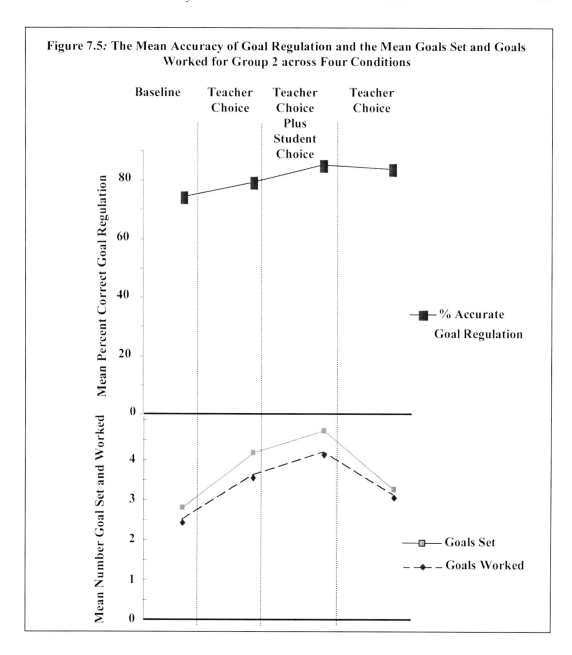

Figure 7.5: The Mean Accuracy of Goal Regulation and the Mean Goals Set and Goals Worked for Group 2 across Four Conditions

goals met, increased steadily across the four conditions, whereas the efficiency of Group 2's work maximized in condition 3 and declined slightly in condition 4. The bottom charts of Figure 7.4 and 7.5, on the other hand, reveal the effects of student-choice in that levels for goals set and goals worked increased dramatically during the student choice and then declined in the final teacher choice condition when student choice was no longer required.

Effects of Instruction and Choice on Practicum Work

Unfortunately, even this study is not without caveats in that it is possible the practicum work levels were highest during the combination condition because teachers had more goals to meet. Indeed, they established goal priorities for their students by the time the professor added Goal #13 to their goal list, which added more work for them to accomplish. Also, it is possible that the teachers were not avoiding Goal #13 so much as choosing other goals they believed to be more important for their students. Indeed, the professor never explained why Goal #13 was important. Hence, it may be that teachers continued to choose other goal options in the final condition because they believed that the content they selected for instruction was more important for students to learn. In an attempt to address these possibilities, another study was conducted to determine whether professor-delivered instruction on the importance of student-directedness would affect the selection of Goal #13. Also, this study included an assessment of instructional philosophies to determine whether teacher beliefs about teacher and student-directedness changed by the end of the study.

Participants and Setting

The 42 preservice teachers who participated in the study were enrolled in two sections of a special education practicum course. The two groups included 3 males and 39 females: 19 from Group 1 and 23 from Group 2. The participants included 14 juniors, 22 seniors, and 6 graduate students. The grade point averages of the students ranged from 1.6 to 3.8. The study took place in the same setting as the previous study. Lectures were conducted at the university and practicum hours were held at two local elementary schools.

General Procedures and Materials

During a 15-minute session that occurred at the beginning and end of the study, participants wrote a paragraph describing their instructional philosophy. Then they were given a 3-ring binder and instructed on its use to regulate their practicum work with students. The binder contained the materials used in the previous studies: data collection sheets, graph paper, as well as instructional materials for use with students (flashcards, workbooks, worksheets, spelling lists, and rewards). The binders also included two choice contracts, one for practicum teachers to use to regulate their goals set, worked, and met during practicum and the other for practicum students to use to regulate their goals set, worked, and met during practicum.

During each in-class session that preceded practicum, the instructor described and demonstrated use of the teacher-choice contract located in the 3-ring binders and then instructed teachers to use it to regulate their work during the practicum that followed. The instructor also described and demonstrated use of the student-choice contract also located in the binders, which allowed practicum students to regulate their goal work. This instruction occurred at the end of the in-class sessions that preceded practicum work with students.

Design

Table 7.2 presents the design of this study. Two groups participated in the same sequence of conditions, which were staggered in a multiple baseline across groups sequence to evaluate the effects of in-class instruction and choice-regulation contracts on beliefs, choices, and work. During the pretest and posttest sessions that preceded and followed the study, participants wrote short instructional philosophy statements. During the first condition, the instructor provided in-class lectures, demonstrations, group work, and case-method instruction on the methods and benefits of student-directed instruction. During the second condition, the practicum professor chose two goals for teachers to work, which were added to the goals they chose to guide their practicum work. During the third condition, the practicum professor only chose Goal #13, the student choice goal, which was added to the goals teachers chose for practicum work. The study ended with a posttest session in which participants wrote their instructional philosophy statements again.

Instructional Philosophy Statements. During the 15-minute session prior to the study, preservice teachers were requested to describe their instructional philosophy. The only instruction provided on the content of these statements was that they were to reflect how they planned to teach. During a second 15-minute session that immediately followed at the end of the study, they were requested to describe their instructional philosophies again. The statements were then analyzed to determine whether the instruction described reflected a teacher-directed or student-directed approach.

In-Class Instruction. During the three-day sessions for Group 1 and the five-day sessions for Group 2, the practicum instructor presented information on student-directed learning as part of a course on the application of behavior principles to classroom settings. Participants were required to read a chapter on cognitive behavior modification from a behavior management text, and then complete homework readings from Agran (1997); Betancourt and Zeiler, (1971); Bolstad and Johnson, (1972); Dickerson and Creedon, (1981); Glynn, Thomas, and Shee, (1973); Hughes, Harmer, Killian and Niarhos, (1995); O'Leary and Dubey, (1979); Sowers, Verdi, Bourbeau, and Sheehan (1985); and Watson and Tharp (1989).

Table 7.2: Pre-Post Test Comparison and Multiple Baseline Across Groups Design

	Instructional Philosophy Statements	Condition I	Condition II	Condition III	Instructional Philosophy Statements
Group 1 N=19	15- minute pre-session All participants write instructional philosophy statements	In-Class Instruction: Lecture Demonstrations Group Work, and Case-Method Instruction Teacher and Student Choice Contracts available w/ no contingency to complete them 3 days	Two-Goal Requirement for Practicum Teacher and Student Choice Contracts available with contingency to complete two random goals 5 days	Student-Choice Contract Goal Requirement for Practicum Teacher and Student Choice Contracts available with contingency to complete Goal #13, Student Contract 5 days	15- minute post-session All participants write instructional philosophy statements
Group 2 N=23	15- minute pre-session All participants write instructional philosophy statements	In-Class Instruction: Lecture Demonstrations Group Work, and Case-Method Instruction Teacher and Student Choice Contracts available w/ no contingency to complete them 5 days	Two-Goal Requirement for Practicum Teacher and Student Choice Contracts available with contingency to complete two random goals 5 days	Student Choice Contract Goal Requirement for Practicum Teacher and Student Choice Contracts available with contingency to complete Goal #13, Student Contract 3 days	15- minute post session All participants write instructional philosophy statements

During class sessions, the instructor presented information on the importance of student-directed learning and then identified differences between student-directed strategies and other behavior management techniques. She explained that use of student-directed methods helped students move from teacher- to student-directed learning, and that too much external control tended to slow that transfer. The strategies used to illustrate self-directed learning included goal setting (Schunk & Swartz, 1993), self-instruction (Hughes, Harmer, Killian, & Niarhos (1995); problem-solving training (Castles & Glass, 1986); self-monitoring (Glynn, Thomas, & Shee, 1973), self-evaluation (Kaufman & O'Leary, 1972), self-reinforcement (Boldstad & Johnson, 1972); and self-selection of performance standards (Dickerson & Creedon, 1981).

The instructor also presented case studies of students with academic and be-havior problems and asked participants to work in groups to identify student-directed strategies that would solve them. At the conclusion of each class, she handed out samples of teacher and student-choice contracts. She demonstrated use of the teacher-choice contract first, by circling one of the 13 goals for practicum work and then by walking through the process of working goals, recording and evaluating results. Then she demonstrated the same goal setting, goal work and evaluation using the student-choice contract that practicum students would use if the teachers chose Goal #13 option.

Two-Goal Choice Requirement. During this condition, there were no lectures or discussions about instructional approaches. The instructor was available to answer questions and discuss problems teachers encountered during their practicum work with students. Teachers continued to hand in their choice contracts after each practicum session. In addition, the instructor randomly selected two goals on their choice contract they were to meet, in addition to the goals they chose. These random selections were from goal options 1–12 only. Therefore, the instructor never chose Goal #13 for teachers to work during practicum. After making goal selections, the participants worked with their practicum students for the 50-minute practicum ses-sion. At the end of the session they turned in their choice contracts to the instructor.

One-Goal Requirement: Student Choice Contract. During this condition the instructor only chose goal option #13, the student-choice contract, for teachers to meet during practicum, which meant that they could introduce the sample student-choice contract in their binder for students to use to meet that goal, or they could create their own version of that contract for students to use. The teachers were also free to choose any of the other 12 goal options to meet as well. As in the previous condition, they handed in their choice contracts at the end of each practicum session.

Belief Indicators

All statements in the teachers' instructional philosophies were classified as being student-directed, teacher directed, or non-directed. A statement was con-sidered teacher-directed if it included words like "teacher directs," "teacher con-trols," or "teacher promotes" to describe a procedure or method to be carried out when teaching. A statement was considered student-directed if it included words like "self," "independence," or "empowerment" to describe a procedure or method to be carried out during instruction. Statements that contained none of these indicator words were classified as non-directed.

Philosophy statements that included one or more student-directed phrases were classified as student-directed; statements that contained one or more teacher-directed phrases and zero student-directed phrases were classified as teacher-directed statements. Philosophy statements that contained neither teacher- nor student-directed phrases were classified as non-directed statements.

Goal Indicators

The goal indicators were the same as in the previous study: goals set, goals worked, and goals met during practicum sessions. Teachers' goal indicators were the number of goals they set, worked and met across the 13 goal options on their choice regulation card; and students' goal indicators were the number of goals practicum students set, worked, and met across five subject matter options identified on their choice regulation card.

Reliability

For philosophy statement data, reliability was the agreement between the practicum supervisor and an independent recorder. For the goals worked data, reliability was the agreement between the practicum supervisor's observations of goals worked and the preservice teachers' record of goals worked. For both cases, reliability was a percent agreement calculated by dividing the number of agreements by the sum of the agreements and disagreements multiplied by 100.

Philosophy Statements. The practicum supervisor and a recorder, who had no knowledge of the study, independently recorded each of the teachers' instructional philosophy statements. They placed each statement in one of three categories: teacher-directed, student-directed, or non-directed. For Group 1, the agreement between the practicum supervisor and the independent recorder was 80 percent, and for Group 2 it was 85 percent. For teacher-directed classifications, the agreement was 85 percent; for student-directed classifications, it was 78 percent; and for non-directed classifications, the agreement was 83 percent.

Goal Regulation Data. The practicum supervisor collected reliability data on the goals participants recorded on their choice cards that they worked each day of practicum. She conducted ten days of reliability checks for each teacher. An agreement occurred when the supervisor observed the teacher working goals that the teacher reported as having worked that day. A non-agreement occurred when the supervisor observed the teacher working goals that were not indicated as having been worked that day. For Group 1, the average agreement between supervisor observations and teacher reports was 94 percent. For Group 2, the average agreement between the supervisor and teacher goal reports was 97 percent.

Results

Figure 7.6 presents data on the number of goals met by the two groups across the three-condition sequence. As indicated in the chart, goals met were lowest during the in-class instructional condition, increased during the 2-goal regulation condition, and increased again in the student-choice condition. The mean rates of

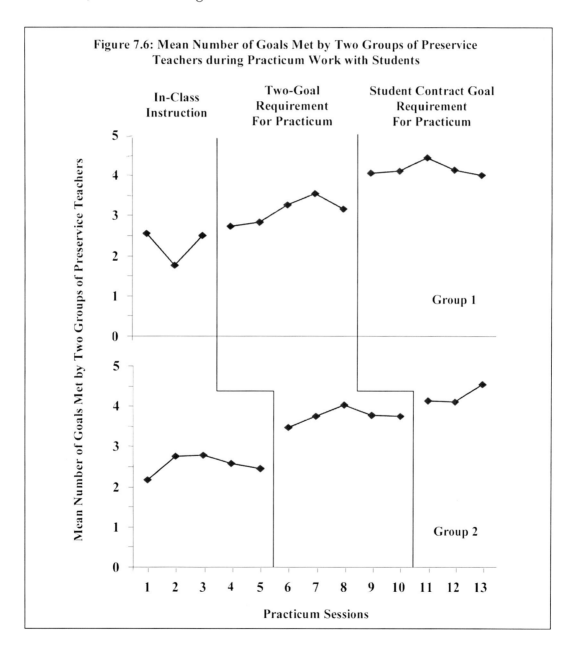

Figure 7.6: Mean Number of Goals Met by Two Groups of Preservice Teachers during Practicum Work with Students

goals met for Group 1 were 2.3 for the instructional condition, 3.1 for the two-goal condition, and 4.1 for the student-choice condition. The mean rates of goals met for Group 2 were 2.6 for the instructional condition, 3.8 for the two-goal condition, and 4.1 for the student-choice condition.

Figure 7.7 presents data on the number of goals worked and met by the students of the two groups of teachers during the three conditions. As indicated in

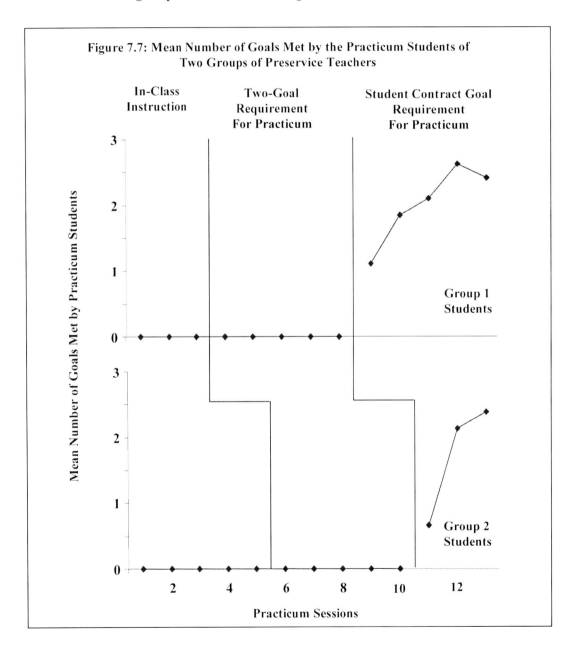

Figure 7.7: Mean Number of Goals Met by the Practicum Students of Two Groups of Preservice Teachers

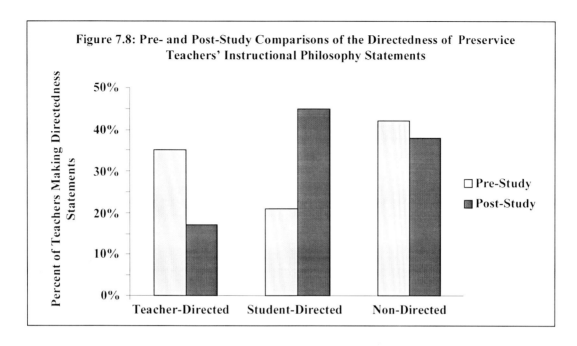

Figure 7.8: Pre- and Post-Study Comparisons of the Directedness of Preservice Teachers' Instructional Philosophy Statements

the chart, none of the students met any of their own goals during the first two conditions because none of their teachers selected goal option #13 on their choice contracts, which would have given students that opportunity. However during the final condition when the instructor assigned that goal option to teachers, students began meeting their own goals, as indicated in the figure.

Figure 7.8 presents a chart showing the proportion of pre- and post-study instructional statements that were classified as teacher-directed, student-directed, and non-directed. As indicated by the pre-test data on the charts, 35 percent of the teachers favored teacher directedness, 21 percent favored student directedness, and 42 percent had no preferences. These proportions changed in the post-test statements, with 17 percent favoring teacher directedness, 45 percent favoring student-directedness, and 38 percent having no preference for instructional directedness.

DISCUSSION

The findings of this study are consistent with those of previous studies in that again preserivce teachers avoided giving their practicum students opportunities to choose learning goals, and that when required to provide those choice opportunities, they met more goals than when they were free to ignore them. Hence, the conclusion suggested here as well as by those studies is that preserivce teachers may have avoided student choice because it required more work. Results of this study supported that conclusion in part by ruling out the possibility that participants avoided goal option #13 because they were unaware of its importance for self-determined learning. During the first condition the practicum professor provided information that justified use of the student self-regulation card. Indeed, she provided information on research-based strategies that promote student-directedness, the problem solving that is involved in student-directed learning, as well use of student-choice contracts to promote it. Nonetheless, these teachers responded as those in previous studies. They avoided goal option #13, only choosing it when required to by their instructor. However, when they finally worked on that goal their goal attainment levels increased substantially, which suggests that they may have avoided that option because it required more work or because the work demanded of them was less predictable than the work they might have chosen.

The problem with this interpretation, of course, is that it does not explain why teachers avoided that option during the conditions that *preceded* the experience of having to help students work on goals they chose. An alternative version of this explanation might be (a) that teachers anticipated that more work would be required if students chose their own goals and that that work would be less controllable and predictable than the work they might choose, (b) that they were more comfortable with the work they were to do with practicum students when they made all the choices, and (c) that their approach to teaching was more teacher- than student-directed anyway, and hence, they felt more empowered when they were in full control of all the instructional choices. Perhaps these factors worked together to motivate participants to control all the choice opportunities during their practicum work with students.

Indeed, data on the instructional philosophies of the participants were at least consistent with this view in that prior to the study 35 percent favored teacher direction as compared with 21 percent who favored student direction, a difference that fell short of significance ($p < .09$). Also, the pattern reversed by the end of the study when they had learned how to accommodate the student choice option. During this posttest period, only 17 percent favored teacher-direction whereas 45 percent favored student direction – a difference that also fell short of significance ($p < .06$).

This interpretation is consistent with these findings. It suggests as well that beginning teachers may need a more convincing argument for student-directed learning if they are to facilitate it in their classrooms. To get them to seriously consider this instructional approach, they may need a full understanding of (a) the theoretical, empirical, and practical differences between direct instruction and self-instruction pedagogy, as explained in Chapter 1, (b) the directedness of their own teaching, as assessed in Chapter 2, and (c) the shifts toward student control that are necessary for self-determined learning to develop in students with disabilities, as described in Chapters 3–6. The next and final chapter of the book describes how information like this can have a positive effect on the willingness of prospective teachers to provide students with choices in the regulation and control of their own learning.

REFERENCES

Agran, M. (1997). *Student-directed learning: Teaching self-determination skills.* Pacific Grove, CA: Brooks/Cole Publishing.

Betancourt, F.W., & Zeiler, M.D. (1971). The choices and preferences of nursery school children. *Journal of Applied Behavior Analysis, 4,* 299–304.

Bolstad, O., & Johnson, S. (1972). Self-regulation in the modification of disruptive classroom behavior. *Journal of Applied Behavior Analysis, 5,* 443–454.

Castles, E.E., & Glass, C.R. (1986). Training in social and interpersonal problem-solving skills for mildly and moderately mentally retarded adults. *American Journal of Mental Deficiency, 91*(1), 35–42.

Dickerson, E.A., & Creedon, C.F. (1981). Self-selection of standards by children: The relative effectiveness of pupil-selected and teacher-selected standards of performance. *Journal of Applied Behavior Analysis, 14,* 425–433.

Glynn, E.L., Thomas, J.D., & Shee, S.M. (1973). Behavioral self-control of on-task behavior in an elementary classroom. *Journal of Applied Behavior Analysis, 6,* 105–113.

Hughes, C., Harmer, M.L., Killian, D.J., & Niarhos, F. (1995). The effects of multiple-examplar self-instructional training on high school students' generalized conversational interactions. *Journal of Applied Behavior Analysis, 28,* 201–218.

Kaufman, K.F., & O'Leary, K.D. (1972). Reward, cost, and self-evaluation procedures for disruptive adolescents in a psychiatric hospital school. *Journal of Applied Behavior Analysis, 5,* 293–309.

Mithaug, D. K. (2002). "Yes" means success: Teaching children with multiple disabilities to self-regulate during independent work. *Teaching Exceptional Children 35*(1), 22–27.

Mithaug, D. K., & Mithaug, D. E. (2003). The effects of choice opportunities on the engagement of prospective teachers in student-determined learning. In Mithaug, D. E., Mithaug, D. K., Agran, M., Martin, J. E., & Wehmeyer, M. L. (Eds.) *Self-determined learning theory: Construction, verification, and evaluation* (pp. 206–219). Mahwah, N. J.: Lawrence Erlbaum Associates.

O'Leary, S.G. & Dubey, D.R. (1979). Applications of self-control procedures by children: A review. *Journal of Applied Behavior Analysis, 12,* 449–465.

Schunk, D. H., & Swartz, C.W. (1993). Goals and progress feedback: Effects of self-efficacy and writing achievement. *Contemporary Educational Psychology, 18,* 337–354.

Sowers, J., Verdi, M., Bourbeau, P., & Sheehan, M. (1985). Teaching job independence and flexibility to mentally retarded students through the use of a self-control package. *Journal of Applied Behavior Analysis, 18,* 81–85.

Chapter 8

WILL YOU CHOOSE SELF-INSTRUCTION PEDAGOGY?

Dennis E. Mithaug
Deirdre K. Mithaug

This book introduced a self-instruction pedagogy that empowers students to become self-determined learners. Chapter 1 compared teacher- with student-directed instruction to show that the former is supported by operant learning theory that justifies teacher control of learning whereas the latter is supported by self-determined learning theory that justifies student control of learning. Chapter 2 demonstrated the significance of this pedagogical comparison by presenting assessment data generated by the *Instruction and Curriculum Scales for Self-Determined Learning* indicating that teachers like yourself are more likely to be teacher-directed than student-directed (Mithaug & Mithaug, Appendix B) and hence unlikely to promote self-determined learning in students. Chapters 3–6 presented a four-step strategy to shift from that baseline to student-directedness. Chapter 7 examined teacher-directedness again by assessing whether that same level of teacher control was present in beginning teachers who had opportunities to give a measure of learning control to their practicum students. The results were sobering in that teacher-directedness persisted in those studies as well. In fact, none of the 118 teachers assessed gave their students choices during their practicum sessions until required to do so by their supervising professor.

Several explanations were offered for this apparent reluctance to cede control. One was that giving students choices introduced a degree of unpredictability in instructional planning and increased the number of subject topics teachers had to prepare prior to teaching. A second was that teachers felt in control when they made all the decisions and this empowered them to persist in that mode of teaching.

There was evidence for both explanations in that the studies reported in Chapter 7 found that when beginning teachers were required to give choices to students, they met more of their instructional goals than when they made those choices for students. Also, Mithaug and Mithaug (Appendix B) reported that teacher ratings on instructional-directedness, self-efficacy, and self-determination were positively correlated and regression analyses showed that teacher-directedness was a significant predictor of self-determination and self-efficacy but student-directedness was not. In other words, teachers were more likely to feel empowered when engaged in teacher-directed instruction than when engaged in student-directed instruction.

So perhaps we should ask whether self-instruction pedagogy could ever be attractive enough for teachers to adopt and use extensively with their students. We think so because we found that when teachers understood the rationale for student-directed learning (Chapter 1), the difference between teacher and student-directedness, and the four steps that shift control to students (Chapters 3–6), they became more student- than teacher-directed in their teaching. Figure 8.1 presents these results for 61 teachers who rated themselves significantly more teacher than student-directed prior to learning about self-instruction pedagogy but then reported being more student than teacher-directed after learning about the pedagogy. Their curricular emphasis also shifted from basic to applied skills (Mithaug & Mithaug, Appendix B).

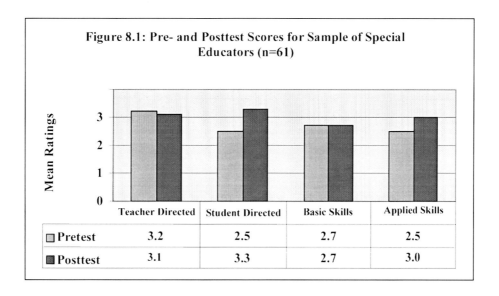

Figure 8.1: Pre- and Posttest Scores for Sample of Special Educators (n=61)

	Teacher Directed	Student Directed	Basic Skills	Applied Skills
Pretest	3.2	2.5	2.7	2.5
Posttest	3.1	3.3	2.7	3.0

We believe these changes were related to their understanding of the differences between direct instruction pedagogy and self-instruction pedagogy as illustrated in Table 8.1 showing that direct instruction involves *external control* of learning whereas self-instruction involves *internal control* of learning. Indeed, direct instruction

prescribes teacher manipulations of antecedent cues and reinforcing consequences to promote learning directly, whereas self-instruction prescribes choice
opportunities, self-instruction strategies, and the matching of results to expectations to promote student persistence in adjusting and learning.

Table 8.1: Comparing Teacher and Student Directedness			
Basis for Teacher Directedness		**Basis for Student Directedness**	
Operant Learning Theory	**Direct Instruction Pedagogy**	**Self-Determined Learning Theory**	**Self-Instruction Pedagogy**
1. Antecedent Events	Stimulus Control Principle	Optimality of Opportunities	Choice Opportunity Principle
2. Behavioral Events	Observable Behavior Principle	Self-regulated Events	Self-Instruction Principle
3. Consequent Events	Contingencies of Reinforcement Principle	Optimality of Adjustments	Matching Expectations Principle
4. Operant Learning	Antecedent, Behavior, Consequent Association Principle	Self-determined Learning	Persistent Adjustment Principle

The four principles in Table 8.2 describe the empowering relationship between
teachers and students that develops when teachers promote student control using
self-instruction pedagogy. The choice principle describes what happens when
teachers provide students with valuable and doable choices for what to learn. The
self-instruction principle describes what happens when they teach students to use
self-instructional strategies to regulate their expectations, choices, actions, and results. The matching principle describes what happens when teachers reward students for matching their results to their own expectations. And the persistence
principle describes what happens when teachers give students opportunities to
adjust repeatedly to those result-expectation matches. In the last row of Table 8.2,

	1. Choice Principle	2. Self-Instruction Principle	3. Matching Principle	4. Persistence Principle
Opportunities:				
Teacher Behavior	Teachers present choice opportunities that match the learner's interests and abilities.	Teachers provide instruction on use of self-instruction strategies to engage choice opportunities.	Teachers provide positive consequences for matching results with expectations for choice opportunities	Teachers provide opportunities for repeated adjustments in order to match results with expectations.
Effects:				
Learner Behavior	*The more valuable and doable a learning opportunity is for the learner, the more likely the learner will engage it by adjusting in some way.*	*The more often learners use strategies to adjust their expectations, choices, and responses to a learning opportunity, the more often they produce results that match their expectations for learning from the opportunity.*	*The more often learners compare their results with their expectations after responding to a learning opportunity, the more often they adjust their expectations, choices, and actions during subsequent attempts to learn from the opportunity.*	*The more often learners adjust their expectations, choices, and actions to produce results they want from a learning opportunity, the closer to maximum is their learning from the opportunity.*
Explanation:				
Self-Determined Learning Theory	The closer to optimal the opportunities for experiencing gain, the more likely the regulation of expectations, choices, and actions to produce gain.	The more often the regulation of expectations, choices, and actions to produce gain, the more likely is it that adjustments optimize as expectations, choices, actions, and results become adaptive, rational, efficient and successful.	The closer to optimal the adjustments to an opportunity, the more persistent is the engagement to produce gain, the greater is the feeling of control over gain production, and the closer to maximum is the learning from that adaptation.	Therefore, the closer to optimal the opportunities for experiencing gain, the more persistent is the engagement, the greater is the sense of control, and the closer to maximum is the learning.

Table 8.2: Opportunities, Effects, and Explanations for the Four Principles of Self-instruction Pedagogy

self-determined learning theory explains why learning maximizes when these principles are in effect.

Choice Principle. This principle, which heads the second column in Table 8.2, represents the first step in empowering self-determined learning. It prescribes opportunities for students to choose what they will learn. This is important for two reasons. First, choice opportunities allow students to select the opportunity that best matches their interests and capabilities and hence, that is most motivating to engage. Second, choice opportunities provoke self-engagement, self-regulation, and adjustment to the opportunity chosen. Indeed, when students are allowed to choose the opportunity that approximates their interests and capabilities, they are provoked into responding, and as predicted by self-determined learning theory, they adjust and then learn from that adjustment. The principle presented below (and the third row of Table 8.2) predicts this outcome.

The Choice Principle

The more valuable and doable the learning opportunity is for the learner, the more likely the learner will engage it by adjusting in some way.

Self-Instruction Principle. The second principle in Table 8.2 describes what happens when students use strategies to help them regulate their expectations, choices, actions, and results in order to adjust to that opportunity. When this happens, students are more likely to (a) set reasonable goals for getting what they want from the opportunity, (b) make good decisions about how to produce that outcome, (c) act in a timely manner on that plan, and (d) adjust optimally to the result they get. In other words, students who use self-instruction strategies are equipped to regulate their expectations, choices, actions, and results in ways that help them learn what they want to know. The principle below describes this outcome.

The Self-Instruction Principle

The more often learners use strategies to adjust their expectations, choices, and responses to a learning opportunity, the more often they produce results that match their expectations for learning from the opportunity.

Matching Principle. The third principle in Table 8.2 explains what happens when students are encouraged to compare their results with their expectations.

When this occurs, they are likely to adjust their expectations, choices, and behaviors whether they get a match or not. This is because getting a match tends to provoke new expectations requiring new adjustments and learning, whereas not getting a match tends to provoke new adjustments until one is found that works as expected. Either way, the process of comparing to produce matches provokes new adjustments and prolongs pursuits, whereas the failure to compare and match discourages adjustments and ends pursuits. In this sense, matching is the lynchpin of persistent adjustment and maximum learning. Regardless of its outcome, adjustment and learning are provoked. The principle below summarizes this effect.

The Matching Principle

The more often learners compare their results with their expectations after responding to a learning opportunity, the more often they adjust their expectations, choices, and actions during subsequent attempts to learn from the opportunity.

Persistence Principle. The last principle described in Table 8.2 predicts that when students have opportunities to adjust repeatedly until they get results they expect, they maximize their learning, as predicted by self-determined learning theory in the third row of the table. The reasons for this are straightforward. When students adjust repeatedly, they tend to move successively closer to their goals because each new adjustment serves as a stepping-stone to the next adjustment and the next until the once intractable situation is a doable opportunity for reaching their desired end. As a result, they experience a changed relationship with their learning opportunity and a corresponding increase in feelings of control over the learning it provoked. They also maximize their learning because, according to self-determined learning theory, all learning is adjustment. Therefore, when their adjustments persist across circumstances, through space, and over time, their learning maximizes, too. The fourth principle captures this culminating effect of self-determined learning.

The Persistent Principle

The more often learners adjust their expectations, choices, and actions to produce results they want from a learning opportunity, the closer to maximum is their learning from the opportunity.

Conclusion

Our view is that understanding these principles is necessary to make an informed decision about whether to control learning directly as prescribed by direct instruction or to teach students to control their learning as prescribed by self-instruction pedagogy. Hopefully, this book will help you make that decision. Of course, at some point all learners must develop this capacity for self-determined learning if they are to succeed at the many challenges that lie ahead. The central argument of this book is that mastering the strategies of self-instruction will develop this capability. It will also trigger the type of learning Candy (1991) described as "learning for oneself the prototype of all learning" (p. 30), and illustrated in the 1830 passage by Craik from *The Pursuit of Knowledge Under Difficulties.*

> Originally, all human knowledge was nothing more than the knowledge of a comparatively small number of such simple facts as those from which Galileo deduced the use of the pendulum for the measurement of time, and Newton the explanation of the system of the heavens. All the rest of our knowledge, and these first rudiments of it also, a succession of individuals have gradually discovered, each his own portion, by their own efforts, and without having any teacher to instruct them. In other words, everything that is actually known has been found out and learned by some person or other, without the aid of an instructor. There is no species of learning, therefore, which self-education may not overtake; for there is none which is not actually overtaken. All discoverers (and the whole of human knowledge that has not been divinely revealed) in the creation of discovery have been self-taught, at least in regard to that which they have discovered . . . [1866, p. 13] (From Candy, 1991, p. 30)

REFERENCE

Candy, P. C. (1991). *Self-direction for lifelong learning: A comprehensive guide to theory and practice.* San Francisco: Jossey-Bass Publishers.

APPENDICES

Appendix A

RESEARCH ON SELF-INSTRUCTION AND DIRECT INSTRUCTION PEDAGOGIES

Research on Self-Instruction Pedagogy

Self-Instruction

Agran, M., Fodor-Davis, J., & Moore, S. (1986). The effects of self-instructional training on job-task sequencing: Suggesting a problem-solving strategy. *Education and Training of the Mentally Retarded, 21*, 273–281.

Agran, M., Fodor-Davis, J., Martella, R., & Moore, S., (1992). The effects of peer-delivered self-instructional training on lunch-making work task for students with severe handicaps. *Education and Training in Mental Retardation, 27*, 230–240.

Agran, M., Salzberg, C. L., & Stowitschek, J. J. (1987). An analysis of the effects of a social skills training program using self-instructions on the acquisition and generalization of two social behaviors in a working setting. *Journal of the Association for Persons with Severe Handicaps, 12*, 131–139.

Ames, C. (1984). Achievement attributions and self-instructions under competitive and individualistic goal structures. *Journal of Educational Psychology, 75*, 478–487.

Asarnow, J. R., & Meichenbaum, D. (1979). Verbal rehearsal and serial recall: The remediational training of kindergarten children. *Child Development, 50*, 1173–1177.

Bem, S., (1967). Verbal self-control: The establishment of effective self-instruction. *Journal of Experimental Psychology, 74*, 485–491.

Bender, N. N. (1977). Verbal mediation as an instructional technique with young trainable mentally retarded children. *Journal of Special Education, 11*, 449–455.

Birch, D. (1966). Verbal control over nonverbal behavior. *Journal of Experimental Child Psychology, 4*, 266–275.

Bornstein, P. H., & Quevillon, R. P. (1976). The effects of a self-instructional package on overactive preschool boys. *Journal of Applied Behavior Analysis, 9*, 179–188.

Burgio, L. D., Whitman, T. L., & Johnson, M. R. (1980). A self-instructional package for increasing attending behavior in educable mentally retarded children. *Journal of Applied Behavior Analysis, 13*, 443–459.

Burron, D., & Bucher, B. (1978). Self-instructions as discriminative cues for rule breaking or rule following. *Journal of Experimental Child Psychology, 26*, 46–57.

Camp, E., Blom, G., Herbert, F., & Van Doorninck, W. (1977). "Think Aloud": A program for developing self-control in young aggressive boys. *Journal of Abnormal Child Psychology, 8*, 157–169.

Copeland, A. P. (1981). The relevance of the subject variables in cognitive self-instructional programs for impulsive children. *Behavior Therapy, 12*, 520–529.

Crouch, D. P., Rusch, F. R., & Karlan, G. R. (1984). Competitive employment utilizing the correspondence training paradigm to enhance productivity. *Education and Training of the Mentally Retarded, 19*, 268–275.

Englert, C. S., Raphael, T., Anderson, L., Anthony, H., & Stevens, D. , & Fear, K. (1991). Making strategies and self-talk visible: Writing instruction in writing in regular and special education classrooms. *American Educational Research Journal, 28*, 337–373.

Fish, M. C., & Mendola, L. R. (1986). The effects of self-instruction training on homework completion in an elementary education class. *School Psychology Review, 15,* 268–276.

Friedling, C., & O'Leary, S. G. (1979). Effects of self-instructional training on second and third-grade hyperactive children: A failure to replicate. *Journal of Applied Behavior Analysis, 12,* 211–219.

Fry, P. S. (1978). Resistance to temptation as a function of the duration of self-verbalizations. *British Journal of Social and Clinical Psychology, 17,* 111–116.

Glenwick, D. S., & Barocas, R. (1979). Training impulsive children in verbal self-control by use of natural change agents. *Journal of Special Education, 13,* 387–398.

Graham, S., & Harris, K. R. (1989b). Improving learning disabled students' skills at composing essays: Self-instructional strategy training. *Exceptional Children, 56,* 201–214.

Graham, S., & MacArthur, C. (1988). Improving learning disabled students' skills at revising essays produced on a word processor: Self-instructional strategy training. *Journal of Special Education, 22,* 133–152.

Graham, S., Harris, K. R., & Sawyer, R. (1987). Composition instruction with learning disabled students: Self-instructional strategy training. *Focus on Exceptional Children, 20,* 1–11.

Guevremont, D. C., Osnes, P. G., & Stokes, T. F. (1986). Programming maintenance after correspondence training interventions with children. *Journal of Applied Behavior Analysis, 19,* 215–219.

Harris, K. R., (1986). The effects of cognitive-behavior modification on private speech and task performance during problem solving among learning disabled and normally achieving students. *Journal of Abnormal Child Psychology, 14,* 63–76.

Harris, K. R., (1990). Developing self-regulated learners: The role of private speech and self-instructions. *Educational Psychologist, 25,* 35–50.

Hartig, M., & Kanfer, F. H. (1973). The role of verbal self-instructions in children's resistance to temptation. *Journal of Personality and Social Psychology, 25,* 259–267.

Higa, W. R., Tharp, R. G., & Calkins, R. P. (1978). Developmental verbal control of behavior: Implications for self-instructional training. *Journal of Experimental Child Psychology, 26,* 439–497.

Hopman, M., & Glynn, T. (1989). The effect of correspondence training on the rate and quality of written expression of four low achieving boys. *Educational Psychology, 9,* 197–213.

Hughes, C. (1992). Teaching self-instruction utilizing multiple exemplars to produce generalized problem-solving by individuals with severe mental retardation. *American Journal on Mental Retardation, 97,* 302–314.

Hughes, C. A., & Agran, M. (1993). Teaching persons with severe disabilities to use self-instruction in community settings: An analysis of applications. *Journal of the Association for Persons with Severe Handicaps, 18,* 261–274.

Hughes, C., & Petersen, D. (1989). Utilizing a self-instructional training package to increase on-task behavior and work performance. *Education and Training in Mental Retardation, 24,* 114–120.

Hughes, C., Harmer, M. L. Killian, D. J., & Niarhos, F. (1995). The effects of multiple-exemplar self-instructional training on high school students' generalized conversational interactions. *Journal of Applied Behavior Analysis, 28,* 201–218.

Israel, A. C. (1978). Some thoughts on correspondence between saying and doing. *Journal of Applied Behavior Analysis, 11,* 271–276.

Israel, A. C., & Brown, M. S. (1977). Correspondence training, prior verbal training, and control of nonverbal behavior via control of verbal behavior. *Journal of Applied Behavior Analysis, 10,* 333–338.

Johnson, M. B., Whitman, T. L., & Johnson, M. (1980). Teaching addition and subtraction to mentally retarded children: A self-instruction program. *Applied Research in Mental Retardation, 1,* 141–160.

Karoly, P., & Dirks, M. J. (1977). Developing self-control in pre-school children through correspondence training. *Behavior Therapy, 8,* 398–405.

Kendall, P. (1977). On the efficacious use of verbal self-instructional procedures with children. *Cognitive Therapy and Research, 1,* 331–341.

Keogh, D. A., Faw, G. D., Whitman, T. L., & Reid, D. (1984). Enhancing leisure skills in severely retarded adolescents through a self-instructional treatment package. *Analysis and Intervention in Developmental Disabilities, 4,* 333–351.

Keogh, D. A., Whitman, T. L., & Maxwell, S. E. (1988). Self-instruction versus external instruction: Individual differences and training effectiveness. *Cognitive Therapy and Research, 12*, 591–610.

Leon, J. A., & Pepe, H. G. (1983). Self-instructional training: Cognitive behavior modification for remediating arithmetic deficits. *Exceptional Children, 50*, 54–60.

Luria, A. R. (1961). *The role of speech in the regulation of normal and abnormal behavior.* New York: Liveright.

Meacham, J. A. (1978). Verbal guidance through remembering the goals of actions. *Child Development, 49*, 188–193.

Meichenbaum, D. (1975). Enhancing creativity by modifying what subjects say to themselves. *American Educational Research Journal, 12*, 129–145.

Meichenbaum, D. H., & Goodman, J. (1969). The developmental control of operant motor responding by verbal operants. *Journal of Experimental Child Psychology, 7*, 533–565.

Meichenbaum, D. H., & Goodman, J. (1971). Training impulsive children to talk to themselves: A means of developing self-control. *Journal of Abnormal Psychology, 77*, 115–126.

Miller, D. T., Weinstein, S. M., & Karniol, R. (1978). Effects of age and self-verbalizations on children's ability to delay gratification. *Developmental Psychology, 14*, 569–570.

Monahan, J., & O'Leary, K. D. (1971). Effects of self-instruction on rule-breaking behavior. *Psychological Reports, 29*, 1059–1066.

Nelson, W. J. Jr., & Birkimer, J. C. (1978). Role of self-instruction and self-reinforcement in the modification of impulsivity. *Journal of Consulting and Clinical Psychology, 46*, 183.

Nelson, W., & O'Leary, D. (1971). Effects of self-instruction on rule-breaking behavior. *Psychological Reports, 29*, 1059–1066.

O'Leary, K. D. (1968). The effects of self-instruction on immoral behavior. *Journal of Experimental Child Psychology, 6*, 297–301.

Palkes, H., Stewart, M., & Kahana, B. (1968). Porteus maze performance of hyperactive boys after training in self-directed verbal commands. *Child Development, 39*, 817–826.

Robin, A. L., Armel, S., & O'Leary, K. D. (1975). The effects of self-instructions on writing deficiencies. *Behavior Therapy, 6*, 178–187.

Rusch, F. R., Martin, J. E., Lagomarcino, T. R., & White, D. M. (1987). Teaching task sequencing via verbal mediation. *Education and Training in Mental Retardation, 22*, 229–235.

Rusch, F. R., McKee, M., Chadsey-Rusch, J. & Renzaglia, A. (1988). Teaching a student with severe handicaps to self-instruct: A brief report. *Education and Training in Mental Retardation, 23*, 51–58.

Rusch, F. R., Morgan, T. K., Martin, J. E., Riva, M., & Agran, M. (1985). Competitive employment: Teaching mentally retarded employees self-instructional strategies. *Applied Research in Mental Retardation, 6*, 389–407.

Sawin, D. B., & Parke, R. D. (1979). Development of self-verbalized control of resistance to deviation. *Developmental Psychology, 15*, 120–127.

Zivin, G. (Ed.) (1979). *The development of self-regulation through private speech.* New York: Wiley.

Self-Regulation

Agran, M., Blanchard, C., & Wehmeyer, M., & Hughes, C. (2001). Teaching students to self-regulate their behavior: The differential effects of students vs. teacher-delivered reinforcement. *Research in Developmental Disabilities, 22*, 319–332.

Agran, M., Martin, J. E., & Mithaug, D. E. (1989). Achieving transition through adaptability instruction. *TEACHING Exceptional Children, 21*, 4–7.

Agran, M., Snow, K., & Swaner, J. (1999). Teacher perceptions of self-determination: Benefits, characteristics, strategies. *Education and Training in Mental Retardation and Developmental Disabilities, 34*, 293–301.

Ames, C. (1992). Classrooms; Goals, structures, and student motivation. *Journal of Educational Psychology 84*, 261–271.

Anderson, L., Fodor, I., & Albert, M. (1976). A comparison of methods for training self-control. *Behavior Therapy, 7*, 649–658.

Bandura, A. (1989). Regulation of cognitive processes through perceived self-efficacy. *Developmental Psychology, 25,* 729–735.

Barkley, R. A., Copeland, A. P., & Sivage, C. (1980). A self-control classroom for hyperactive children. *Journal of Autism and Developmental Disorders, 10,* 75–89.

Blackwood, R. (1970). The operant conditioning of verbally mediated self-control in the classroom. *Journal of School Psychology, 8,* 251–258.

Bolstad, O. D., & Johnson, S. M. (1972). Self-regulation in the modification of disruptive classroom behavior. *Journal of Applied Behavior Analysis, 5,* 443–454.

Borkowski, J. A., Estrada, M. T., Milstead, M., & Hale, C. A. (1989). General problem-solving skills: Relations between metacognition and strategic processing. *Learning Disability Quarterly, 12,* 57–70.

Briggs, A., Alberto, P., Sharpton, W., Berlin, D., McKinley, C., & Ritts, C. (1990) Generalized use of a self-operated audio prompt system. *Education and Training in Mental Retardation, 25,* 381–389.

Camp, E., Blom, G., Herbert, F., & Van Doorninck, W. (1977). "Think Aloud": A program for developing self-control in young aggressive boys. *Journal of Abnormal Child Psychology, 8,* 157–169.

Carter, D. B., Patterson, C. J., & Quasebarth, S. J. (1979). Development of children's use of plans for self-control. *Cognitive Therapy and Research, 3,* 407–413.

Coleman, R. S., & Whitman, T. L. (1984). Developing, generalizing, and maintaining physical fitness in mentally retarded adults: Toward a self-directed program. *Analysis and Intervention in Developmental Disabilities, 4,* 109–127.

Collet-Klingenberg, L., & Chadsey-Rusch, J. (1991). Using a cognitive-process approach to teach social skills. *Education and Training in Mental Retardation, 26,* 258–270.

Columbus, M.A., & Mithaug, D. E. (2003). The effects of self-regulation problem-solving instruction on the self-determination of secondary students with disabilities. In D. E. Mithaug, D. K. Mithaug, M. Agran, J. E. Martin, & M. L. Wehmeyer (Eds.). *Self-determined learning theory: Construction, verification, and evaluation* (pp. 172–187). Mahway, NJ: Lawrence Erlbaum Associates.

Danoff, B., Harris, K. R., & Graham, S. (1993). Incorporating strategy instruction within the writing process in the regular classroom: Effects on the writing of students with and without learning disabilities. *Journal of Reading Behavior, 25,* 295–322.

De La Paz, S. (1999). Self-regulated strategy instruction in regular education settings: Improving outcomes for students with and without learning disabilities. *Learning Disabilities Research and Practice, 14,* 92–106.

Derry, S. J. (1990). Remediating academic difficulties through strategy training: The acquisition of useful knowledge. *Remedial and Special Education, 11*(6), 19–31.

Deshler, D. D., & Schumaker, J. B. (1986). Learning strategies: An instructional alternative for low-achieving adolescents. *Exceptional Children, 52,* 583–590.

Deshler, D. D., & Schumaker, J. B., & Lenz, B. K. (1984). Academic and cognitive interventions for LD adolescents: Part I. *Journal of Learning Disabilities, 17,* 108–117.

Douglas, V. I., Parry, P., Marton, P., & Garson, C. (1976). Assessment of a cognitive training program for hyperactive children. *Journal of Abnormal Child Psychology, 4*(4), 389–407.

Drabman, R. S., Spitalnik, R., & O'Leary, K. D. (1973). Teaching self-control to disruptive children. *Journal of Abnormal Psychology, 82,* 10–16.

Dweck, C. S., & Leggett, E. L. (1999). A social-cognitive approach to motivation and personality. *Psychological Review, 95,* 256–273.

Ellis, E. S. (1986). The role of motivation and pedagogy on the generalization of cognitive training by the mildly handicapped. *Journal of Learning Disabilities, 19,* 66–70.

Ellis, E. S., Deshler, D. D., & Schumaker, J. B. (1989). Teaching adolescents with learning disabililties to generate and use task-specific strategies. *Journal of Learning Disabilities, 22,* 108–119.

Ellis, E. S., Lenz, B. K., & Sabornie, E. J. (1987). Generalization and adaptation of learning strategies to natural environments: Part 1: Critical agents. *Remedial and Special Education, 8*(1), 6–20.

Englert, C. S., Raphael, T., Fear, K., & Anderson, L. (1988). Students' metacognitive knowledge about how to write informational texts. *Learning Disability Quarterly, 11,* 18–46.

Epstein, R., & Goss, C. M. (1978). A self-control procedure for the maintenance of nondisruptive behavior in an elementary school child. *Behaviour Therapy, 9*, 109–117.

Fagen, S. A., & Long, N. J. (1976). Teaching children self-control: A new responsibility for teachers. *Focus on Exceptional Children, 7*(8), 1–12.

Fagen, S. A., & Long, N. J. (1979). A psychoeducational curriculum approach to teaching self-control. *Behavior Disorders, 4*, 68–82.

Fantuzzo, J., Harrell, K., & McLeoud, M. (1979). Across-subject generalization of attending behavior as a function of self-regulation training. *Child Behavior Therapy, 1*, 313–321.

Garner, R. (1990). When children and adults do not use learning strategies: Toward a theory of settings. *Review of Educational Research, 60*, 517–529.

Garner, R., & Alexander, P. A. (1989). Metacognition: Answered and unanswered questions. *Educational Psychologist, 24*(2), 143–158.

Gettinger, M. (1985). Effects of teacher-directed versus student-directed instruction and cues versus no cues for improving spelling performance. *Journal of Applied Behavior Analysis, 18*, 167–171.

Glenwick, D. S., & Barocas, R. (1979). Training impulsive children in verbal self-control by use of natural change agents. *Journal of Special Education, 13*, 387–398.

Glynn, E. L., & Thomas, J. D. (1974). Effect of cueing on self-control of classroom behavior. *Journal of Applied Behavior Analysis, 7*, 299–306.

Glynn, E. L., & Thomas, J. D., & Shee, S. M. (1973). Behavioral self-control of on-task behavior in an elementary classroom. *Journal of Applied Behavior Analysis, 6*, 105–113.

Goetz, E. M., & Etzel, B. C. (1978). A brief review of self-control procedures: Problems and solutions. *Behavior Therapists, 1*, 5–8.

Goldfried, M., Decenteceo, E., & Weinberg, . (1974). Systematic rational restructuring as a self-control technique. *Behavior Therapy, 5*, 247–254.

Grace, N., Cowart, C., & Matson, J. L. (1988). Reinforcement and self-control for treating a chronic case of self-injury in Lesch-Nyhan syndrome. *Journal of the Multihandicapped Person, 1*, 53–59.

Graham, S. (1997). Executive control in the revising of students with learning and writing difficulties. *Journal of Education Psychology, 89*, 223–234.

Graham, S., & Harris, K. R. (1989a). A components analysis of cognitive strategy training: Effects on learning disabled students' compositions and self-efficacy. *Journal of Educational Psychology, 81*, 353–361.

Graham, S., & Harris, K. R. (1993). Self-regulated strategy development: Helping students with learning problems develop as writers. *Elementary School Journal, 94*, 169–181.

Graham, S., & Harris, K. R. (1997). Self-regulation and writing: Where do we go from here? *Contemporary Educational Psychology, 22*, 102–114.

Graham, S., Harris, K. R., & Reid, R. (1992). Developing self-regulated learners. *Focus on Exceptional Children, 24*(6), 1–16.

Graham, S., Harris, K. R., & Troia, G. A. (2000). Self-regulated strategy development revised: Teaching writing strategies to struggling writers. *Topics in Language Disorders, 20*(4), 1–14.

Harris, K. (1982). Cognitive behavior modification: Application with exceptional children. *Focus on Exceptional Children, 15*, 1–16.

Harris, K. R. (1980). The sustained effects of cognitive communication apprehension. *Communication Quarterly, 24*, 47–57.

Harris, K. R. (1982). Cognitive-behavior modification: Application with exceptional children. *Focus on Exceptional Children, 15*(2), 1–16.

Harris, K. R., & Brown, R. (1982). Cognitive modification and informed teacher treatments for shy children. *Journal of Experimental Education, 50*, 137–144.

Harris, K. R., & Graham, S. (1985). Improving students' composition skills: Self-control strategy training. *Learning Disability Quarterly, 8*, 27–38.

Harris, K. R., & Pressley, M. (1991). The nature of cognitive strategy instruction: Interactive strategy construction. *Exceptional Children, 57*, 392–405.

Harris, K. R., (1988). Learning disabilities research: The need, the integrity, and the challenge. *Journal of Learning Disabilities, 21*, 267–270, 274.

Harris, K. R., (1990). Developing self-regulated learners: The role of private speech and self-instructions. *Educational Psychologist, 25*, 35–50.

Hinshaw, S. P., Henker, B., & Whalen, C. W. (1984). Self-control in hyperactive boys in anger-inducing situations: Effects of cognitive-behavioral training and of methylpendate. *Journal of Abnormal Child Psychology, 12*, 55–78.

Karoly, P. & Kanfer, F. H. (1974). Effects of prior contractual experiences on self-control in children. *Developmental Psychology, 10*, 459–460.

Karoly, P., & Dirks, M. J. (1977). Developing self-control in pre-school children through correspondence training. *Behavior Therapy, 8*, 398–405.

Kendall, P. C., & Finch, A. J. (1978). A cognitive-behavioral treatment for impulsivity: A group comparison study. *Journal of Consulting and Clinical Psychology, 46*, 110–118.

Kendall, P. C., & Wilcox, L. E. (1980). A cognitive-behavioral treatment for impulsivity: Concrete versus conceptual training in non-self-controlled problem children. *Journal of Consulting and Clinical Psychology, 48*, 80–91.

Kendall, P., & Finch, A. (1976). A cognitive-behavioral treatment for impulse control: A case study. *Journal of Consulting and Clinical Psychology, 44*, 852–859.

Kurtz, P. D., & Neisworth, J. T. (1976). Self-control possibilities for exceptional children. *Exceptional Children, 42*, 212–217.

Litrownik, A. J., Cleary, C. P., Lecklitner, G. L., & Fanzini, L. R. (1978). Self-regulation in retarded persons: Acquisition of standards for performance. *American Journal of Mental Deficiency, 83*, 149–506.

Litrownik, A. J., Franzini, L. R., Geller, S., & Geller, M. (1977). Delay of gratification: Decisional self-control and experience with delay intervals. *American Journal of Mental Deficiency, 82*, 149–154.

Lloyd, J. (1980). Academic instruction and cognitive behavior modification: The need for attack strategy training. *Exceptional Education Quarterly, 1*, 53–63.

Mahoney, M. J., & Mahoney, K. (1976). Self-control techniques with the mentally retarded. *Exceptional Children, 42*, 338–339.

Martin, J. E., Rusch, F. R., James, V. L., Decker, P. J., & Trtol, K. A. (1982). The use of picture cues to establish self-control in the preparation of complex meals by mentally retarded adults. *Applied Research in Mental Retardation, 3*, 105–119.

McKinney, J. d., & Haskins, R. (1980). Cognitive training and the development of problem-solving strategies. *Exceptional Education Quarterly, 1*, 41–51.

Meichenbaum, D. (1972). Cognitive modifications of test anxious college students. *Journal of Consulting and Clinical Psychology, 39*, 370–382.

Meichenbaum, D. (1977). *Cognitive-behavior modification: An integrative approach.* New York: Plenum.

Meichenbaum, D. (1980). Cognitive behavior modification with exceptional children: A promise yet unfulfilled. *Exceptional Education Quarterly, 1*, 83–88.

Miller, D. T., Weinstein, S. M., & Karniol, R. (1978). Effects of age and self-verbalizations on children's ability to delay gratification. *Developmental Psychology, 14*, 569–570.

Mischel, W., & Patterson, C. J. (1976). Substantive and structural elements of effective plans for self-control. *Journal of Personality and Social Psychology, 34*, 942–950.

Mithaug, D. E. (1993). *Self-regulation theory: How optimal adjustment maximizes gain.* Westport, CT: Praeger.

Mithaug, D. E., Martin, J. E., & Agran, M. (1987). Adaptability instruction: The goal of transitional programming. *Exceptional Children, 53*, 500–505.

Mithaug, D. E., & Mithaug, D. K. (2004). Self-determined learning. In S. Farmer & S. Stein (Eds.). *Connotative learning.* Washington, D.C.: Kendall/Hunt Publishing Company.

Mithaug, D. E., Mithaug, D. K., Martin, J. E., Agran, M., & Wehmeyer, M. L. (2003) (Eds.). *Self-determined learning theory: Construction, predictions, and evaluation.* Mahway, NJ: Lawrence Erlbaum Associates.

Mithaug, D. K. (2002). "Yes" means success: Teaching children with multiple disabilities to self-regulate during independent word. *TEACHING Exceptional Children, 35*(1), 22–27.

Mithaug, D. K., & Mithaug, D. E. (2003). The effects of teacher-directed versus student-directed instruction on the self-management of young children with disabilities. *Journal of Applied Behavior Analysis, 36*, 133–136.

O'Leary, S. G., & Dubey, D. R. (1979). Applications of self-control procedures by children: A review. *Journal of Applied Behavior Analysis, 12*, 449–465.

Paris, S. G., & Winograd, P. (1990). Promoting metacognition and motivation of exceptional children. *Remedial and Special Education, 11*(6), 7–15.

Patterson, C. J., & Carter, D. B. (1979). Attentional determinants of children's self-control in waiting and working situations. *Child Development, 50*, 272–275.

Pearl, R. (1985). Cognitive behavioral interventions for increasing motivation. *Journal of Abnormal Child Psychology, 13*, 443–454.

Rachlin, H. (1974). Self-control. *Behaviorism, 2*, 94–107.

Reid, M., & Borkowski, J. G. (1987). Causal attributions of hyperactive children: Implications for teaching strategies and self-control. *Journal of Educational Psychology, 79*, 296–307.

Sagotsky, G., Patterson, C. J., & Lepper, M. R. (1978). Training children's self-control: A field experiment in self-monitoring and goal-setting in the classroom. *Journal of Experimental Child Psychology, 25*, 242–253.

Sawin, D. B., & Parke, R. D. (1979). Development of self-verbalized control of resistance to deviation. *Developmental Psychology, 15*, 120–127.

Sawyer, R., Graham, S., & Harris, K. R. (1992). Direct teaching, strategy instruction, and strategy instruction with explicit self-regulation: Effects on learning disabled students' composition skills and self-efficacy. *Journal of Educational Psychology, 84*, 340–352.

Sexton, M., Harris, K. R., & Graham, S. (1998). Self-regulated strategy development and the writing process: Effects on essay writing and attributions. *Exceptional Children, 64*, 295–311.

Shure, M., & Spivack, G. (1972). Means-ends thinking, adjustment and social class among elementary school-aged children. *Journal of Consulting and Clinical Psychology, 38*, 438–353.

Solomon, G., & Globerson, T. (1987). Skill may not be enough: The role of mindfulness in learning and transfer. *International Journal of Educational Research, 11*, 623–637.

Sowers, J., Verdi, M., Bourbeau, P., & Sheehan, M. (1985). Teaching job independence and flexibility to mentally retarded students through the use of a self-control package. *Journal of Applied Behavior Analysis, 18*, 81–85.

Spates, C. R., & Kanfer, F. H. (1977). Self-monitoring, self-evaluation, and self-reinforcement in children's learning: A test of a multistage self-regulation model. *Behavior Therapy, 8*, 9–16.

Spivack, G., & Shire, M. (1974). *Social adjustment of young children: A cognitive approach to solving real-life problems.* San Francisco: Jossey-Bass.

Stevenson, H. C., & Fantuzzo, J. W. (1984). Application of the "generalization map" to a self-control intervention with school-aged children. *Journal of Applied Behavior Analysis, 17*, 203–212.

Stevenson, H. C., & Fantuzzo, J. W. (1986). The generality of social validity of a competency-based self-control training intervention for underachieving students. *Journal of Applied Behavior Analysis, 19*, 269–276.

Toner, I. J., Holstein, R. B., & Hetherington, E. M. (1977). Reflection-impulsivity and self-control in preschool children. *Child Development, 48*, 239–245.

Trask-Tyler, S.A., Grossi, T.A., & Heward, W.L. (1994). Teaching young adults with developmental disabilities and visual impairments to use tape-recorded recipes: Acquisition, generalization, and maintenance of cooking skills. *Journal of Behavioral Education, 4*, 283–311.

Turkowitz, H., O'Leary, K. D., & Ironsmith, M. (1975). Generalization and maintenance of appropriate behavior through self-control. *Journal of Consulting and Clinical Psychology, 43*, 577–583.

Wallace, I., & Pear, J. (1977). Self-control techniques of famous novelists. *Journal of Applied Behavior Analysis, 10*, 515–525.

Watson, D. L., & Tharp, R. G. (1977). *Self-directed behavior: Self-modification for personal adjustment* (2nd Ed.). Monterey, CA: Brooks/Cole.

Wehmeyer, M. L., Agran, M., & Hughes, C.A. (2000). A national survey of teachers' promotion of self-determination and student-directed learning. *The Journal of Special Education 34*, 58–68.

Wehmeyer, M. L., Palmer, S.B., Agran M., Mithaug, D.E., & Martin, J.E. (2000). Promoting causal agency: The Self-Determined Learning Model of Instruction. *Exceptional Children, 66*, 430–453.

Wehmeyer, M. L., & Schwartz, M. (1997). Self-determination and positive adult outcomes: A follow-up study of youth with mental retardation or learning disabilities. *Exceptional Children, 63*, 245–255.

Whitman, T. L., (1990). Self-regulation and mental retardation. *American Journal on Mental Retardation, 94*(3), 347–362.

Williams, D. Y., & Akamatsu, T. J. (1978). Cognitive self-guidance training with juvenile delinquents: Applicability and generalization. *Cognitive Therapy and Research, 2*, 285–288.

Wong, B. Y. L. (1994). Instructional parameters promoting transfer of learned strategies in students with learning disabilities. *Learning Disability Quarterly, 17*, 110–120.

Wong, B. Y., L. (2000). Writing strategies instruction for expository essays for adolescents with and without learning disabilities. *Topics in Language Disorders, 20*(4), 29–44).

Zimmerman, B. J. (1989). A social cognitive view of self-regulated academic learning. *Journal of Educational Psychology, 81*, 329–339.

Zivin, G. (Ed.) (1979). *The development of self-regulation through private speech.* New York: Wiley.

Self-Management

Agran, M., Fodor-Davis, J., Moore, S., & Deer, M. (1989). The application of a self-management program on instruction-following skills. *Journal of the Association for Persons with Severe Handicaps, 14*, 147–154.

Alberto, P. A., & Sharpton, W. (1987). Prompting strategies that promote student self-management. *TEACHING Exceptional Children, 19*(4), 54–57.

Browder, D. M., & Shapiro, E. S. (1985). Application of self-management to individuals with severe handicaps: A review. *Journal of the Association for Persons with Severe Handicaps, 10*, 200–208.

Dalton, T., Martella, R.C., & Marchard-Martella, N.E. (1999). The effects of a self-management program in reducing off-task behavior. *Journal of Behavioral Education, 9*, 157–176.

Digangi, S. A., & Maag, J. W. (1992). A component analysis of self-management training with behaviorally disordered youth. *Behavioral Disorders, 17*, 281–290.

Ferretti, R.P., Cavalier, A.R., Murphy, M.J., & Murphy, R. (1993). The self-management of skills by persons with mental retardation. *Research in Developmental Disabilities, 14*, 184–205.

Firman, K. B., Bere, P., & Loyd, R. (2002). Enhancing self-management in students with mental retardation: Extrinsic versus intrinsic procedures. *Education and Training in Mental Retardation and Developmental Disabilities, 37*(2), 163–171.

Fowler, S. F. (1984). Introductory comments: The pragmatics of self-management for the developmentally disabled. *Analysis and Intervention in Developmental Disabilities, 4*, 85–89.

Gardner, W. I., Cole, C. L., Berry, D. L., & Nowinski, J. M. (1983). Reduction of disruptive behaviors in mentally retarded adults: A self-management approach. *Behavior Modification, 7*, 76–96.

Garff, J. T., & Storey, K. (1998). The use of self-management strategies for increasing the appropriate hygiene of persons with disabilities in supported employment settings. *Education and Training in Mental Retardation and Developmental Disabilities, 33*(2), 179–188.

Glomb, N., & West, R. P. (1990). Teaching behaviorally disordered adolescents to use self-management skills for improving the completeness, accuracy, and neatness of creative writing assignments. *Behavioral Disorders, 15*, 233–242.

Gross, A. M., Bringham, T. A., Hopper, C., & Bologna, N. C. (1980). Self-management and social skills training: A study with predelinquent and delinquent youth. *Criminal Justice and Behavior, 7*, 161–184.

Harchik, A. E., Sherman, J. A., & Sheldon, J. B. (1992). The use of self-management procedures by people with developmental disabilities: A brief review. *Research in Developmental Disabilities, 13*, 211–227.

Hoff, K.E., & DuPaul, G.J. (1998). Reducing disruptive behavior in general education classrooms: The use of self-management strategies. *School Psychology Review, 27*, 290–303.

Hughes, C. A., Korinek, L., & Gorman, J. (1991). Self-management for students with mental retardation in public school settings: A research review. *Education and Training in Mental Retardation, 26,* 271–291.

Hughes, C. A., Ruhl, K. L., & Peterson, S. K. (1988). Teaching self-management skills: Promising practices. *TEACHING Exceptional Children, 20*(2), 70–72.

Hughes, C., & Lloyd, J. W. (1993). An analysis of self-management. *Journal of Behavioral Education, 3,* 405–425.

Hughes, C., & Scott, S. V. (1997). Teaching self-management in employment settings. *Journal of Vocational Rehabilitation, 8,* 43–53.

Humphrey, L. L., Karoly, P., & Kirschembaum, D. S. (1978). Self-management in the classroom: Self-imposed response cost versus self-reward. *Behavior Therapy, 9,* 591–601.

Irvine, B. A., Erickson, A. M., Singer, G., & Stahlberg, D. (1992). A coordinated program to transfer self-management skills from school to home. *Education and Training in Mental Retardation, 27*(3), 241–254.

King-Sears, M. E. (1999). Teacher and researcher co-design self-management content for an inclusive setting: Research training, intervention, and generalization effects on student performance. *Education and Training in Mental Retardation and Developmental Disabilities, 34,* 134–156.

Koegel, L.K., Koegel, R.L., Hurley, C., & Frea, W. D. (1992). Improving social skills and disruptive behavior in children with autism through self-management. *Journal of Applied Behavior Analysis, 25,* 341–353.

Koegel, R.L., & Koegel, L.K. (1990). Extended reductions in stereotypic behavior of students with autism through a self-management treatment package. *Journal of Applied Behavior Analysis, 23,* 119–127.

Lagomarcino, T. R., & Rusch, F. R. (1989). Utilizing self-management procedures to teach independent performance. *Education and Training in Mental Retardation, 24,* 297–305.

Lovett, D. L., & Haring, K. A. (1989) The effects of self-management training on the daily living of adults with mental retardation. *Education and Training in Mental Retardation, 24,* 306–323.

Lovitt, T. C. (1973). Self-management projects with children with behavioral disorders. *Journal of Learning Disabilities, 6,* 138–150.

Malott, R. W. (1984). Rule-governed behavior, self-management, and the developmentally disabled: A theoretical analysis. *Analysis and Intervention in Developmental Disabilities, 4,* 199–209.

McAdam, D. B., & Cuvo, A. J. (1994). Textual prompts as an antecedent cue self-management strategy for persons with mild disabilities. *Behavior Modification, 18*(1), 47–65.

McDougall, D., Brady, M. P. (1998). Initiating and fading self-management interventions to increase math fluency in general education classes. *Exceptional Children, 64*(2), 151–166.

McNally, R. J., Kompik, J. J., & Sherman, G. (1984). Increasing the productivity of mentally retarded workers through self-management. *Analysis and Intervention in Developmental Disabilities, 4,* 129–135.

Moore, S. C., Agran, M., & Fodor-Davis, J. (1989). Using self-management strategies to increase the production rates of workers with severe handicaps. *Education and Training in Mental Retardation, 24,* 324–332.

Nelson, J. R., Smith, D. J., Young, R. K., & Dodd, J. M. (1991). A review of self-management outcome research conducted with students who exhibit behavior disorders. *Behavioral Disorders, 16*(3), 169–179.

Newman, B., Ryan, C. S., Tuntigian, L., & Reinecke, D. R. (1997). Self-management of a DRO procedure by three students with autism. *Behavioral Interventions, 12,* 149–156.

Ninness, H. A. C., Fuerst, J., & Rutherford, R. D. (1991). Effects of self-management training and reinforcement on the transfer of improved conduct in the absence of supervision. *Journal of Applied Behavior Analysis, 24,* 499–508.

Ninness, H.A. C., Ellis, J., Miller, W.B., Baker, D., & Rutherford, R. (1995). The effect of a self-management training package on the transfer of aggression control procedures in the absence of supervision. *Behavior Modification, 19,* 464–490.

Peterson, L.D., Young, K.R., West, R.P., & Peterson, M.H. (1999). Effects of student self-management on generalization of student performance to regular classrooms. *Education and Treatment of Children, 22,* 357–372.

Pierce, K. L., & Schreibman, L. (1994). Teaching daily living skills to children with autism in unsupervised settings through pictorial self-management. *Journal of Applied Behavior Analysis, 27,* 471–481.

Reinecke, D.R., Newman, B., & Meinberg, D.L. (1999). Self-management of sharing in three pre-schoolers with autism. *Education and Training in Mental Retardation and Developmental Disabilities, 34,* 312–317.

Rumsey, I. & Ballard, K. (1985). Teaching self-management strategies for independent story writing to children with classroom behavior difficulties. *Educational Psychology, 5,* 147–157.

Schloss, P. (1987). Self-management strategies for adolescents entering the work force. *TEACHING Exceptional Children 19*(9), 39–43.

Shapiro, E. S. (1989). Teaching self-management skills to learning disabled adolescents. *Learning Disability Quarterly, 12,* 275.

Shapiro, E. S., Browder, D. M., & D'Huyvetters, K. K. (1984). Increasing academic productivity of severely ill multihandicapped children with self-management: Idiosyncratic effects. *Analysis and Intervention in Developmental Disabilities, 4,* 171–188.

Shapiro, E.S., DuPaul, G.J., & Bradley-Klug, K.L. (1998). Self-management as a strategy to improve the classroom behavior of adolescents with ADHD. *Journal of Learning Disabilities, 31,* 545–555.

Shaprio, E. S., & Klein, R. D. (1980). Self-management of classroom behavior with retarded/disturbed children. *Behavior Modification, 4,* 83–97.

Smith, D. J., Young, K. R., Nelson, J. R., & West, R. P. (1992). The effect of a self-management procedure on the classroom and academic behavior of students with mild handicaps. *School Psychology Review, 21*(1), 59–72.

Smith, D. J., Young, K. R., West, R. P., Morgan, D. P., & Rhode, G. (1988). Reducing the disruptive behavior of junior high school students: A classroom self-management procedures. *Behavioral Disorders, 13*(4), 231–239.

Srikameswaran, S., & Martin, G. L. (1984). A component analysis of a self-management program for improving work rates of mentally handicapped persons. *Mental Retardation and Learning Disability Bulletin, 12,* 39–52.

Stahmer, A.C., & Schreibman, L. (1992). Teaching children with autism appropriate play in unsupervised environments using a self-management treatment package. *Journal of Applied Behavior Analysis, 25,* 447–459.

Thierman, G. J., & Martin, G. L. (1989). Self-management with picture prompts to improve quality of household cleaning by severely mentally handicapped persons. *International Journal of Rehabilitation Research, 12*(1), 27–39.

Goal Setting

Ames, C. (1992). Classrooms; Goals, structures, and student motivation. *Journal of Educational Psychology 84,* 261–271.

Brownell, K.D., Colletti, G., Ersner-Hershfield, R., Hershfield, S. M., & Wilson, G. T. (1977). Self-control in school children: Stringency and leniency in self-determined and externally imposed performed standards. *Behavior Theory, 8,* 442–455.

Childers, J. H. (1987, May). Goal-setting in counseling: steps, strategies, and roadblocks. *The School Counselor,* 362–368.

Dickerson, E. A., & Creedon, C. F. (1981). Self-selection of standards by children: The relative effectiveness of pupil-selected and teacher-selected standards of performance. *Journal of Applied Behavior Analysis, 14,* 423–233.

Flexer, R., Newbery, J., & Martin, A. (1979). Use of goal setting procedures in increasing task assembly rate of severely retarded workers. *Education and Training of the Mentally Retarded, 14*(3), 177–184.

Fuchs, L. S., Fuchs, D., Hamelett, C., & Whinnery, K. W. (1991). Effects of goal line feedback on level, slope, and stability of performance within curriculum-based measurement. *Learning Disabilities Research & Practice, 6,* 66–74.

Graham, S., MacArthur, C. A., & Schwartz, S. S. (1995). The effects of goal setting and procedural facilitation on the revising behavior and writing performance of students with writing and learning problems. *Journal of Educational Psychology, 87,* 230–240.

Graham, S., MacArthur, C., Schwartz, S., & Page, V. (1992). Improving the compositions of students with learning disabilities using a strategy involving product and process goal setting. *Exceptional Children, 58,* 322–334.

Hanel, F., & Martin, G. (1980). Self-monitoring, self-administration of token reinforcement, and goal setting to improve work rates with retarded clients. *International Journal of Rehabilitation Research, 3*, 505–517.

Kazdin, A. (1974). Reactive self-monitoring: The effects of response desirability, goal setting, and feedback. *Journal of Consulting and Clinical Psychology, 42*, 704–716.

Kim, J. S., & Hamner, W. C. (1976). Effect of performance feedback and goal setting on productivity and satisfction in an organizational setting. *Journal of Applied Psychology, 61*, 48–57.

Lenz, B. K., Ehren, B. J., & Smiley, L. R. (1991). A goal attainment approach to improve completion of project-type assignments by adolescents with learning disabilities. *Learning Disabilities Research and Practice, 6*, 166–176.

Litrownik, A. J., Cleary, C. P., Lecklitner, G. L., & Fanzini, L. R. (1978). Self-regulation in retarded persons: Acquisition of standards for performance. *American Journal of Mental Deficiency, 83*, 149–506.

Locke, E. A., Shaw, K. N., Saari, L. M., & Latham, G. P. (1981). Goal setting and task performance: 1969–1980. *Psychological Bulletin, 90*, 125–152.

Lovitt, T. C., & Curtiss, K. A. (1969). Academic response rate as a function of teacher and self-imposed contingencies. *Journal of Applied Behavior Analysis, 2*, 49–53.

Martino, L. R. (1993). A goal-setting model for young adolescent at risk students. *Middle School Journal, 24*, 19–22.

Meacham, J. A. (1978). Verbal guidance through remembering the goals of actions. *Child Development, 49*, 188–193.

Page-Voth, V., & Graham, S. (1999). Effects of goal setting and strategy use on the writing performance and self-efficacy of students with writing and learning problems. *Journal of Educational Psychology, 91*, 230–240.

Sagotsky, G., Patterson, C. J., & Lepper, M. R. (1978). Training children's self-control: A field experiment in self-monitoring and goal-setting in the classroom. *Journal of Experimental Child Psychology, 25*, 242–253.

Schunk, D. H. (1985). Participation in goal setting: Effects on self-efficacy and skills of learning-disabled children. *Journal of Special Education, 19*, 307–317.

Schunk, D. H., & Schwartz, C. W. (1993). Writing strategy instruction with gifted students: Effects of goals and feedback on self-efficacy and skills. *Roeper Review, 15*, 225–230.

Terborg, J. R. (1976). Motivational components of goal setting. *Journal of Applied Psychology, 61*, 613–621.

Tollefson, N., Tracey, D. B., Johnson, E. P., & Charman, J. (1986). Teaching learning disabled students goal-implementation skills. *Psychology in the Schools, 23*, 194–204.

Self-Planning/Scheduling

Bambara, L. M., & Ager, C. (1992). Using self-scheduling to promote self-directed leisure activity in home and community settings. *Journal of the Association for Persons with Severe Handicaps, 17*(2), 67–76.

Carter, D. B., Patterson, C. J., & Quasebarth, S. J. (1979). Development of children's use of plans for self-control. *Cognitive Therapy and Research, 3*, 407–413.

De La Paz, S., & Graham, S. (1997a). Effects of dictation and advanced planning instruction on the composing of students with writing and learning problems. *Journal of Educational Psychology, 89*, 203–222.

De La Paz, S., & Graham, S. (1997b). Strategy instruction in planning: Effects on the writing performance and behavior of students with learning difficulties. *Exceptional Children, 63*, 167–181.

Karoly, P. & Kanfer, F. H. (1974). Effects of prior contractual experiences on self-control in children. *Developmental Psychology, 10*, 459–460.

Martin, J. E., Elias-Burger, S., & Mithaug, D. E. (1987). Acquisition and maintenance of time-based task change sequence. *Education and Training in Mental Retardation, 22*, 250–255.

Martin, J. E., Mithaug, D. E., Burger, D. L., (1990). Effects of visual cues upon the vocational task performance of students with mental retardation. *Exceptionality, 1*(1), 41–59.

Martin, J. E., Mithaug, D. E., & Frazier, E. S. (1992). Effects of picture referencing on PVC chair, Love Seat, and Settee assemblies by students with mental retardation. *Research in Developmental Disabilities, 13*, 267–286.

Mischel, W., & Patternson, C. J. (1976). Substantive and structural elements of effective plans for self-control. *Journal of Personality and Social Psychology, 34*, 942–950.

Mithaug, D. E., & Mar, D. K. (1980). The relation between choosing and working prevocational tasks in two severely retarded young adults. *Journal of Applied Behavior Analysis, 13*, 177–182.

Montague, M., Graves, A., & Leavell, A. (1991). Planning, procedural facilitation, and narrative composition of junior high students with learning disabilities. *Learning Disabilities Research and Practice, 6*, 219–224.

Patterson, C., & Mischel, W. (1975). Plans to resist distraction. *Developmental Psychology, 11*, 369–378.

Torrance, M., Thomas, G. V., & Robinson, E. J. (1991). Strategies for answering examination essay questions: Is it helpful to write a plan? *British Journal of Educational Psychology, 61*, 46–54.

Troia, G. A., Graham, S., Harris, K. R. (1999). Teaching students with learning disabilities to mindfully plan when writing. *Exceptional Children, 65*, 235–252.

Wong, B. Y. L., Butler, D. L., Ficzere, S. A., & Kuperis, S. (1996). Teaching low achievers and students with learning disabilities to plan, write, and revise essays. *Journal of Learning Disabilities, 29*, 197–212.

Wong, B. Y. L., Butler, D. L., Ficzere, S. A., & Kuperis, S. (1996). Teaching low achievers and students with learning disabilities to plan, write, and revise essays. *Journal of Learning Disabilities, 29*, 197–212.

Self-Monitoring

Ackerman, A., & Shapiro, E. S. (1984). Self-monitoring and work productivity with mentally retarded adults. *Journal of Applied Behavior Analysis, 17*, 403–407.

Alberto, P. A., Sharpton, W. R., Briggs, A., & Stright, M. H. (1986). Facilitating task acquisition through the use of a self-operated auditory prompting system. *Journal of the Association for Persons with Severe Handicaps, 11*(2), 85–91.

Bandura, A., & Perloff, B. (1976). Relative efficacy of self-monitored and externally imposed reinforcement systems. *Journal of Personality and Social Psychology, 7*, 111–116.

Bandura, A., Grusec, J. E., and Menlove, F. L. (1967). Some social determinants of self-monitoring reinforcement systems. *Journal of Personality and Social Psychology, 5*, 449–455.

Digangi, S. A., Maag, J. W., & Rutherford, R. B., Jr. (1991). Self-graphing of on-task behavior: Enhancing the reactive effects of self-monitoring on on-task behavior and academic performance. *Learning Disability Quarterly, 14*, 221–230.

Dunlap, L. K., Dunlap, G., Doegel, L. K., & Koegel, R. L. (1991). Using self-monitoring to increase independence. *TEACHING Exceptional Children, 23*(3), 17–22.

Dunlap, l., & Dunlap, G. (1989). Self-monitoring of subtraction problems by students with learning disabilities. *Journal of Applied Behavior Analysis, 22*, 309–314.

Fowler, S. A. (1986). Peer-monitoring and self-monitoring: Alternatives to traditional teacher management. *Exceptional Children, 52*, 573–581.

Frith, G. H. Armstrong, S. W. (1986). Self-monitoring for behaviorally disordered students. *TEACHING Exceptional Children, 18*, 144–148.

Gajar, A., Schloss, P. J., Schloss, C. N., & Thompson, C. K. (1984). Effects of feedback and self-monitoring on head trauma youths' conversational skills. *Journal of Applied Behavior Analysis, 17*(3), 353–358.

Gambrell, L. B., & Bates, R. J. (1986). Mental imagery and the comprehension-monitoring performance of fourth- and fifth-grade poor readers. *Reading Research Quarterly, 21*, 454–464.

Gilberts, G.H., Agran, M., Hughes, C., & Wehmeyer, M. (2001). The effects of peer-delivered self-monitoring strategies on the participation of students with severe disabilities in general education classrooms. *Journal of The Association for Persons with Severe Handicaps, 26*, 25–36.

Gottman, J. M., & McFall, R. M. (1972). Self-monitoring effects in a program for potential high school dropouts: A time series analysis. *Journal of Consulting and Clinical Psychology, 39*, 273–281.

Harris, K. R., Graham, S., Reid, R., McElroy, K., & Hamby, R. (1994). Self-monitoring of attention versus self-monitoring of performance: Replication and cross-task comparison studies. *Learning Disability Quarterly, 17*, 121–139.

Hayes, S. C., & Nelson, r. C. (1983). Similar reactivity produced by external cues and self-monitoring. *Behavior Modification, 7,* 183–196.

Heins, E. D., Lloyd, J. W., & Hallahan, D. P. (1986). Cued and noncued self-recording of attention to task. *Behavior Modification, 10,* 235–254.

Hinshaw, S. P., & Melnick, S. (1992). Self-monitoring therapies and attention deficit hyperactivity disorder. *Behavior Modification, 16*(2), 253–273.

Holman, J., & Baer, D. M. (1979). Facilitating generalization of on-task behavior through self-monitoring of academic tasks. *Journal of Autism and Developmental Disabilities, 9,* 429–446.

Hughes, C. A., & Hendrickson, J. A. (1987). Self-monitoring with at-risk students in the regular class setting. *Education and Treatment of Children, 10*(3), 225–236.

Hughes, C., Copeland, S. R., Agran, M., Wehmeyer, M. L., Rodi, M. S., & Presley, J. A. (2002). Using self-monitoring to improve performance in general education high school classes. *Education and Training in Mental Retardation and Developmental Disabilities, 37*(3), 262–272.

Hughes, C., Rung, L., Wehmeyer, M.L., Agran, M., Copeland, S.R., & Hwang, B. (2000). Self-prompted communication book use to increase social interaction among high school students. *Education and Training in Mental Retardation and Developmental Disabilities, 25,* 153–166.

Hughes, C.A., & Boyle, J.R. (1991). Effects of self-monitoring for on-task behavior and task productivity on elementary students with moderate mental retardation. *Education and Treatment of Children, 14,* 96–111.

Kazdin, A. (1974). Reactive self-monitoring: The effects of response desirability, goal setting, and feedback. *Journal of Consulting and Clinical Psychology, 42,* 704–716.

Kern, L., Dunlap, G., Childs, K. E., & Clarke, S. (1994). Use of a classwide self-monitoring program to improve the behavior of students with emotional and behavioral disorders. *Education and Treatment of Children, 17*(3), 445–458.

McCarl, J. J., Svobodny, L., & Boare, P. L. (1991). Self-recording in a classroom for students with mild to moderate handicaps: Effects on productivity and on-task behavior. *Education and Training in Mental Retardation, 26,* 79–83.

McDougall, D., & Brady, M.P. (2001). Using audio-cued self-monitoring for students with severe behavior disorders. *The Journal of Educational Research, 88,* 309–317.

McKenzie, T. L., & Rushall, B. S. (1974). Effects of self-recording on attendance and performance in a competitive swimming environment. *Journal of Applied Behavior Analysis, 7,* 199–206.

McLaughlin, T. F. (1983). Effects of self-recording for on-task and academic responding: A long-term analysis. *Journal of Special Education Technology, 6,* 5–12.

McLaughlin, T. F. (1984). A comparison of self-monitoring and self-monitoring plus consequences for on-task and assignment completion. *Contemporary Educational Psychology, 9,* 185–192.

McLaughlin, T. F., & Truhlicka, M. (1983). Effects on academic performance of self-recording and self-recording and matching with behaviorally disordered students: A replication. *Behavioral Engineering, 8,* 69–74.

Mechling, L. C., & Gast, D. L. (1997). Combination audio/visual self-prompting system for teaching chained tasks to students with intellectual disabilities. *Education and Training in Mental Retardation and Developmental Disabilities, 32,* 138–153.

Miner, S. (1990). Use of a self-recording procedure to decrease the time taken by behaviorally disordered students to walk to special classes. *Behavioral Disorders, 15,* 210–216.

Misra, A. (1992). Generalization of social skills through self-monitoring by adults with mild retardation. *Exceptional Children, 58,* 495–507.

Moxley, R. A. (1998). Treatment-only designs and student self-recording as strategies for public school teachers. *Education and Treatment of Children, 21,* 37–61.

Nelson, R. O., & Hayes, S. C. (1981). Theoretical explanations for reactivity in self-monitoring. *Behavior Modification, 5*(1), 3–14.

Nelson, R. O., Hay, R. L., Devany, J., & Koslow-Green, L. (1980). The reactivity and accuracy of children's self-monitoring: Three experiments. *Child Behavior Therapy, 2*(3), 1–24.

Nelson, R. O., Lipinski, D. P., & Black, J. L. (1975). The effects of expectancy in the reactivity of self-recording. *Behavior Therapy, 6,* 337–349.

Nelson, R. O., Lipinski, D. P., & Boykin, R. A. (1978). The effects of self-recording training and the obtrusiveness of the self-recording device on the accuracy and reactivity of self-monitoring. *Behavior Therapy, 9*, 200–208.

Newman, B., Buffington, D. M., O'Grady, M. A., McDonald, M. E., Poulson, C. L., & Hemmes, N. S. (1995). Self-management of schedule-following in three teenagers with autism. *Behavioral Disorders, 20*, 195–201.

Ollendick, T. (1981). Self-monitoring and self-administered overcorrection: The modification of nervous tics in children. *Behavior Modification, 5*, 75–84.

Peacock, R., Layman, R. D., Rickard, H. C. (1978). Correspondence between self-report and observer report as a function of task difficulty. *Behavior Therapy, 9*, 578–583.

Thinesen, P. J., & Bryan, A. J. (1981). The use of sequential pictorial cues in the initiation and maintenance of grooming behaviors with mentally retarded adults. *Mental Retardation, 5*, 247–250.

Trammel, D. L., Schloss, P. T., & Alper, S. (1994). Using self-recording evaluation, and graphing to increase completion of homework assignments. *Journal of Learning Disabilities, 27*(2), 75–81.

Trask-Tyler, S.A., Grossi, T.A., & Heward, W.L. (1994). Teaching young adults with developmental disabilities and visual impairments to use tape-recorded recipes: Acquisition, generalization, and maintenance of cooking skills. *Journal of Behavioral Education, 4*, 283–311.

Webber, J., Scheuermann, B., McCall, C., & Coleman, M. (1993). Research on self-monitoring as a behavior management technique in special education classrooms: A descriptive review. *Remedial and Special Education, 14*, 38–56.

Zegiob, L., Klukas, N., & Juniger, J. (1978). Reactivity of self-monitoring procedures with retarded adolescents. *American Journal of Mental Deficiency, 83*, 156–163.

Zohn, C. J., & Bornstein, P. H. (1980). Self-monitoring of work performance with mentally retarded adults: Effects upon work productivity, work quality, and on-task behavior. *Mental Retardation, 18*, 19–25.

Self-Evaluation

Alvarez, V., & Adelman, H. S. (1986). Over-statements of self-evaluations by students with psychoeducational problems. *Journal of Learning Disabilities, 19*, 567–571.

Grossi, T. A., & Heward, W. L. (1998). Using self-evaluation to improve the work productivity of trainees in a community-based restaurant training program. *Education and Training in Mental Retardation and Developmental Disabilities, 33*(3), 248–263.

Hundert, J., & Altstone, D. (1978). A practical procedure to maintain pupil's accurate self-rating in a classroom token program. *Behavior Modification, 2*, 93–112.

Kaufman, K. F., & O'Leary, K. D. (1972). Reward, cost and self-evaluation procedures for disruptive adolescents in a psychiatric hospital school. *Journal of Applied Behavior Analysis, 5*, 292–309.

Lloyd, J. W., Hallahan, D. P., Kosiewicz, M. M., & Kneedler, R. D. (1982). Reactive effects of self-assessment and self-recording on attention to task and academic productivity. *Learning Disabilities Quarterly, 5*, 216–227.

Mank, D. M., & Horner, R. H. (1987). Self-recruited feedback: A cost effective procedure for maintaining behavior. *Research in Developmental Disabilities, 8*, 91–112.

Masters, J. C., Furman, W., & Barden, R. C. (1977). Effects of achievement standards, tangible rewards and self-dispensed achievement evaluations on children's task mastery. *Child Development, 48*, 217–224.

Nelson, J. R., Smith, D. J., & Colvin, G. (1995). The effects of a peer-mediated self-evaluation procedures on playground behavior. *Journal of Remedial and Special Education 16*, 117–125.

Rhode, G., Morgan, D. P., & Young, K. R. (1983). Generalization and maintenance of treatment gains of behaviorally handicapped students from resource rooms to regular classrooms using self-evaluation procedures. *Journal of Applied Behavior Analysis, 16*, 1781–187.

Ringel, B. A., & Springer, C. J. (1980), On knowing how well one is remembering: The persistence of strategy use during transfer. *Journal of Experimental Child Psychology, 29*, 322–333.

Rosen, M., Diggory, J. C., Floor, L., & Nowakiwska, M. (1971). Self-evaluation, expectancy, and performance in the mentally subnormal. *Journal of Mental Deficiency Research, 15*, 81–95.

Sainato, D. M., Strain, P. S., Lefebvre, D., & Rapp, N. (1990). The effects of self-evaluation package on the independent work skills of handicapped preschool children. *Exceptional Children, 56,* 540–549.

Santogrossi, D. A., O'Leary, K. D., Romanczyk, R. G., & Kaufman, K. F. (1973). Self-evaluation by adolescents in a psychiatric hospital school token program. *Journal of Applied Behavior Analysis, 6,* 277–287.

Shapiro, E. S., McGonigle, J. J., & Ollendick, T. H. (1980). An analysis of self-assessment and self-reinforcement in a self-managed token economy with mentally retarded children. *Applied Research in Mental Retardation, 1,* 227–240.

Spates, C. R., & Kanfer, F. H. (1977). Self-monitoring, self-evaluation, and self-reinforcement in children's learning: A test of a multistage self-regulation model. *Behavior Therapy, 8,* 9–16.

Thomas, J. D. (1976). Accuracy of self-assessment of on-task behavior by elementary school children. *Journal of Applied Behavior Analysis, 9,* 209–210.

Trammel, D. L., Schloss, P. T., & Alper, S. (1994). Using self-recording evaluation, and graphing to increase completion of homework assignments. *Journal of Learning Disabilities, 27*(2), 75–81.

Wood, R., & Flynn, J. M. (1978). A self-evaluation token system versus an external evaluation token system alone in a residential setting with predelinquent youths. *Journal of Applied Behavior Analysis, 11,* 503–512.

Self-Reinforcement

Barling, J., & Patz, M. (1980). Differences following self- and external reinforcement as a function of locus of control and age: A social learning analysis. *Personality and Individual Differences, 1,* 79–85.

Castro, L., & Rachline, (1980). Self-reward, self-monitoring, and self-punishment as feedback in weight control. *Behavior Therapy, 11,* 38–48.

Crandall, V. C., Katkovsky, W., & Crandall, V. G. (1965). Children's belief in their own control of reinforcements in intellectual-academic achievement situations. *Child Development, 36,* 91–109.

Fantuzzo, J. W., & Clement, P. W. (1981). Generalization of the effects of teacher and self-administered token reinforcers to nontreated students. *Journal of Applied Behavior Analysis, 14,* 435–447.

Fredericksen, L. W., & Frederiksen, C. B. (1975). Teacher determined and self-determined token reinforcement in a special education classroom. *Behavior Therapy, 6,* 310–314.

Glynn, E. L. (1970). Classroom applications of self-determined reinforcement. *Journal of Applied Behavior Analysis, 3,* 123–132.

Hanel, F., & Martin, G. (1980). Self-monitoring, self-administration of token reinforcement, and goal setting to improve work rates with retarded clients. *International Journal of Rehabilitation Research, 3,* 505–517.

Helland, C. D., Paluck, R. J., & Klein, M. (1976). A comparison of self- and external reinforcement with the trainable mentally retarded. *Mental Retardation, 14,* 22–23.

Hildelbrandt, D. E., Feldman, S. E., & Ditrichs, R. (1973). Rules, models, and self-reinforcement in children. *Journal of Personality and Social Psychology, 25,* 1–5.

Humphrey, L. L., Karoly, P., & Kirschembaum, D. S. (1978). Self-management in the classroom: Self-imposed response cost versus self-reward. *Behavior Therapy, 9,* 591–601.

Jones, R. T., Nelson, R. E., & Kazdin, A. E. (1977). The role of external variables in self-reinforcement. *Behavior Modification, 1,* 147–178.

Lovitt, T. C., & Curtiss, K. A. (1969). Academic response rate as a function of teacher and self-imposed contingencies. *Journal of Applied Behavior Analysis, 2,* 49–53.

Mahoney, M. J., & Mahoney, K. (1976). Self-control techniques with the mentally retarded. *Exceptional Children, 42,* 338–339.

Mahoney, M. J., Moura, N. G. M., & Wade, T. C. (1973). The relative efficacy of self-reward, self-punishment and self-monitoring techniques for weight loss. *Journal of Consulting and Clinical Psychology, 40,* 404–407.

Martin, G. L., & Hrydowy, E. R. (1989). Self-monitoring and self-managed reinforcement procedures for improving work productivity of developmentally disabled workers. *Behavior Modification, 13,* 323–339.

Masters, J. C. (1968). Effects of social comparison upon subsequent self-reinforcement behavior in children. *Journal of Personality and Social Psychology, 10,* 391–401.

Masters, J. C. (1972). Effects of success, failure, and reward-outcome on contingent and non-contingent self-reinforcement. *Developmental Psychology, 7*, 110–118.

Masters, J. C. (1973). Effects of age and social comparison upon children's noncontingent self-reinforcement and the value of a reinforcer. *Child Development, 45*, 9–13.

Masters, J. C., & Christy, M. D. (1974). Achievement standards for contingent self-reinforcement: Effects of task length and task difficulty. *Child Development, 45*, 9–13.

Masters, J. C., & Peskay, J. (1972). Effects of race, socioeconomic status, and success or failure on contingent and non-contingent self-reinforcement in children. *Developmental Psychology, 7*, 139–145.

Mischel, W., & Liebert, R. M. (1967). The role of power in the adoption of self-reward patterns. *Child Development, 38*, 673–683.

Nelson, W. J. Jr., & Birkimer, J. C. (1978). Role of self-instruction and self-reinforcement in the modification of impulsivity. *Journal of Consulting and Clinical Psychology, 46*, 183.

Newman, B., Buffington, D. M., & Hemmers, N. S. (1996). External and self-reinforcement used to increase the appropriate conversation of autistic teenagers. *Education and Training in Mental Retardation and Developmental Disabilities, 31*, 304–309.

Shapiro, E. S., McGonigle, J. J., & Ollendick, T. H. (1980). An analysis of self-assessment and self-reinforcement in a self-managed token economy with mentally retarded children. *Applied Research in Mental Retardation, 1*, 227–240.

Spates, C. R., & Kanfer, F. H. (1977). Self-monitoring, self-evaluation, and self-reinforcement in children's learning: A test of a multistage self-regulation model. *Behavior Therapy, 8*, 9–16.

Research on Direct Instruction Pedagogy

Direct Instruction

Adams, G., & Engelmann, S. (1996). *Research on Direct Instruction: 25 years beyond DISTAR.* Seattle: Educational Achievement Systems.

Becker, W. (1992). Direct Instruction: A twenty-year review. In R. West & L. Hammerlynck (Eds.), *Design for educational excellence: The legacy of B.F. Skinner.* Longmont CO: Sopris West.

Becker, W. C. (1977). Teaching reading and language to the disadvantaged – what we have learned from field research. *Harvard Educational Review, 47*, 518–543.

Becker, W. C., & Gersten, R. (1982). A follow-up of follow through: Meta-analysis of the later effects of the Direct Instruction Model. *American Educational Research Journal, 19*, 75–93.

Bereiter, C., & Engelmann, S. (1966). *Teaching disadvantaged children in the preschool.* Englewood Cliffs, NJ: Prentice-Hall.

Bock, G., Stebbins, L., & Proper, E. C. (1996). Excerpts from the Abt reports: Descriptions of the models and the results. *Effective School Practices, 15*(1), 10–16.

Carnine, D. W., & Fink, W. T. (1978). Increasing rates of presentation and use of signals in elementary classroom teachers. *Journal of Behavior Analysis, 11*, 35–46.

Carnine, D. W., Silbert, J., & Kameenui, E. J. (1998). *Direct instruction reading* (3rd Ed). Upper Saddle River, NJ: Merrill/Prentice Hall.

Darch, C., Gersten, R., & Taylor, R. (1987). Evaluation of Williamsburg County Direct Instruction program: Factors leading to success in rural elementary programs. *Research in Rural Education, 4*, 111–118.

Engelmann, S., & Bruner, E. C. (1988). *Reading mastery: Fast cycle (DISTAR).* Chicago: Science Research Associates.

Engelmann, S., & Carnine, D. (1982). *Theory of instruction: Principles and application.* New York: Irvington.

Engleman, S., & Carnine, D. (1992). *Connecting math concepts.* Chicago: Science Research Associates.

Englemann, S., Granzin, A., & Severson, H. (1979). Diagnosing instruction. *Journal of Special Education, 13*, 355–363.

Englemann, S., Haddox, P., & Bruner, E. (1983). *Teach your child to read in 100 easy lessons.* New York: Simon & Schuster.

Gersten, R. (1998). Recent advances in instructional research for students with learning disabilities: An overview. *Learning Disabilities Research and Practice, 13*, 162–170.

Gersten, R. M., Maggs, A. (1982). Five-year longitudinal study of cognitive development of moderately retarded children in a Direct Instruction program. *Analysis and Intervention in Developmental Disabilities, 2*, 329–343.

Gersten, R., & Keating, T (1987a). Long-term benefits from Direct Instruction. *Educational Leadership, 44*(6), 28–29.

Gersten, R., & Keating, T. (1987b). Improving high school performance of "at risk" students: A study of long-term benefits of direct instruction. *Educational Leadership, 44*(6), 28–31.

Gersten, R., Carnine, D., & Woodward, J. (1987). Direct Instruction research: The third decade. *Remedial and Special Education, 8*(6), 48–56.

Gersten, R., Keating, T., & Becker, W. (1988). The continued impact of the Direct Instruction Model: Longitudinal studies of follow through students. *Education and Treatment of Children, 11*(4), 318–327.

Gersten, R., Woodward, J., & Darch, G. (1986). Direct Instruction: A research-based approach to curriculum design and teaching. *Exceptional Children, 53*(1), 17–31.

Kameenui, E. J., & Carnine, D. W. (1998). *Effective teaching strategies that accommodate diverse learners.* Upper Saddle River, NJ: Merrill/Prentice Hall.

Kameenui, E. J., & Simmons, D. C. (1990). *Destining instructional strategies: The prevention of academic learning problems.* Upper Saddle River, NJ: Merrill/Prentice-Hall.

Lloyd, J. W., & Carnine, D. W. (Eds.). (1981). Forward to structured instruction: Effective teaching of essential skills. *Exceptional Education Quarterly, 2*(1), vii–ix.

Lockery, M., & Maggs, A. (1982). Direct Instruction research in Australia: A ten-year analysis. *Educational Psychology, 2*, 263–288.

Meyer, L. A. (1984). Long-term academic effects of the direct instruction Project Follow Through. *Elementary School Journal, 84*, 380–394.

Meyer, L., Gersten, R., & Gutkin, J. (1983). Direct Instruction: A project follow through success story in an inner-city school. *Elementary School Journal, 84*, 241–252.

Moore, J. (1986). Direct instruction: A model for instructional design. *Educational Psychology, 6*(3), 201–230.

Stein, M., Silbert, J., & Carnine, D. W., (1997). *Designing effective mathematics instruction: A Direct Instruction approach* (3rd Ed.). Upper Saddle, River, NJ: Merrill/Prentice Hall.

Tarver, S. G. (1998). Myths and truths about Direct Instruction. *Effective School Practices, 17*(1), 18–22.

White, W. A. T. (1988). Meta-analysis of the effects of direct instruction in special education. *Education and Treatment of Children, 11*, 364–374.

Direct Instruction Derivatives

Donley, C. R., & Greer, R. D. (1993). Setting events controlling social verbal exchanges between students with developmental delays. *Journal of Behavioral Education, 3*, 387–401.

Greenwood, C. R., Carta, J. J., Arreaga-Mayer, C., & Rager, A. (1991). The Behavior Analyst Consulting Model: Identifying and validating naturally effective instructional models. *Journal of Behavioral Education, 1*, 165–192.

Greer, R. D. (1991). The teacher as strategic scientist: A solution to our educational crisis? *Behavior and Social Issues, 1*, 25–41.

Greer, R. D. (1994). A systems analysis of the behaviors of schooling. *Journal of Behavior Education, 4*, 255–264.

Greer, R. D. (2002). *Designing teaching strategies: An applied behavior analysis systems approach.* San Diego, CA: Academic Press.

Greer, R. D., McCorkle, N. P., & Williams, G. (1989). A sustained analysis of the behaviors of schooling. *Behavioral Residential Treatment, 4*, 113–141.

Ingham, P., & Greer, R. D. (1992). Changes in student and teacher responses in observed and generalized settings as a function of supervisor observations. *Journal of Applied Behavior Analysis, 25*, 153–164.

Jenkins, J., Deno, S. L., Mirkin, P. K. (1979). Measuring pupil progress in the least restrictive alternative. *Learning Disability Quarterly, 2*, 81–92.

Jones, E. D., & Drouse, J. P. (1988). The effectiveness of data-based instruction by student teachers in classrooms for pupils with mild handicaps. *Teacher Education and Special Education, 11*(1), 9–19.

Lamm, N., & Greer, R. D., (1991). A systematic replication of CABAS in Italy. *Journal of Behavioral Education, 1*, 427–444.

Malott, R. W., & Heward, W. L. (1995). Saving the world by teaching behavior analysis: A behavioral systems approach. *The Behavior Analyst, 18*, 341–354.

Polirstok, S. R., & Greer, R. D., (1977). Remediation of a mutually aversive interaction between a problem student and four teachers by training the student in reinforcement techniques. *Journal of Applied Behavior Analysis, 10*, 573–582.

Selinske, J., Greer, R. D., & Lodhi, S. (1991). A functional analysis of the Comprehensive Application of Behavior Analysis to Schooling. *Journal of Applied Behavior Analysis, 13*, 645–654.

Precision Teaching

Binder, C. (1996). Behavioral fluency: Evolution of a new paradigm. *The Behavior Analyst, 19*, 163–197.

Binder, C., & Watkins, C. L. (1989). Promoting effective instructional methods: Solutions to America's educational crisis. *Future Choices, 1*(3), 33–39.

Binder, C., & Watkins, C. L. (1990). Precision Teaching and Direct Instruction: Measurably superior instructional technology in schools. *Performance Improvement Quarterly, 3*(4), 74–96.

Binder, C., Haughton, E., & Van Eyk, D. (1990). Increasing endurance by building fluency: Precision teaching attention span. *TEACHING Exceptional Children, 22*(3), 24–27.

Koorland, M. A., Keel, M. C., & Ueberhorst, P. (1990). Setting aims for precision learning. *TEACHING Exceptional Children, 22*(3), 64–66.

Liberty, K. A., & Haring, N. G. (1990). Introduction to decision rule systems. *Remedial and Special Education, 11*(1), 32–41.

Lindsley, O. R. (1990a). Our aims, discoveries, failures, and problems. *Journal of Precision Teaching, 7*, 7–17.

Lindsley, O. R. (1990b). Precision Teaching: By teachers for children. *TEACHING Exceptional Children, 22*(3), 10–15.

Lindsley, O. R. (1991). Precision Teaching's unique legacy from B. F. Skinner. *Journal of Behavioral Educational, 1*, 253–266.

Lindsley, O. R. (1992a). Precision Teaching: Discoveries and effects. *Journal of Applied Behavior Analysis, 25*, 51–57.

Lindsley, O. R. (1992b). Why aren't effective teaching tools widely adopted? *Journal of Applied Behavior Analysis, 25*, 21–26.

Lindsley, O. R. (1995). Ten products of fluency. *Journal of Precision Teaching, 13*(1), 2–11.

McDade, C. E. (1992). Computer-based precision learning: A course builder application. *Behavior Research Methods, Instruments, & Computers, 24*, 269–272.

McDade, C. E., & Olander, C. P. (1987). Precision management of instructional technology: A program update. *Educational Technology, 27*, 44–46.

McGreevy, P. (1984). Frequency and the Standard Celeratino Chart: Necessary components of Precision Teaching. *Journal of Precision Teaching, 5*(2), 28–36.

Mercer, C. D., Mercer, A. R., & Evans, S. E. (1982). The use of frequency in establishing instructional aims. *Journal of Precision Teaching, 3*(3), 57–63.

Mirkin, P., Deno, S., Tindal, G., & Kuehnle, K. (1982). Frequency of measurement and data utilization strategies as factors in standardized behavior assessment of academic skill. *Journal of Behavioral Assessment, 4*(4), 361–370.

White, O. R., Haring, N. G. (1980). *Exceptional teaching.* Columbus, OH: Charles E. Merrill.

Curriculum Based Instruction

Blankenship, C. S. (1985). Using curriculum-based assessment data to make instructional decisions. *Exceptional Children, 52*(3), 233–238.

Coulter, W. A. (1985). Implementing curriculum-based assessment: Considerations for pupil appraisal professionals. *Exceptional Children, 52*(3), 277–281.

Deno, S. L. (1985). Curriculum-based measurement: The emerging alternative. *Exceptional Children, 52*(3), 219–232.

Deno, S. L. (1986). Formative evaluation of individual student programs: A new role for school psychologists. *School Psychology Review, 15*, 358–374.

Deno, S. L. (1987). Curriculum-based measurement. *TEACHING Exceptional Children, 20*(1), 41–42.

Deno, S. L., & Fuchs, L. S. (1987). Developing curriculum-based measurement systems for data-based special education problem solving. *Focus on Exceptional Children, 19*(8), 1–16.

Deno, S. L., Marston, D., & Mirkin, P. (1982). Valid measurement procedures for continuous evaluation of written expression. *Exceptional Children, 48*(4), 368–371.

Deno, S. L., Marston, D., Shinn, M., & Tindal, G. (1983). Oral reading fluency: A simple datum for scaling reading disability. *Topics in Learning and Learning Disabilities, 2*(4), 53–59.

Deno, S. L., Mirkin, P. K., & Wesson, C. (1984). Procedures for writing data-based IEPs. *TEACHING Exceptional Children, 16*(2), 94–104.

Deno, S. Mirkin, P. K., & Chiang, B. (1982). Identifying valid measures of reading. *Exceptional Children, 49*(1), 36–45.

Ferguson, C., & Fuchs, L. S. (1991). Scoring accuracy within curriculum-based measurement: The emerging alternative. *Exceptional Children, 52*, 219–232.

Fuchs, L. S. (1986). Monitoring the performance of mildly handicapped students. Review of current practice and research. *Remedial and Special Education, 7*, 5–12.

Fuchs, L. S. (1988). Effects of computer-managed instruction on teachers' implementation of systematic monitoring programs and student achievement. *Journal of Educational Research, 81*, 294–304.

Fuchs, L. S., & Deno, S. (1992). Effects of curriculum within curriculum-based measurement. *Exceptional Children, 58*(3), 232–243.

Fuchs, L. S., & Fuchs, D. (1984). Criterion-referenced assessment without measurement: How accurate for special education? *Remedial and Special Education, 5*(4), 29–32.

Fuchs, L. S., & Fuchs, D. (1986). Effects of systematic formative evaluation: A meta-analysis. *Exceptional Children, 53*(3), 199–208.

Fuchs, L. S., Allinder, R. M., Hamlett, C. L., & Fuchs, D. (1990). An analysis of spelling curricula and teachers' skills in identifying error types. *Remedial and Special Education, 11*(1), 42–53.

Fuchs, L. S., Deno, S. L., & Mirkin, P. K. (1984). The effects of frequent curriculum-based measurement and evaluation on pedagogy, student achievement and student awareness of learning. *American Educational Research Journal, 21*(2), 449–460.

Fuchs, L. S., Deno, S., & Marston, D. (1983). Improving the reliability of curriculum-based measures of academic skills for psycho-educational decision making. *Diagnostique, 8*, 135–149.

Fuchs, L. S., Fuchs, D., & Deno, S. L. (1982). Reliability and validity of curriculum-based informal reading inventories. *Reading Research Quarterly, 18*, 6–26.

Fuchs, L. S., Fuchs, D., & Deno, S. L. (1985). The importance of goal ambitiousness and goal mastery to student achievement. *Exceptional Children, 52*, 63–71.

Fuchs, L. S., Fuchs, D., & Hamlet, C. L. (1992). Computer applications to facilitate curriculum-based measurement. *Teaching Exceptional Children, 24*(4), 58–60.

Fuchs, L. S., Fuchs, D., & Hamlet, C. L. (1994). Strengthening the connection between assessment and instructional planning with expert systems. *Exceptional Children, 61*(2), 138–146.

Fuchs, L. S., Fuchs, D., & Hamlett, C. L. (1989). Effects of alternative goal structures within curriculum-based measurement. *Exceptional Children, 55*(5), 429–438.

Fuchs, L. S., Fuchs, D., & Maxwell, L. (1988). The validity of informal reading comprehension measures. *Remedial and Special Education, 9*(2), 20–28.

Fuchs, L. S., Fuchs, D., Hamlett, C. L., & Allinder, R. M. (1991). Effects of expert system advice within curriculum-based measurement on teacher planning and student achievement. *School Psychology Review, 20,* 49–66.

Fuchs, L. S., Fuchs, D., Hamlett, C. L., & Ferguson, C. (1992). Effects of expert system consultation within curriculum-based measurement using a reading maze task. *Exceptional Children, 58,* 436–450.

Fuchs, L. S., Fuchs, D., Hamlett, C. L., & Stecker, P. M. (1991). Effects of curriculum-based measurement and consultation on teacher planning and student achievement. *American Educational Research Journal, 28,* 617–641.

Fuchs, L. S., Fuchs, D., Hamlett, C. L., Phillips, N., & Benz, J. (1994). Classwide curriculum-based measurement: Helping general educators meet the challenge of student diversity. *Exceptional Children, 60,* 518–537.

Fuchs, L. S., Hamlett, C., Fuchs, D., Stecker, P. M., & Ferguson, C. (1988). Conducting curriculum-based measurement with computerized data collection: Effects on efficiency and teacher satisfaction. *Journal of Special Education Technology, 9*(2), 73–86.

German, G., & Tindal, G. (1985). An application of curriculum-based assessment: The use of direct and repeated measurement. *Exceptional Children, 52*(3), 244–265.

Marston, D., & Magnusson, D. (1985). Implementing curriculum-based measurement in special and regular education settings. *Exceptional Children, 52*(3), 266–276.

Marston, D., Mirkin, P. K., & Deno, S. (1984). Curriculum-based measurement of academic skills: An alternative to traditional screening, referral, and identification of learning disabled students. *Journal of Special Education, 18,* 109–118.

Marston, D., Tindal, G., & Deno, S. L. (1984). Eligibility for learning disability services: A direct and repeated measurement approach. *Exceptional Children, 50,* 6, 554–556.

Potter, M. L., & Wamre, H. M. (1990). Curriculum-based measurement and developmental reading models: Opportunities for cross-validation. *Exceptional Children, 57*(1), 16–25).

Rosenfield, S., & Rubinson, F. (1985). Introducing curriculum-based assessment through consultation. *Exceptional Children, 52*(3), 282–287.

Shinn, M. R. (1988). Development of curriculum-based local norms for use in special education decision making. *School Psychology Review, 17,* 61–80.

Shinn, M. R., Ysseldyke, J. E., Deno, S. L., & Tindal, G. A. (1986). A comparison of differences between students labeled learning disabled and low achieving on measures of classroom performance. *Journal of Learning Disabilities, 19,* 545–552.

Shinn, M., & Marston, D. (1985). Assessing mildly handicapped, low achieving and regular education students: A curriculum-based approach. *Remedial and Special Education, 6,* 31–38.

Taylor, R. L., Willits, P. P., & Richards, S. B. (1988). Curriculum-based assessment: Considerations and concerns. *Diagnostique, 14,* 14–21.

Tucker, J. A. (1985). Curriculum-based assessment: An introduction. *Exceptional Children, 52*(3), 199–204.

Wesson, C. L. (1991). Curriculum-based measurement and two models of follow-up consolation. *Exceptional Children, 57,* 246–257.

Wesson, C. L. Skiba, R., Sevick, B., King, R., & Deno, S. (1984). The effects of technically adequate instructional data on achievement. *Remedial and Special Education, 5,* 17–22.

Wesson, C. S., Fuchs, L. S., Tindal, G., Mirkin, P. K., & Deno, S. L. (1986). Facilitating the efficiency of ongoing curriculum-based measurement. *Teacher Education and Special Education, 9,* 166–172.

Wesson, C., King, R. P., & Deno, S. L. (1984). Direct and frequent measurement of student performance: If it's good for us, why don't we do it? *Learning Disability Quarterly, 7*(1), 45–48.

INSTRUCTION AND CURRICULUM SCALES
FOR SELF-DETERMINED LEARNING

DENNIS E. MITHAUG
DEIRDRE K. MITHAUG

The *Instruction and Curriculum Scales for Self-Determined Learning* assess whether the instruction and curriculum used to educate students with disabilities are likely to promote self-determined learning. They evaluate whether the causal agency of teaching is teacher or student-directed and whether the content of the curriculum is basic or applied. According to self-determined learning theory, when students regulate their adjustments to learning opportunities – when their instruction is student-directed – and when those opportunities are consistent with their needs, interests, and abilities – when the curriculum has an applied focus – then their learning maximizes (Mithaug, Mithaug, Agran, Martin, & Wehmeyer, 2003).

Table B-1 presents four scales that assess these factors. The two instructional scales reflect causal agency of teachers and students during instruction and the curriculum scales reflect the acquisition and application of knowledge and skills being taught. Each scale consists of 12 items. Table B-2 presents the 24 items comprising the two instructional scales, with 12 items assessing teacher-directed instruction (left column) and 12 items assessing student-directed instruction (right column). Table B-3 presents the 24 items comprising the two curriculum scales, with 12 items assessing the acquisition of basic skills and knowledge (left column), and 12 items assessing the application of skills and knowledge (right column).

The rating items for instructional directedness cover student needs, interests, and abilities (items 1–3), the setting of instructional goals based on those assessments (items 4–5), the development of plans to meet goals (items 6–7), the taking of action, monitoring of actions, evaluations of results (items 8–10), and the adjustments made based on those evaluations (items 11–12). The rating items for the curriculum cover computational skills (items 1–4 in the basic skills column and items 13–16 in the applied skills column); reading and writing (items 5–9 in the basic skills column and items 17–21 in the applied skills column); and social

Table B 1: Assessing Instruction and Curriculum for Self-Determined Learning

1. I learn what my students like so I can make decisions based on their preferences. 0 1 2 3 4
2. My students learn to read words to solve everyday problems. 0 1 2 3 4
3. There are instructional opportunities for students to adjust their plans frequently and repeatedly in order to improve their results. 0 1 2 3 4
4. My students learn to add numbers during drill and practice exercises. 0 1 2 3 4
5. My students learn to write words at their developmental level. 0 1 2 3 4
6. I learn what students can do so that I can make decisions based on their abilities. 0 1 2 3 4
7. My students learn to add numbers to solve everyday problems. 0 1 2 3 4
8. My students learn to write words that solve everyday problems. 0 1 2 3 4
9. I set goals for students based on what they need or want and what they are able to do to satisfy those needs and wants. 0 1 2 3 4
10. My students learn to subtract numbers during drill and practice exercises. 0 1 2 3 4
11. There are instructional opportunities for students to act independently on their plans to meet their learning goals. 0 1 2 3 4
12. My students learn to read phrases at their developmental level. 0 1 2 3 4
13. I make plans for how students will meet learning and behavior goals. 0 1 2 3 4
14. My students learn to subtract numbers to solve everyday problems. 0 1 2 3 4
15. There are instructional opportunities for students to construct plans to meet their learning and behavior goals. 0 1 2 3 4
16. My students learn to divide numbers during drill and practice exercises. 0 1 2 3 4
17. My students monitor their results by comparing them with goals in order to determine whether their plans are working. 0 1 2 3 4
18. My students learn to write and read English compositions at their developmental level. 0 1 2 3 4
19. There are instructional opportunities for students to set goals for what they want to learn and what they want to do. 0 1 2 3 4
20. My students learn to divide numbers to solve everyday problems. 0 1 2 3 4
21. I use my evaluations of student results to adjust their goals, plans, and actions so that they will improve next time. 0 1 2 3 4
22. My students learn to adjust to signs in their communities. 0 1 2 3 4
23. I have frequent opportunities to set goals for what students need and want to learn. 0 1 2 3 4
24. My students learn to multiply numbers during drill and practice exercises. 0 1 2 3 4
25. My students learn by adjusting to their results until they know what choices and actions produce the results they want. 0 1 2 3 4
26. My students learn science concepts at their developmental level. 0 1 2 3 4
27. I learn about my students by adjusting to results repeatedly until I know what decisions and actions produce the results want for them. 0 1 2 3 4
28. My students learn to multiply numbers to solve everyday problems. 0 1 2 3 4
29. There are instructional opportunities for students to discover for themselves what they like, what they want, and what they can do to satisfy their interests and needs. 0 1 2 3 4
30. My students learn how to improve their adjustments at home.
31. There are instructional opportunities for me to discover what students like, what they want, and what they can do to satisfy their interests and needs. 0 1 2 3 4
32. I monitor students' results by comparing them with their goals in order to determine whether my plans are working for them. 0 1 2 3 4
33. My students learn social studies at their developmental level. 0 1 2 3 4
34. My students use their evaluations of results to adjust their plans to improve next time. 0 1 2 3 4
35. There are instructional opportunities for me to construct plans for students to meet their learning goals. 0 1 2 3 4
36. My students learn how to improve their adjustments at work. 0 1 2 3 4
37. There are instructional opportunities for me to follow through on plans I construct for students to meet their learning goals. 0 1 2 3 4
38. My students make their own plans to meet their goals. 0 1 2 3 4
39. My students learn to recognize phrases that solve everyday problems. 0 1 2 3 4
40. My students learn to set goals based on what they need or want and what they are able to do to satisfy their needs and wants. 0 1 2 3 4
41. My students learn to spell words at their developmental level. 0 1 2 3 4
42. My students learn to solve reading, math, and science problems at their developmental level. 0 1 2 3 4
43 My students learn what they can do so they can make choices based on their abilities. 0 1 2 3 4
44. My students learn to spell words that solve everyday problems. 0 1 2 3 4
45. There are instructional opportunities for me to adjust student plans frequently and repeatedly in order to improve their results. 0 1 2 3 4
46. My students learn how to adjust to different situations in the community. 0 1 2 3 4
47. My students learn what they like so they can make choices based on that knowledge. 0 1 2 3 4
48. My students learn to read words at their developmental level. 0 1 2 3 4

0=Never, 1=Almost Never, 2=Sometimes, 3=Almost Always, 4=Always

studies, science and problem solving (items 10–12 in the basic skills column and items 22–24 in the applied skills column).

Teachers rate themselves by indicating how frequently they teach in the manner identified by the 48 items in the instrument. The rating frequencies of the scale are: never, almost never, sometimes, almost always, and always. Hence,

	Teacher Directedness		**Student Directedness**
	Table B 2: The 24 Items of the Instructional Directedness Scale		
1	I learn what my students like so I can make decisions based on their preferences (1)	13	My students learn what they like so they can make choices based on that knowledge. (59)
2	I learn what students can do so that I can make decisions based on their abilities. (7)	14	My students learn what they can do so they can make choices based on their abilities. (55)
3	There are instructional opportunities for me to discover what students like, what they want, and what they can do to satisfy their interests and needs. (35)	15	There are instructional opportunities for students to discover for themselves what they like, what they want, and what they can do to satisfy their interests and needs. (33)
4	I set goals for students based on what they need or want and what they are able to do to satisfy those needs and wants. (11)	16	My students learn to set goals based on what they need or want and what they are able to do to satisfy their needs and wants. (51)
5	I have frequent opportunities to set goals for what students need and want to learn. (27)	17	There are instructional opportunities for students to set goals for what they want to learn and what they want to do. (23)
6	I make plans for how students will meet learning and behavior goals. (15)	18	My students make their own plans to meet their goals. (47)
7	There are instructional opportunities for me to construct plans for students to meet their learning goals. (41)	19	There are instructional opportunities for students to construct plans to meet their learning and behavior goals. (19)
8	There are instructional opportunities for me to follow through on plans I construct for students to meet their learning goals. (45)	20	There are instructional opportunities for students to act independently on their plans to meet their learning goals. (13)
9	I monitor students' results by comparing them with their goals in order to determine whether my plans are working for them. (37)	21	My students monitor their results by comparing them with goals in order to determine whether their plans are working. (21)
10	I use my evaluations of student results to adjust their goals, plans, and actions so that they will improve next time. (25)	22	My students use their evaluations of results to adjust their plans to improve next time. (39)
11	I learn about my students by adjusting to results repeatedly until I know what decisions and actions produce the results I want for them. (31)	23	My students learn by adjusting to their results until they know what choices and actions produce the results they want. (29)
12	There are instructional opportunities for me to adjust student plans frequently and repeatedly in order to improve their results. (57)	24	There are instructional opportunities for students to adjust their plans frequently and repeatedly in order to improve their results. (3)

item ratings in Table B-2 reflect the frequency that a teacher instructs in a teacher-directed or student-directed manner, and item ratings in Table B-3 indicate the frequency that the teacher's curriculum focuses on learning basic or applied skills and knowledge.

Table B 3: The 24 Items of the Curricular Content Scale			
	Basic Skills Column		**Applied Skills Column**
1	My students learn to add numbers during drill and practice exercises. (4)	13	My students learn to add numbers to solve everyday problems. (8)
2	My students learn to subtract numbers during drill and practice exercises. (12)	14	My students learn to subtract numbers to solve everyday problems. (16)
3	My students learn to multiple numbers during drill and practice exercises. (28)	15	My students learn to multiply numbers to solve everyday problems. (32)
4	My students learn to divide numbers during drill and practice exercises. (20)	16	My students learn to divide numbers to solve everyday problems. (24)
5	My students learn to read words at their developmental level. (60)	17	My students learn to read words to solve everyday problems. (2)
6	My students learn to read phrases at their developmental level. (14)	18	My students learn to recognize phrases that solve everyday problems. (48)
7	My students learn to spell words at their developmental level. (52)	19	My students learn to spell words that solve everyday problems. (56)
8	My students learn to write words at their developmental level. (6)	20	My students learn to write words that solve everyday problems. (10)
9	My students learn to write and read English compositions at their developmental level. (22)	21	My students learn to adjust to signs in their communities. (26)
10	My students learn social studies at their developmental level. (38)	22	My students learn how to improve their adjustments at home. (34)
11	My students learn science concepts at their developmental level. (30)	23	My students learn how to adjust to different situations in the community. (58)
12	My students learn to solve reading, math, and science problems at their developmental level. (54)	24	My students learn how to improve their adjustments at work. (42)

Reliability

The reliability of the scale was evaluated by determining the consistency of 30 teachers' self-ratings conducted twice over a 60-day period. Chronbach's test indicated that for this group, the coefficient of reliability and standardized alpha for the 48-item scale were both .93. For the 24-item instructional-directedness scale (Table B-2 items), Chronbach's alpha was .91 and the standardized item alpha was .93. For the 24-item curriculum content scale (Table B-3 items), Chronbach's alpha was .94 and the standardized item alpha was .95. For the instructional-directedness subscales, Chronbach and standardized item alphas for teacher-directedness were .76 and .85 respectively, and they were .87 and .88 respectively for student-directedness. For the curricular content subscales, the Chronbach and standardized item alphas were .96 and .95 respectively for basic skills, and .90 and .96 respectively for applied skills. Table B-4 presents these results.

Table B 4: Chronbach's Alpha and Standardized Item Alpha for the 60-day Test-Retest Reliability Tests on the Instruction and Curriculum Rating Scale		
Instruction and Curriculum Scale for Self-Determined Learning	Scale Alpha	Standardized Item Alpha
Full Scale (48 items)	.9319	.9333
Instructional Directedness Scale (24 Items)	.9144	.9273
Teacher Instructional Directedness (12 Items)	.7560	.8541
Student Instructional Directedness (12 Items)	.8685	.8750
Curriculum Content Scale (24 Items)	.9388	.9492
Basic Skills Curriculum (12 Items)	.9608	.9616
Applied Skills Curriculum (12 Items)	.9011	.9588

Validity

Three analyses determined whether the scale items of the instrument measured what they were intended to measure, namely instructional-directedness and curricular content. The first set of evaluations determined whether Table B-2 items for teacher and student-directedness correlated significantly, whether Table B-3 items for basic and applied skills curriculum correlated significantly, and whether items for student-directedness and applied skills correlated significantly. The second evaluation determined whether these correlations were robust enough to predict student-directedness in the learning of applied skills. The last evaluation determined whether the four scales cohered in a single instruction and curriculum factor to explain most of the variance in the 48 item ratings.

Correlation Analyses

The first question was addressed with a correlation analysis to determine whether teacher ratings on teacher-directedness, student-directedness, basic skills, and applied skills were significantly correlated. Table B-5 presents results for 253 experienced teachers who rated themselves on the four scales. As indicated in the table, the ratings on the four scales were significantly correlated. Teacher and student-directedness ratings correlated significantly at .584. Teacher-directedness ratings correlated significantly with basic skills ratings at .313, and with applied skills ratings at .358 and student-directedness ratings correlated significantly with basic skills ratings at .556 and with applied skills ratings at .712. Finally, ratings on the basic and applied skills scales correlated significantly at .792. These results are consistent with the expectation that teacher and student-directedness ratings would correlate significantly, that basic and applied skill ratings would correlate significantly, and that student-directedness and applied skill ratings would correlate significantly.

Scales	Student Directedness	Basic Skills	Applied Skills
Table B 5: Significant Correlations (2-tailed at .000) among the Four Instruction and Curriculum Scales for a Sample of 253 Teachers			
Teacher Directedness	.584	.313	.358
Student Directedness		.556	.712
Basic Skills			.792

Regression Analyses

The second question on whether these correlations are robust enough to predict student-directedness in an applied skills curriculum was addressed with four regression analyses, which identified significant predictors for each scale. Here, three of the scales were entered as predictor variables and the fourth as the predicted variable. The results of these analyses follow.

Scale Predictors of Teacher-Directedness. In this analysis, item ratings by 253 experienced teachers on student-directedness, applied skills, and basic skills were entered as possible predictors of teacher-directedness, the dependent variable. As indicated in the model in Table B-6, this regression model explained 34 percent of the variance in teacher-directedness, which according to the ANOVA in Table B-7 was significant at $p < .001$. Table B-8 identifies the significant predictor of teacher-directedness to be student-directedness, which was significant at $p < .001$. Note, also that item ratings for applied skills approached significance but as a negative predictor of teacher-directedness at $p < .06$, which means that

Model	R	R Square	Adjusted R Square	Std. Error of the Estimate
Table B 6: Regression Model Summary for Teacher Directedness				
1	.593	.351	.344	.4604

a Predictors: (Constant), Student, Basic, Applied

Table B 7: ANOVA of Regression Model for Teacher Directedness

Model		Sum of Squares	df	Mean Square	F	Sig.
1	Regression	28.596	3	9.532	44.977	.000
	Residual	52.771	249	.212		
	Total	81.367	252			

a Predictors: (Constant), Student, Basic, Applied
b Dependent Variable: Teacher Directed

Table B 8: Significant Predictors of Teacher Directedness

Model		Unstandardized Coefficients		Standardized Coefficients	t	Sig.
		B	Std. Error	Beta		
1	(Constant)	1.963	.113		17.379	.000
	Basic	6.750E-02	.060	.095	1.133	.258
	Applied	-.148	.076	-.194	-1.962	.051
	Student Directed	.544	.059	.670	9.213	.000

a Dependent Variable: Teacher Directed

the lower the applied skills ratings by teachers, the higher the predicted ratings for their teacher-directedness.

Figure B-1 summarizes the main result of this regression model, indicating that student-directedness was a significant predictor of teacher-directedness. The Beta coefficient of .670 indicates the proportion of change in teacher-directedness ratings predicted for each unit of change in student-directedness ratings.

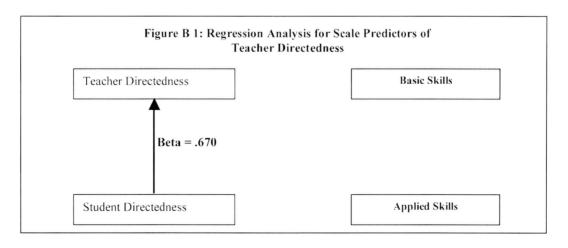

Figure B 1: Regression Analysis for Scale Predictors of Teacher Directedness

Scale Predictors of Student Directedness. The second analysis identified significant predictors of student-directedness ratings, with teacher-directedness, basic skills and applied skill ratings entered as predictor variables. As indicated in Table B-9, this regression explained 62.8 percent of the variance in student-directedness and as indicated in the ANOVA in Table B-10 was significant at p < .001. Table B-11 presents data on predictor variables that show teacher-directedness and applied skills ratings to be significant predictors of student-directedness at p < .001.

Table B 9: Regression Model Summary for Student Directedness

Model	R	R Square	Adjusted R Square	Std. Error of the Estimate
1	.795	.632	.628	.4264

a Predictors: (Constant), Teacher Directed, Basic, Applied

Table B 10: ANOVA of Regression Model for Student Directedness

Model		Sum of Squares	df	Mean Square	F	Sig.
1	Regression	77.905	3	25.968	142.814	.000
	Residual	45.277	249	.182		
	Total	123.182	252			

a Predictors: (Constant), Teacher Directed, Basic, Applied
b Dependent Variable: Student Directed

Table B 11: Significant Predictors of Student Directedness

		Unstandardized Coefficients		Standardized Coefficients	t	Sig.
Model		B	Std. Error	Beta		
1	(Constant)	-.313	.154		-2.031	.043
	Basic	-4.535E-02	.055	-.052	-.821	.413
	Applied	.580	.060	.617	9.626	.000
	Teacher Directed	.467	.051	.380	9.213	.000

a Dependent Variable: Student Directed

Figure B-2 builds on the causal model started in Figure B-1 by showing that in addition to the significant prediction of teacher-directedness by student-directedness, there was a significant relationship between directedness and applied skill content in that teacher-directedness predicted student-directedness with a Beta coefficient of .380, and applied skills content predicted student-directedness with a Beta coefficient of .617. The emboldened arrows in the figure identify these relationships.

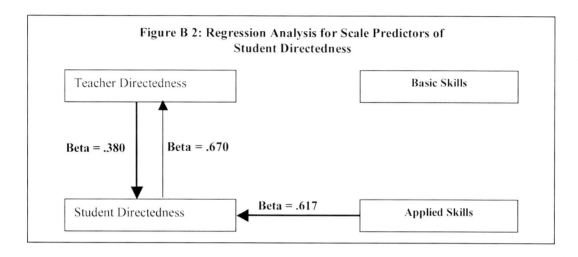

Figure B 2: Regression Analysis for Scale Predictors of Student Directedness

Scale Predictors of Basic Skills. The third analysis identified predictors of basic skills content, with teacher-directedness, student-directedness, and applied skill ratings entered as predictor variables. As indicated in Table B-12, this regression explained 62.5 percent of the variance in basic skill ratings with the ANOVA in Table B-13 significant at $p < .001$. Table B-14 identified the significant correlates to be applied skill ratings, which were significant predictors of basic skills content at $p < .001$.

Figure B-3 adds this finding to the causal model, this time showing a predictive relationship between applied and basic skill ratings. Here applied skill ratings predicted basic skill ratings with a Beta coefficient of .810. The emboldened arrow in the figure adds this predictor relationship to the emerging causal model.

Table B 12: Regression Model Summary for Basic Skills

Model	R	R Square	Adjusted R Square	Std. Error of the Estimate
1	.794	.630	.625	.4884

a Predictors: (Constant), Student Directed, Teacher Directed, Applied Skills

Table B 13: ANOVA for Regression Model on Basic Skills

Model		Sum of Squares	df	Mean Square	F	Sig.
1	Regression	101.036	3	33.679	141.194	.000
	Residual	59.393	249	.239		
	Total	160.429	252			

a Predictors: (Constant), Student Directed, Teacher Directed, Applied Skills
b Dependent Variable: Basic Skills

Table B 14: Significant Predictors of Basic Skills

Model		Unstandardized Coefficients		Standardized Coefficients	t	Sig.
		B	Std. Error	Beta		
1	(Constant)	.377	.177		2.132	.034
	Applied	.869	.059	.810	14.674	.000
	Teacher Directed	7.598E-02	.067	.054	1.133	.258
	Student Directed	-5.948E-02	.072	-.052	-.821	.413

a Dependent Variable: Basic Skills

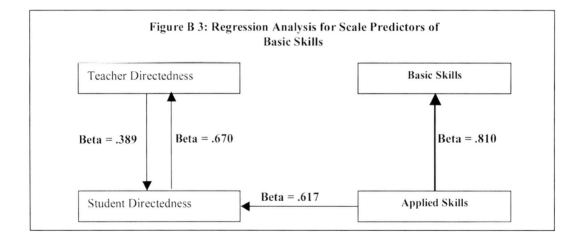

Figure B 3: Regression Analysis for Scale Predictors of Basic Skills

Scale Predictors of Applied Skills. The last analysis identified the significant predictors of applied skills ratings, with teacher-directedness, student-directedness, and basic skills ratings entered as predictor variables. Table B-15 presents these findings showing a regression equation that explained 73.5 percent of the variance in applied skill content and an ANOVA in Table B-16 indicating a significance level at or less than .001. Table B-17 presents results on the predictor variables indicating that student-directedness and basic skills content were significant predictors of applied skill content at p < .001. Figure B-4 updates the causal model with these findings by showing these relationships between student-directedness, applied skills, and basic skills. Here basic skills predicted applied skills with a Beta coefficient of .572, and student-directedness predicted applied skills with a Beta of .439. The emboldened arrows identify these relationships in the now-completed causal model representing the four scales of the instrument.

Table B 15: Regression Model Summary for Applied Skills

Model	R	R Square	Adjusted R Square	Std. Error of the Estimate
1	.859	.738	.735	.3829

a Predictors: (Constant), Basic Skills, Teacher Directed, Student Directed

Table B 16: ANOVA for Regression Model on Applied Skills

Model		Sum of Squares	df	Mean Square	F	Sig.
1	Regression	103.044	3	34.348	234.244	.000
	Residual	36.512	249	.147		
	Total	139.555	252			

a Predictors: (Constant), Basic, Teacher Directed, Student
b Dependent Variable: Applied Skills

Table B 17: Significant Predictors of Applied Skills

		Unstandardized Coefficients		Standardized Coefficients	t	Sig.
Model		B	Std. Error	Beta		
1	(Constant)	.228	.139		1.638	.103
	Teacher Directed	-.103	.052	-.078	-1.962	.051
	Student Directed	.468	.049	.439	9.626	.000
	Basic	.534	.036	.572	14.674	.000

a Dependent Variable: Applied Skills

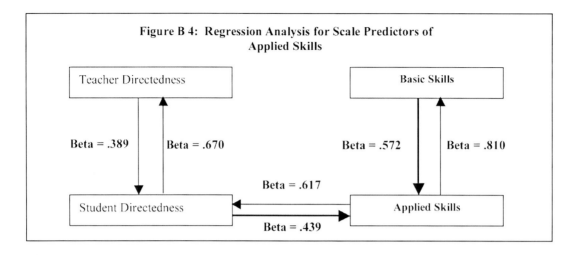

Figure B 4: Regression Analysis for Scale Predictors of Applied Skills

Evaluation of the Model. According to these regression analyses, the causal model for the *Instruction and Curriculum Scales for Self-Determined Learning* in Figure B-4 is consistent with the pedagogical claims of this book that teacher and student-directedness are functionally related as are basic and applied skills. It is also consistent with the prediction from self-determined learning theory that when students have opportunities to direct learning that is consistent with their needs and interests, they are engaged in self-determined learning.

The model is consistent with the first claim in showing that teacher and student-directedness were significant predictors of each other just as basic and applied skills were significant predictors of each other. It is also consistent with the second claim in that student-directedness and applied skills were significant predictors of each other. Indeed, the bi-directional arrows for those variables graphically depict this interaction suggesting that the more student-directed the learning is, the more likely its content is relevant to students' needs and interests (applied skills), and conversely, the more relevant that content is to those needs and interests, the more likely students self-direct when learning (student-directedness).

Finally, the name given these four scales – the *Instruction and Curriculum Scales of Self-Determined Learning* – seems fully justified in that the focus of the assessment is decidedly self-determined learning as suggested by the causal model showing that teacher-directedness and basic skills content were not significantly correlated whereas student-directedness and applied skills content ratings were. Moreover, the explained variance of the 48 items in this instrument reflected a self-determined learning focus with student-directedness explaining more item variance than teacher-directedness (.628 vs. .344) and applied skills content explaining more variance than basis skills content (.735 vs. .625). Table B-18 presents these data.

	Table B 18: Summary of Explained Variance by the Four Regression Models	
Regression Model	Dependent Variable	Explained Variance
1	Teacher Directedness	.344
2	**Student Directedness**	**.628**
3	Basic Skills	.625
4	**Applied Skills**	**.735**

Factor Analysis

The last analysis evaluates the extent that the four scales function together as a single instruction-curriculum construct to explain most of the variance in the 48-item instrument. A factor analysis, which extracted the components of the instrument that explain most of the variance in 48 item ratings, provided this answer. Table B-19 presents the first step of the analysis, which reports variance for each of the four scales that was shared by the other scales. This is called its communality or shared variance (the difference between the common variance and 1.00, which is the variance due to a single scale). In this case, teacher-directedness shared .420 of its variance with the others scales, student-directedness shared .770 of the variance with the others, basic skills shared .691 of its variance with the others, and applied skills content shared .806 of its variance with the other scales. This sharing of significant levels of variance suggests that the instrument assesses a common instruction and curriculum factor rather than several independent factors.

Table B 19: Communalities		
	Initial	Extraction
Teacher Directedness	1.000	.420
Student Directedness	**1.000**	**.770**
Basic Skills	1.000	.691
Applied Skills	**1.000**	**.806**

Extraction Method: Principal Component Analysis

Table B-20 presents results of the second step that identifies the amount of variance explained by each extracted component as well as their respective Eigenvalues (the variances explained by extracted factors). The decision on the number of factors represented by the data is guided by Eigenvalues. The rule is to identify all factors with values greater than one. In this case, however, there was only one factor with a value greater than one: it had a value of 2.678. This justifies the conclusion that the 48-item instrument measures a single factor that explains 67.19 percent of the item variance. Component factor 1 in Table B-21 represents this finding by showing correlations between the four scale variables and that extracted factor. As indicated in the table all scales correlated significantly with the extracted factor at values greater than .5. Hence, they are significant components of that common instruction and curriculum factor.

Table B 20: Explained Variance of Component Factors

Component	Initial Eigenvalues			Extraction Sums of Squared Loadings		
	Total	% of Variance	Cumulative %	Total	% of Variance	Cumulative %
1	2.687	67.187	67.187	2.687	67.187	67.187
2	.812	20.292	87.479			
3	.341	8.519	95.998			
4	.160	4.002	100.000			

Extraction Method: Principal Component Analysis.

Table B 21: Component Matrix:
Scale Correlations with Extracted Component

	Component 1
Teacher Directedness	.648
Student Directedness	**.877**
Basic Skills	.831
Applied Skills	**.898**

Extraction Method: Principal Component Analysis.
a 1 component extracted.

Validity of Scale

Taken together these analyses support the claim that the *Instruction and Curriculum Scales for Self-Determined Learning* measure what they were intended to measure – the instruction and curricular approaches that are consistent with self-determined learning. The four scales were shown to be significantly inter-correlated (first analysis); predictive of student-directedness of practical skill acquisitions (second analysis), and functionally interrelated as a single assessment unit that accounted for more than two thirds of the 48-item variance (third analysis). In other words, the *Instruction and Curriculum Scales for Self-Determined Learning* appears to be a valid method of assessing teaching approaches that promote self-determined learning.

Utility

This section evaluates whether the instrument is useful in a practical sense by determining the extent that it reflects important teaching differences among experienced teachers. One of these determines, for example, whether the scales identify the causal agency and applied content of the teaching of different groups of teachers. A second evaluates whether the scales discriminate between the instruction and curriculum approaches of teachers from different educational and cultural backgrounds. A third determines whether the scales detect changes in instruction and curriculum of teachers who have been exposed to self-instruction pedagogy. And a fourth determines whether the scale ratings correlate significantly with teachers' levels of self-efficacy and self-determination.

Use in Identifying Instruction and Curriculum Patterns of Teachers

This section presents instruction and curriculum data generated by a sample of 31 general education teachers and 45 special education teachers from the U.S. and 28 special education teachers from the West Indies. These groups used the *Instruction and Curriculum Scales for Self-Determined Learning* to rate the instructional agency and curricular emphasis of their instruction. Figure B-5 presents mean group ratings for the four scales, indicating that teachers reported more frequent teacher- than student-directedness and more frequent teaching of basic than applied skills. Table B-22 presents statistics on the significance of these ratings, and Table B-23 presents t-test results indicating that teacher-directedness was rated significantly more often than student-directedness ($t_{103} = 12.31$; $p < .001$) and basic skills content was rated significantly more often than applied skills content ($t_{103} = 3.133$; $p < .003$).

Within-Group Teaching Variations for General Educators. There were within-group differences as well. Figure B-6 presents these findings for the general education sample. Table B-24 presents statistical comparisons for teacher- and student-directedness and for basic and applied skills content. And Table B-25 presents t-test results indicating that teacher-directedness ratings were significantly

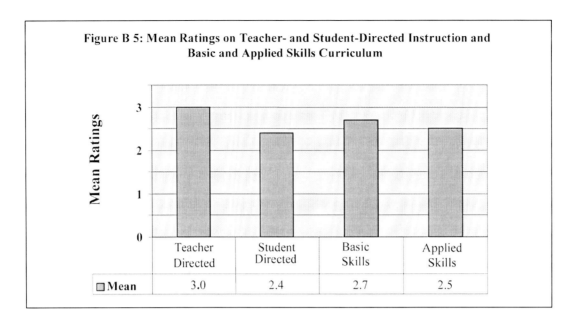

Figure B 5: Mean Ratings on Teacher- and Student-Directed Instruction and Basic and Applied Skills Curriculum

	Teacher Directed	Student Directed	Basic Skills	Applied Skills
☐ Mean	3.0	2.4	2.7	2.5

Table B 22: Descriptive Statistics for the Four Instruction and Curriculum Scales

	N	Minimum	Maximum	Mean	Std. Deviation
Teacher-Directed Instruction	104	1.67	3.92	2.9586	.5395
Student-Directed Instruction	104	.83	3.75	2.4083	.6276
Basic Skills Curriculum	104	.00	4.00	2.6572	.7951
Applied Skills Curriculum	104	.45	3.92	2.5073	.7254

Table B 23: t-Test Statistics Comparing Teacher with Student-Directed Instruction and Basic Skills with Applied Skills Curriculum

	Paired Differences					t	df	Sig. (2-tailed)
	Mean	Std. Deviation	Std. Error Mean	95% Confidence Interval of the Difference				
Pair Comparisons				Lower	Upper			
Teacher -Student Directed Instruction	.5503	.4558	4.469E-02	.4617	.6390	12.314	103	.000
Basic-Applied Skills Curriculum	.1498	.4878	4.783E-02	5.498E-02	.2447	3.133	103	.002

higher than were student-directedness ratings (t_{103} = 4.115; p < .001), but there were no significant differences in ratings for basic and applied skills (t_{103} = .594; p = .557).

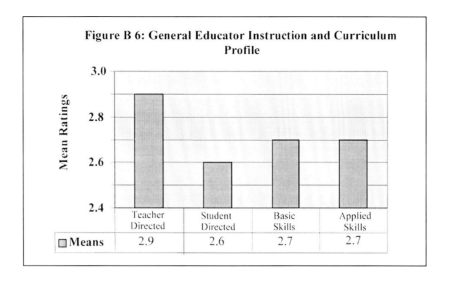

Figure B 6: General Educator Instruction and Curriculum Profile

	Teacher Directed	Student Directed	Basic Skills	Applied Skills
☐ Means	2.9	2.6	2.7	2.7

Table B 24: Descriptive Statistics for General Educator Self-Ratings on the Instruction and Curriculum Scale

General Educator Ratings	Mean	N	Std. Deviation	Std. Error Mean
Teacher Directed Instruction Rating	2.9179	31	.4456	8.003E-02
Student Directed Instruction Rating	2.6058	31	.5714	.1026
Basic Skills Curriculum Rating	2.7141	31	.4298	7.720E-02
Applied Skills Curriculum Rating	2.6783	31	.5127	9.208E-02

Table B 25: General Educator t-Test Statistics Comparing Teacher- and Student-Directed Instruction

	Paired Differences					t	df	Sig. (2-tailed)
	Mean	Std. Deviation	Std. Error Mean	95% Confidence Interval of the Difference				
Pair Comparisons				Lower	Upper			
Teacher- vs. Student-Directed Instruction	.3121	.4182	7.511E-02	.1587	.4655	4.155	30	.000
Basic Skills vs. Applied Skills	3.575E-02	.3349	6.014E-02	-8.7079E-02	.1586	.594	30	.557

Within-Group Teaching Variations for U.S. Special Educators. Figure B-7 presents the instruction and curriculum profile for the U.S. special educators of this sample. Table B-26 presents statistics on their ratings on teacher- and student-directedness, and on basic and applied skills content. Table B-27 presents t-test results for the instruction and curriculum scales. For this group, self-ratings for teacher-directedness were significantly higher than for student-directedness (t_{103} = 9.577; p < .001), but there were no significant differences between ratings for basic and applied skills (t_{103} = .842; p = .405).

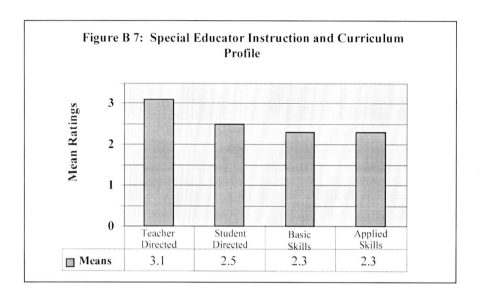

Figure B 7: Special Educator Instruction and Curriculum Profile

	Teacher Directed	Student Directed	Basic Skills	Applied Skills
□ Means	3.1	2.5	2.3	2.3

Table B 26: Descriptive Statistics for Special Educator Self-Ratings on the Instruction and Curriculum Scale

Special Education Ratings	Mean	N	Std. Deviation	Std. Error Mean
Teacher Directed Instruction	3.1380	45	.5269	7.855E-02
Student Directed Instruction	2.4806	45	.5981	8.915E-02
Basic Skills Curriculum	2.3426	45	.8973	.1338
Applied Skills Curriculum	2.2746	45	.8327	.1241

Table B 27: Special Educator t-Test Statistics Comparing Differences in Instruction and Curriculum

	Paired Differences					t	df	Sig. (2-tailed)
	Mean	Std. Deviation	Std. Error Mean	95% Confidence Interval of the Difference				
Pair Comparisons				Lower	Upper			
Teacher- vs. Student-Directed Instruction	.6574	.4605	6.865E-02	.5191	.7958	9.577	44	.000
Basic vs. Applied Skills Curriculum	6.801E-02	.5422	8.082E-02	-9.4875E-02	.2309	.842	44	.405

Within-Group Teaching Variations for West Indies Special Educators.
Figure B-8 presents the instruction and curriculum profile for the West Indies special education teachers. Table B-28 presents statistics for their ratings on teacher- and student-directedness and basic and applied skills content. Table B-29 presents

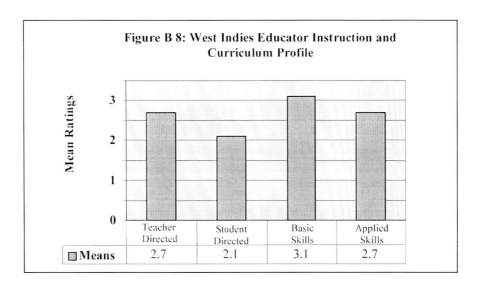

Figure B 8: West Indies Educator Instruction and Curriculum Profile

	Teacher Directed	Student Directed	Basic Skills	Applied Skills
Means	2.7	2.1	3.1	2.7

Table B 28: Descriptive Statistics for West Indies Educators' Instruction and Curriculum Self-Ratings

	Mean	N	Std. Deviation	Std. Error Mean
Teacher Directed Instruction	2.7154	28	.5660	.1070
Student Directed Instruction	2.0734	28	.6223	.1176
Basic Skills Curriculum	3.0997	28	.7228	.1366
Applied Skills Curriculum	2.6920	28	.6530	.1234

Table B 29: West Indies Special Educator t-Test Statistics Comparing Differences in Instruction and Curriculum

	Paired Differences					t	df	Sig. (2-tailed)
	Mean	Std. Deviation	Std. Error Mean	95% Confidence Interval of the Difference				
Pair Comparisons				Lower	Upper			
Teacher- vs. Student-Directed Instruction	.6420	.3994	7.549E-02	.4871	.7969	8.505	27	.000
Basic vs. Applied Skills Curriculum	.4077	.4570	8.637E-02	.2304	.5849	4.720	27	.000

t-test results indicating significantly higher ratings for teacher-directedness than for student-directedness ($t_{103} = 8.505$; $p < .001$), and significantly higher ratings for basic skills than for applied skills content ($t_{103} = 4.720$; $p < .001$).

Use in Identifying Group Differences in Instruction and Curriculum Ratings

This section evaluates whether the scales also identified group differences in instructional-directedness and curricular content. Figure B-9 presents these comparisons indicating that U.S. general and special educators rated their instructional approaches higher than did West Indies special educators, and West Indies special educators rated their curricular approaches higher than did U.S. special and general educators.

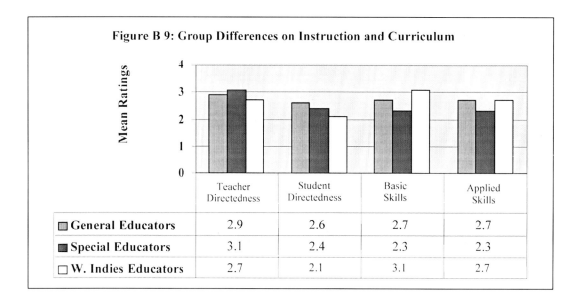

Figure B 9: Group Differences on Instruction and Curriculum

	Teacher Directedness	Student Directedness	Basic Skills	Applied Skills
General Educators	2.9	2.6	2.7	2.7
Special Educators	3.1	2.4	2.3	2.3
W. Indies Educators	2.7	2.1	3.1	2.7

Group Differences on Teacher-Directedness. A statistical analysis indicated that these differences were significant. Table B-30, for example, presents teacher-directedness data for the three groups, and Table B-31 presents results of an analysis of variance indicating the significant differences ($p < .005$). The Tukey analysis in Table B-32 identified the group ratings responsible for the difference to be between special educators from the U.S. and from the West Indies. U.S special educators rated teacher-directedness significantly more often than did West Indies special educators ($p < .005$).

Group Differences on Student-Directedness. Table B-33 presents student-directedness data for the three groups, and Table B-34 presents results of an analy-

Table B 30: Group Statistics for Teacher-Directedness Ratings

	N	Mean	Std. Deviation	Std. Error	95% Confidence Interval for Mean		Minimum	Maximum
					Lower Bound	Upper Bound		
General	31	2.9179	.4456	8.003E-02	2.7545	3.0813	1.67	3.75
Special	45	3.1380	.5269	7.855E-02	2.9797	3.2963	2.00	3.92
West Indies	28	2.7154	.5660	.1070	2.4959	2.9349	1.67	3.58
Total	104	2.9586	.5395	5.290E-02	2.8537	3.0635	1.67	3.92

Table B 31: ANOVA for Group Differences on Teacher-Directedness Ratings

	Sum of Squares	df	Mean Square	F	Sig.
Between Groups	3.157	2	1.578	5.944	.004
Within Groups	26.822	101	.266		
Total	29.979	103			

Table B 32: Multiple Group Comparisons for Teacher-Directedness Using Tukey HSD

(I) Special	(J) Special	Mean Difference (I-J)	Std. Error	Sig.	95% Confidence Interval	
					Lower Bound	Upper Bound
General	Special	-.2202	.120	.165	-.5063	6.597E-02
	West Indies	.2025	.134	.292	-.1171	.5221
Special	General	.2202	.120	.165	-6.5968E-02	.5063
	West Indies	.4227	.124	.003	.1276	.7177
West Indies	General	-.2025	.134	.292	-.5221	.1171
	Special	-.4227	.124	.003	-.7177	-.1276

Table B 33: Group Statistics for Student-Directedness Ratings

	N	Mean	Std. Deviation	Std. Error	95% Confidence Interval for Mean		Minimum	Maximum
					Lower Bound	Upper Bound		
General	31	2.6058	.5714	.1026	2.3962	2.8154	1.42	3.67
Special	45	2.4806	.5981	8.915E-02	2.3009	2.6603	1.17	3.75
West Indies	28	2.0734	.6223	.1176	1.8321	2.3147	.83	3.17
Total	104	2.4083	.6276	6.154E-02	2.2862	2.5303	.83	3.75

Table B 34: ANOVA for Group Differences on Student-Directed Instruction Ratings

	Sum of Squares	df	Mean Square	F	Sig.
Between Groups	4.586	2	2.293	6.435	.002
Within Groups	35.987	101	.356		
Total	40.573	103			

Table B 35: Multiple Group Comparisons for Student-Directedness Using Tukey HSD

(I) Special	(J) Special	Mean Difference (I-J)	Std. Error	Sig.	95% Confidence Interval Lower Bound	95% Confidence Interval Upper Bound
General	Special	.1252	.139	.642	-.2062	.4566
	West Indies	.5324	.156	.003	.1622	.9026
Special	General	-.1252	.139	.642	-.4566	.2062
	West Indies	.4072	.144	.015	6.545E-02	.7490
West Indies	General	-.5324	.156	.003	-.9026	-.1622
	Special	-.4072	.144	.015	-.7490	-6.5455E-02

Table B 36: Group Statistics for Basic Skills Curriculum Ratings

	N	Mean	Std. Deviation	Std. Error	95% Confidence Interval for Mean Lower Bound	95% Confidence Interval for Mean Upper Bound	Minimum	Maximum
General	31	2.7141	.4298	7.720E-02	2.5564	2.8718	1.91	3.50
Special	45	2.3426	.8973	.1338	2.0730	2.6122	.00	4.00
West Indies	28	3.0997	.7228	.1366	2.8194	3.3800	1.00	4.00
Total	104	2.6572	.7951	7.797E-02	2.5025	2.8118	.00	4.00

sis of variance indicating there were significant group differences ($p < .005$). The Tukey analysis in Table B-35 identified the group ratings responsible to be between U.S. and West Indies educators. Both groups of U.S educators rated student-directedness significantly higher than did West Indies special educators ($p < .005$ for general educators and $p < .05$ for special educators).

Group Differences on Basic Skills Curricula. Table B-36 presents basic skills rating data for the three groups, and Table B-37 presents results of an analysis of variance indicating significant group differences ($p < .005$). The Tukey analysis in Table B-38 identifies the group ratings responsible for the difference to be between special educators from the U.S. and special educators from the West Indies. U.S. special educators rated basic skills content significantly lower than did West Indies special educators ($p < .005$).

Table B 37: ANOVA for Group Differences on Basic Skill Curriculum Ratings

	Sum of Squares	df	Mean Square	F	Sig.
Between Groups	10.037	2	5.018	9.203	.000
Within Groups	55.077	101	.545		
Total	65.114	103			

Table B 38: Multiple Group Comparisons for Basic Skills Curriculum Using Tukey HSD

(I) Special	(J) Special	Mean Difference (I-J)	Std. Error	Sig.	95% Confidence Interval	
					Lower Bound	Upper Bound
General	Special	.3715	.172	.084	-3.8510E-02	.7815
	West Indies	-.3856	.193	.117	-.8436	7.236E-02
Special	General	-.3715	.172	.084	-.7815	3.851E-02
	West Indies	-.7571	.178	.000	-1.1799	-.3343
West Indies	General	.3856	.193	.117	-7.2364E-02	.8436
	Special	.7571	.178	.000	.3343	1.1799

Group Differences on Applied Skills Curricula. Table B-39 presents applied skills curriculum data for the three groups, and Table B-40 presents results from an analysis of variance indicating significant group differences ($p < .05$). The Tukey analysis in Table B-41 identifies the group ratings responsible for the difference to be between U.S. special educators who rated applied skills content significant lower than did U.S. general educators ($p < .05$) or than did West Indies special educators ($p < .05$).

Table B 39: Group Statistics for Applied Skills Curriculum Ratings

	N	Mean	Std. Deviation	Std. Error	95% Confidence Interval for Mean		Minimum	Maximum
					Lower Bound	Upper Bound		
General	31	2.6783	.5127	9.208E-02	2.4903	2.8664	1.67	3.67
Special	45	2.2746	.8327	.1241	2.0244	2.5247	.45	3.83
West Indies	28	2.6920	.6530	.1234	2.4389	2.9452	.92	3.92
Total	104	2.5073	.7254	7.114E-02	2.3662	2.6484	.45	3.92

Table B 40: ANOVA for Group Differences on Applied Skills Curriculum Ratings

	Sum of Squares	df	Mean Square	F	Sig.
Between Groups	4.300	2	2.150	4.351	.015
Within Groups	49.906	101	.494		
Total	54.205	103			

Table B 41: Multiple Group Comparisons for Applied Skills Curriculum Using Tukey HSD

(I) Special	(J) Special	Mean Difference (I-J)	Std. Error	Sig.	95% Confidence Interval Lower Bound	Upper Bound
General	Special	.4038	.164	.041	1.347E-02	.7941
	West Indies	-1.3704E-02	.183	.997	-.4496	.4222
Special	General	-.4038	.164	.041	-.7941	-1.3474E-02
	West Indies	-.4175	.169	.040	-.8199	-1.4988E-02
West Indies	General	1.370E-02	.183	.997	-.4222	.4496
	Special	.4175	.169	.040	1.499E-02	.8199

Use in Detecting Changes in Instructional and Curriculum Baselines

The last evaluation determined whether the instruction and curriculum ratings would reflect changes in teaching after teachers learned about self-instruction pedagogy. This evaluation was based on instrument ratings of 61 experienced special education teachers who completed the self-assessments before and then after they learned about the pedagogy. Table B-42 presents these pre and posttest results and Table B-43 presents statistical analyses indicating significant differences between them.

On pretest assessments, teacher-directedness was rated significantly more often than was student-directed instruction ($t_{60} = 11.113$; $p < .005$) but on posttest assessments, student-directedness was rated significantly more often than was teacher-directedness ($t_{60} = -2.663$; $p < .05$). On pretest ratings of the curriculum, there were no significant differences between basic or applied skills ratings ($t_{60} = 1.178$; $p = .243$). On posttest ratings, however, applied skills were rated significantly more often than were basic skills ($t_{60} = -3.685$; $p < .005$).

Tables B-44 and B-45 present data on the pre- and posttest assessments. Table B-44 presents means for these assessments, and Table B-45 identifies significant differences between them. For instructional-directedness, the difference between

Table B 42: Instruction and Curriculum Rating Statistics for Pre and Posttests		Mean	N	Std. Deviation	Std. Error Mean
Pretest	Teacher Directed Instruction	3.2983	61	.5137	6.577E-02
	Student Directed Instruction	2.5339	61	.6689	8.564E-02
Pretest	Basic Skills Curriculum	2.6261	61	.7029	9.000E-02
	Applied Skills Curriculum	2.5291	61	.5819	7.450E-02
Posttest	Teacher Directed Instruction	3.0834	61	.6087	7.794E-02
	Student Directed Instruction	3.3290	61	.5427	6.949E-02
Posttest	Basic Skills Curriculum	2.7926	61	.6362	8.146E-02
	Applied Skills Curriculum	3.0231	61	.5133	6.572E-02

Table B 43: Within Condition Differences on Instruction and Curriculum Scale Ratings

		Paired Differences					t	df	Sig. (2-tailed)
		Mean	Std. Deviation	Std. Error Mean	95% Confidence Interval of the Difference				
	Within Condition Differences				Lower	Upper			
Pretest Comparison	Teacher vs Student Directed Instruction	.7644	.5373	6.879E-02	.6268	.9020	11.113	60	**.000**
Posttest Comparison	Teacher vs Student Directed Instruction	-.2456	.7203	9.222E-02	-.4301	-6.1155E-02	-2.663	60	**.010**
Pretest Comparison	Basic vs. Applied Instruction	9.708E-02	.6436	8.240E-02	-6.7754E-02	.2619	1.178	60	.243
Posttest Comparison	Basic vs. Applied Instruction	-.2304	.4884	6.253E-02	-.3555	-.1054	-3.685	60	**.000**

Table B 44: Pre and Posttest Statistics for Instruction and Curriculum Ratings					
		Mean	N	Std. Deviation	Std. Error Mean
Pretest	Teacher Directed Instruction	3.2983	61	.5137	6.577E-02
Posttest	Teacher Directed Instruction	3.0834	61	.6087	7.794E-02
Pretest	Student Directed Instruction	2.5339	61	.6689	8.564E-02
Posttest	Student Directed Instruction	3.3290	61	.5427	6.949E-02
Pretest	Basic Skills Curriculum	2.6261	61	.7029	9.000E-02
Posttest	Basic Skills Curriculum	2.7926	61	.6362	8.146E-02
Pretest	Applied Skills Curriculum	2.5291	61	.5819	7.450E-02
Posttest	Applied Skills Curriculum	3.0231	61	.5133	6.572E-02

Table B 45: Between Condition Differences for Instruction and Curriculum Ratings								
		Paired Differences					t	df	Sig. (2-tailed)
	Between Condition Differences	Mean	Std. Deviation	Std. Error Mean	95% Confidence Interval of the Difference				
					Lower	Upper			
Pre-Post Test Comparison	Teacher Directed Instruction	.2150	.7361	9.425E-02	2.642E-02	.4035	2.281	60	**.026**
Pre-Post Test Comparison	Student Directed Instruction	-.7951	.7759	9.934E-02	-.9938	-.5964	-8.004	60	**.000**
Pre-Post Test Comparison	Basic Skills Curriculum	-.1665	.7042	9.017E-02	-.3468	1.388E-02	-1.846	60	.070
Pre-Post Test Comparison	Applied Skills Curriculum	-.4940	.6570	8.412E-02	-.6623	-.3257	-5.872	60	**.000**

the pretest mean of 3.3 and posttest mean of 3.1 for teacher-directedness was significant ($t_{60} = 2.281$; $p < .05$) as was the difference between the pretest mean of 2.5 and posttest mean of 3.3 for student-directedness ($t_{60} = -8.005$; $p < .005$). For curricular emphasis, there were no significant differences in pre and posttest assessments on basic skills ($t_{60} = -1.846$; $p > .05$), but there was for the applied skills pretest rating of 2.5 and posttest rating of 3.0 ($t_{60} = -5.872$; $p < .005$). Figure B-10 illustrates these changes from teacher- to student-directedness and from basic to applied skills.

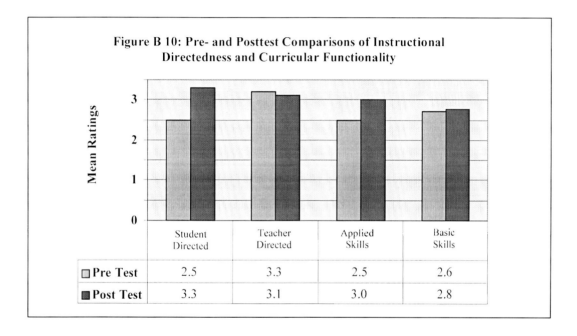

Figure B 10: Pre- and Posttest Comparisons of Instructional Directedness and Curricular Functionality

	Student Directed	Teacher Directed	Applied Skills	Basic Skills
Pre Test	2.5	3.3	2.5	2.6
Post Test	3.3	3.1	3.0	2.8

Use in Explaining Teacher-Directedness with Self-Efficacy and Self-Determination

The final analysis evaluates whether self-ratings on the directedness scales of the instrument correlate with teacher empowerment during instruction and hence, with the persistence of their control over student learning as suggested in Chapter 7. Perhaps teachers choose teaching methods that are consistent with their goals and therefore reflect their self-determination and feelings of self-efficacy. This explanation can be evaluated to some extent by correlating the directedness of instruction with levels of self-efficacy and self-determination. The following sections report analyses of these relationships.

Correlations between Instructional-Directedness and Empowerment. Table B-46 presents correlations between teacher-directedness, student-directedness, self-efficacy, and self-determination and their significance. It shows that teacher and student-directedness were correlated (r = .721; p < .005) but self-efficacy and self-determination were not (r = .174, p > .100). It also shows that teacher-directedness was significantly correlated with self-efficacy (r = .284, p < .01), and self-determination (r = .339, p < .005). But student-directedness was only correlated significantly with self-determination (r = .270, p < .05). Its correlation with self-efficacy was not significant (r = .149, p > .100).

Although this preliminary analysis is consistent with the hypothesized association that teacher-directedness is associated with teacher empowerment, it is still unclear how these correlations function in a prediction analysis, given that self-determination also correlated significantly with student-directedness.

To identify the directions of these associations, six regression analyses were conducted to determine the significant predictors among these correlations. The first regression identified significant instructional-directedness predictors of self-efficacy. The second identified significant instructional-directedness predictors of self-determination. The third identified significant empowerment predictors of teacher-directedness. The fourth identified significant empowerment predictors of student-directedness. The fifth determined whether the instructional indicators predicted each other, and the sixth determined whether the empowerment indicators predicted each other. The results of each regression analysis contributed to the development of a causal model that might better explain these correlations between directedness and empowerment.

Table B 46: Correlations between C&T Scales and Empowerment Scales
(n = 91)

	Teacher Directedness	Student Directedness	Self Efficacy	Self-Determination
Teacher Directedness	1.000	**.721**	**.284**	**.339**
Significance		.000	.007	.001
Student Directedness	**.721**	1.000	.149	**.270**
Significance	.000		.160	.011
Self Efficacy	**.284**	.149	1.000	.174
Significance	.007	.160		.106
Self-Determination	**.339**	**.270**	.174	1.000
Significance	.001	.011	.106	

Instructional Predictors of Self-Efficacy. In this analysis, the item ratings by 91 experienced teachers on instructional-directedness were entered as possible predictors of their self-efficacy ratings, the dependent variable. The model in Table B-47 presents the results for this regression model. It explained 6.6 percent of the variance in self-efficacy, which according to the ANOVA in Table B-48 was significant at $p < .02$. Table B-49 identifies the significant predictor of self-efficacy to be teacher-directedness, which was significant at $p < .02$. Student-directedness was not a significant predictor of self-efficacy.

Figure B-11 presents the first step in building a causal model from these investigations. It shows that teacher-directedness was a significant predictor of self-efficacy in that the more teacher-directedness reported by teachers, the higher the predicted change in self-efficacy (a Beta of .367).

Table B 47: Model Summary

Model	R	R Square	Adjusted R Square	Std. Error of the Estimate
1	.295	.087	.066	.4127

a Predictors: (Constant), Student Directedness, Teacher Directedness

Table B 48: ANOVA

Model	R	Sum of Squares	df	Mean Square	F	Sig.
1	Regression	1.409	2	.705	4.136	.019
	Residual	14.821	87	.170		
	Total	16.230	89			

a Predictors: (Constant), Student Directedness, Teacher Directedness
b Dependent Variable: Self Efficacy

Table B 49: Coefficients

Model		Unstandardized Coefficients		Standardized Coefficients	t	Sig.
		B	Std. Error	Beta		
1	(Constant)	2.198	.238		9.253	.000
	Teacher Directedness	.285	.115	.367	2.480	.015
	Student Directedness	-7.677E-02	.099	-.115	-.779	.438

a Dependent Variable: Self Efficacy

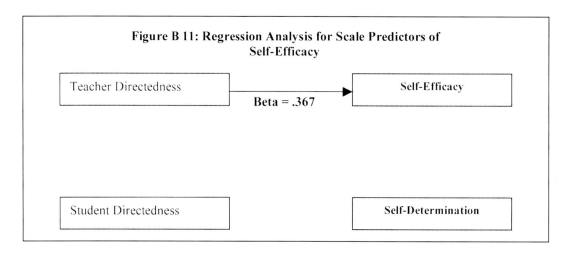

Figure B 11: Regression Analysis for Scale Predictors of Self-Efficacy

Instructional Predictors of Self-Determination. This analysis used the same ratings to identify the instructional predictors of self-determination. Here teacher-directedness and student-directedness were entered as possible predictors of self-determination, the dependent variable. Table B-50 presents this regression model. It explained 9.5 percent of the variance in the self-determination ratings of teachers, which according to the ANOVA in Table B-51 was significant at p < .01. Table B-52 identifies the predictor of those ratings to be teacher-directedness but not student-directedness. This regression was significant at p < .05. Figure B-12 reflects this contribution to the developing causal model showing that teacher-directedness also predicts change in self-determination at a Beta of .305.

Table B 50: Model Summary

Model	R	R Square	Adjusted R Square	Std. Error of the Estimate
1	.340	.116	.095	.4280

a Predictors: (Constant), Student Directedness, Teacher Directedness

Table B 51: ANOVA

Model		Sum of Squares	df	Mean Square	F	Sig.
1	Regression	2.037	2	1.018	5.558	.005
	Residual	15.573	85	.183		
	Total	17.609	87			

a Predictors: (Constant), Student Directedness, Teacher Directedness
b Dependent Variable: Self-Determination

Table B 52: Coefficients

Model		Unstandardized Coefficients		Standardized Coefficients	t	Sig.
		B	Std. Error	Beta		
1	(Constant)	3.052	.250		12.196	.000
	Teacher Directedness	.251	.123	.305	2.032	.045
	Student Directedness	3.210E-02	.106	.046	.303	.762

a Dependent Variable: Self-Determination

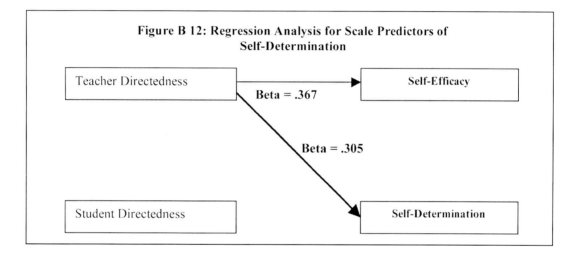

Figure B 12: Regression Analysis for Scale Predictors of Self-Determination

Empowerment Predictors of Teacher-Directedness. This analysis investigates whether the two empowerment variables, self-efficacy and self-determination, predict variations in the directedness of instruction. Table B-53 presents this regression model, which explained 13.7 percent of the variance in teacher-directedness ratings and according to the ANOVA in Table B-54 was significant at p < .005. Table B-55 identifies the significant predictors of directedness ratings to be self-efficacy, which was significant at p < .05 and self-determination, which was significant at p < .005.

Figure B-13 illustrating the emerging causal model shows a predictive relationship between self-efficacy and self-determination and teacher-directedness, with Beta scores of .209 and .302 respectively, a model that is fully consistent with the hypothesis presented that teachers' instructional-directedness would be significantly related to feelings of empowerment. According to this model, however, the association is reciprocal in that teacher-directedness predicts empowerment

Table B 53: Model Summary

Model	R	R Square	Adjusted R Square	Std. Error of the Estimate
1	.396	.157	.137	.5088

a Predictors: (Constant), Self-Determination, Self Efficacy

Table B 54: ANOVA

Model		Sum of Squares	df	Mean Square	F	Sig.
1	Regression	4.096	2	2.048	7.911	.001
	Residual	22.004	85	.259		
	Total	26.100	87			

a Predictors: (Constant), Self-Determination, Self Efficacy
b Dependent Variable: Teacher Directedness

Table B 55: Coefficients

Model		Unstandardized Coefficients		Standardized Coefficients	t	Sig.
		B	Std. Error	Beta		
1	(Constant)	.743	.554		1.343	.183
	Self Efficacy	.269	.131	.209	2.063	.042
	Self-Determination	.368	.123	.302	2.991	.004

a Dependent Variable: Teacher Directedness

Figure B 13: Regression Analysis for Empowerment Predictors of Teacher Directedness

and empowerment predicts teacher-directedness. Of course, other predictive relationships have yet to be considered before this analysis is complete.

Empowerment Predictors of Student-Directedness. One of these is between student-directedness and the empowerment indicators. In this analysis, self-efficacy and self-determination ratings were entered as predictor candidates and student-directedness as the dependent variable. Table B-56 presents this regression model, which explained 6.2 percent of the variance in student-directedness and according to the ANOVA in Table B-57 was significant at $p < .05$. Table B-58 identifies the significant predictor in this analysis to be self-determination, which was significant at $p < .05$. Self-efficacy was not a significant predictor. Figure B-14 presents the causal model with this relationship added. It shows that the only predictive relationship between student-directedness and empowerment was with self-determination, which predicted change in student-directedness at a Beta of .251.

Table B 56: Model Summary

Model	R	R Square	Adjusted R Square	Std. Error of the Estimate
1	.289	.084	.062	.6184

a Predictors: (Constant), Self-Determination, Self Efficacy

Table B 57: ANOVA

Model		Sum of Squares	df	Mean Square	F	Sig.
1	Regression	2.964	2	1.482	3.876	.025
	Residual	32.506	85	.382		
	Total	35.470	87			

a Predictors: (Constant), Self-Determination, Self Efficacy
b Dependent Variable: Student Directedness

Table B 58: Coefficients

Model		Unstandardized Coefficients B	Std. Error	Standardized Coefficients Beta	t	Sig.
1	(Constant)	.588	.673		.873	.385
	Self-Efficacy	.159	.159	.106	1.005	.318
	Self-Determination	.356	.150	.251	2.382	.019

a Dependent Variable: Student Directedness

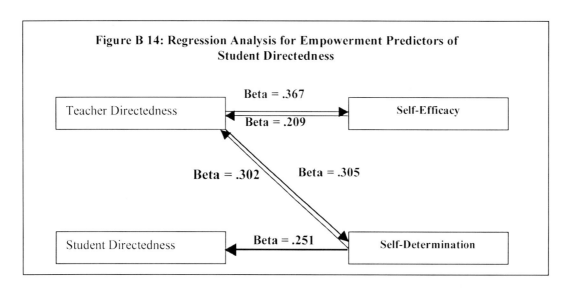

Figure B 14: Regression Analysis for Empowerment Predictors of Student Directedness

Reciprocal Predictors of Teacher Empowerment. This analysis investigated whether self-efficacy and self-determination were significant predictors of each other, but they were not. When self-determination or self-efficacy was entered as a predictor of the other, the regression model explained less than two percent of the variance (Table B-59) and was not significant (Table B-60). Hence, neither was a significant predictor of the other (Table B-61).

Reciprocal Predictors of Instructional-Directedness. The final analysis determined whether teacher and student-directedness predicted each other. It

Table B 59: Model Summary

Model	R	R Square	Adjusted R Square	Std. Error of the Estimate
1	.174	.030	.019	.4203

a Predictors: (Constant), Self-Determination

Table B 60: ANOVA

Model		Sum of Squares	df	Mean Square	F	Sig.
1	Regression	.472	1	.472	2.671	.106
	Residual	15.196	86	.177		
	Total	15.667	87			

a Predictors: (Constant), Self-Determination
b Dependent Variable: Self Efficacy

Table B 61: Coefficients

Model		Unstandardized Coefficients		Standardized Coefficients	t	Sig.
		B	Std. Error	Beta		
1	(Constant)	2.218	.390		5.690	.000
	Self-Determination	.164	.100	.174	1.634	.106

a Dependent Variable: Self Efficacy

showed that when either variable was entered as predictor, 51.5 percent of the variance in the other indicator was explained by a regression (Table B-62) that was significant at a p < .001 (Table B-63), with the predictor (teacher or student-directedness) being significant at p < .001 (Table B-64), and the Beta for explained change in the dependent variable at .721.

Figure B-15 adds these relationships to the final causal model showing predictive relationships between teacher-directedness, student-directedness and the empowerment indicators. According to the model, teacher and student-directedness are reciprocal predictors and teacher-directedness, self-efficacy, and self-determination are reciprocal predictors. Student-directedness and the empowerment indicators are not, however, because change in teachers' self-determination predicted change in student-directedness but change in student-directedness did not predict change in self-determination. Finally, the empowerment indicators appeared

Table B 62: Model Summary

Model	R	R Square	Adjusted R Square	Std. Error of the Estimate
1	.721	.520	.515	.4466

a Predictors: (Constant), Teacher Directedness

Table B 63: ANOVA

Model		Sum of Squares	df	Mean Square	F	Sig.
1	Regression	19.031	1	19.031	95.428	.000
	Residual	17.549	88	.199		
	Total	36.580	89			

a Predictors: (Constant), Teacher Directedness
b Dependent Variable: Student Directedness

Table B 64: Coefficients

Model		Unstandardized Coefficients		Standardized Coefficients	t	Sig.
		B	Std. Error	Beta		
1	(Constant)	-6.378E-02	.257		-.248	.804
	Teacher Directedness	.842	.086	.721	9.769	.000

a Dependent Variable: Student Directedness

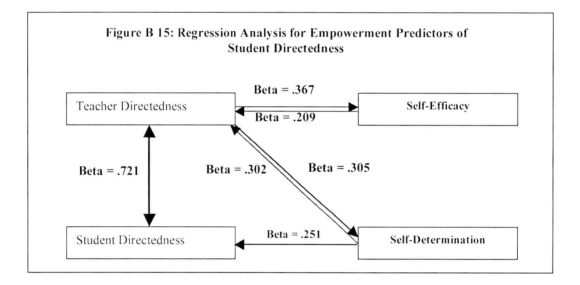

Figure B 15: Regression Analysis for Empowerment Predictors of Student Directedness

to function independently in that there were no predictive relationships between them. Of course, this was not the case for instructional indicators, which function reciprocally. Here a change in either teacher or student-directedness predicted a change in the other. This relationship was also very robust, explaining more than two thirds of the variance of those self-ratings.

CONCLUSION

The purpose of the *Instruction and Curriculum Scales of Self-Determined Learning* is to determine whether the instructional approaches used by teachers of students with disabilities encourage self-determined learning. The basis of this is the claim from self-determined learning theory that learning maximizes when opportunities and self-regulated adjustments optimize. This occurs when (a) learning opportunities are perceived by learners to be valuable *and* doable occasions for gaining something *they* need or want, and (b) when learners regulate their adjustments to those opportunities as effectively as possible under the circumstances.

This assessment instrument was constructed to measure the teaching behaviors most likely to correlate with these conditions, with basic and applied skill/knowledge items reflecting the value and manageability of learning opportunities and teacher and student-directedness items reflecting the agency of control over that learning. The expectation was that instrument ratings favoring student-directedness and applied skills would be more in line with student-determined learning than would ratings favoring teacher-directedness and basic skills. In other words, to the extent that students have opportunities to direct learning that is consistent with *their perceived* needs, interests, and abilities, they engage in self-determined learning. Of course, this theoretical claim was not tested by the evaluations reported here. Rather, it was the basis for those evaluations, which attempted to determine whether the instrument assessed the presence or absence of those learning conditions during instruction. On that score, reliability, validity, and utility tests were conducted to determine whether the instrument measured the extent that teachers or students directed the learning process and the extent that the content of learning was immediately consistent with teacher or student needs and interests.

The reliability tests, which determined whether the instrument ratings were consistent over time, were conducted 60 days apart with experienced teachers using the four scales to rate their instruction and curricular approaches with students. The validity tests, which determined whether the instrument measured what it was intended to measure, consisted of inter-scale correlations to identify significant relationships among the four scales, regression analyses to identify predictive relationships among the scales, and a factor analysis to identify the factor or factors explaining most of the variance in item ratings. Last, the utility tests, which determined whether the instrument identified expected instruction and curriculum differences among different groups of teachers, were conducted with various samples of general and special education teachers from the U.S. and the West Indies. The following findings summarize the results of these evaluations.

1. The reliability for the full scale was .93; the reliability of the instructional-directedness scale was .91; and the reliability of the curriculum focus scale was .94.
2. Student-directedness and applied skills were the central predictors of the four scales.
3. The instrument's instruction-curriculum factor explained 67 percent of the variance in its item ratings.

4. The instrument was useful in identifying different instructional-directedness and curricular content patterns of general and special education teachers in the U.S. and West Indies.
5. The instrument was useful in identifying differences in the instructional-directedness and curricular content of general and special education teachers in the U.S. and the West Indies.
6. The instrument was useful in identifying changes in the instructional-directedness and curricular content of teachers who learned about self-instruction pedagogy.
7. The teacher-directedness scale of the instrument was correlated with teachers' levels of self-efficacy and self-determination, which were reciprocally predictive of teacher directedness.
8. Teacher-directedness and student-directedness were reciprocally predictive: with teacher-directedness increasing (or decreasing) when student-directedness increased (or decreased), and with student-directedness increasing (or decreasing), when teacher-directedness increased (or decreased).

In other words, the *Instruction and Curriculum Scales for Self-Determined Learning* provide a reliable, valid, and useful measure of one important factor in the teaching of students with disabilities: whether it is likely to encourage self-determined learning. The instrument consistently and predictably identified two contrasting patterns of teaching, one focusing on teacher-directed learning of basic skills and knowledge and the other focusing on student-directed learning of applied skills and knowledge. The claim in this book and elsewhere is that the latter is more consistent with self-determined learning than is the former. With this in mind, the following conclusions can be drawn from this set of test evaluations: (a) teachers who rate themselves high on all four scales are likely to be encouraging some level of self-determined learning; (b) teachers who rate themselves significantly higher on teacher-directedness than on student-directedness are likely to be encouraging more teacher-determined than student-determined learning; (c) teachers who rate themselves higher on student-directedness than on teacher-directedness are likely to be encouraging student-directed learning of applied skills; and (d) teachers who rate themselves low on all four scales are unlikely to be encouraging teacher- or student-directed learning.

REFERENCES

Mithaug, D. E., Mithaug, D. K., Agran, M. Martin, J. E., & Wehmeyer, M. L., (2003). *Self-determined learning theory: Construction, verification, evaluation.* Mahwah, N. J.: Lawrence Erlbaum Associates.
Mithaug, D. E., Mithaug, D. K., Agran, M. Martin, J. E., & Wehmeyer, M. L., (2007). *Self-instruction pedagogy: How to teach self-determined learning.* Springfield, IL: Charles C Thomas.

NAME INDEX

A

Abery, B., 105
Ackerman, A., 16, 170
Adams, G., 13, 174
Adelman, H.S., 16, 172
Ager, C., 17, 169
Agran, J., 67, 87
Agran, Martin, 7, 9, 16–17, 20, 27, 29, 32, 44–52, 54–56, 59–65, 67–68, 75, 85–87, 91, 100–102, 104–105, 108, 118, 128, 141, 149, 159–161, 164–167, 170–171, 179, 217
Akamatsu, T.J., 15, 20, 30, 166
Albert, M., 15, 161
Alberto, P.A., 16–17, 20, 27, 162, 166
Alexander, P.A., 16, 163
Algozzine, B., 4, 29
Allen, S.K., 115, 127
Allinder, R.M., 13, 177–178
Alper, C., 63
Alper, S., 17, 51, 62, 172–173
Altstone, D., 15, 172
Alvarez, V., 16, 172
American Youth Policy Forum (AYPF), 108, 127
Ames, C., 16–17, 159, 161, 168
Anastasiow, N.J., 5, 28
Anderegg, M.L., 4, 30
Anderson-Inman, 16
Anderson, L., 15, 17, 159, 161–162
Andrews, D., 68, 87
Anthony, H., 17, 159
Armel, S., 15, 161
Armstrong, S.W., 16, 170
Arreaga-Mayer, C., 13, 175
Artuso, A.K., 5, 7, 28
Asarnow, J.R., 159

B

Baer, D.M., 15, 171
Bahr, 16
Baker, D., 17, 20, 29, 167

Ballard, K., 16, 168
Bambara, L.M., 17, 169
Bandura, A.B., 7, 16, 58, 63, 89, 104, 162, 170
Barden, R.C., 15, 172
Barkley, R.A., 16, 162
Barling, J., 173
Barocas, R., 15, 160, 163
Bassett, D.S., 107, 113, 127
Bateman, 16
Bates, R.J., 16, 170
Beal, 16
Beare, P.L., 17, 49, 64
Becker, W.C., 13, 174–175
Bem, S., 7, 159
Bender, N.N., 15, 159
Benson, H.A., 44
Benz, J., 13, 178
Bere, P., 17, 166
Bereiter, C., 5, 7, 27, 174
Berg, W.K., 16–17, 20, 30
Berger, L.H., 6, 28
Berlin, D., 17, 20, 27, 162
Berrie, P., 16, 20, 30
Berry, D.L., 16, 166
Bertrando, R., 47, 63
Betancourt, F.W., 141, 149
Bickel, D.D., 31, 44
Bickel, W.E., 31, 44
Binder, C., 13, 176
Birch, D., 7, 159
Birkimer, J.C., 15, 161, 174
Black, J.L., 15, 171
Blackwood, R., 15, 162
Blanchard, C., 50, 55, 62, 91, 101–102, 104, 161
Blankenship, C.S., 4, 13, 27, 177
Blenkinsop, 16
Blick, 16
Blom, G., 15, 159, 162
Boag, P.G., 6, 28
Boare, P.L., 171
Bock, G., 13, 174
Bolding, N., 55, 65

Bologna, N.C., 166
Bolstad, O.D., 15, 141, 143, 149, 162
Borden, 15
Borkowski, J.A., 16, 162
Borkowski, J.G., 16, 165
Borland, B.J., 110, 128
Bornstein, P.H., 15–16, 159, 172
Bos, C.S., 5, 30, 75, 85, 115, 129
Bourbeau, P., 16, 141, 149, 165
Boykin, R.A., 15, 172
Boyle, J.R., 17, 171
Bradley-Klug, K.L., 17, 168
Brady, M.P., 17, 19, 29, 167, 171
Bransford, J.D., 91, 104
Briggs, A., 17, 20, 27, 162, 170
Bringham, T.A., 166
Brooks, David, v, viii
Brougher, 17
Browder, D.M., 16, 166, 168
Brown, M.S., 15, 160
Brown, R., 163
Brownell, K.D., 15, 49, 63, 168
Bruner, E.C., 13, 174
Bryan, A.J., 20, 30, 172
Bucher, B., 15, 159
Buffington, D.M., 17, 172, 174
Burger, D.L., 169
Burgio, L.D., 159
Burron, D., 15, 159
Bursuck, W.D., 4–5, 27
Burta, 17
Butler, D.L., 17, 170

C

Cai, X., 63
Calkins, R.P., 15, 160
Camp, E., 15, 159, 162
Campeau, P.L., 21, 29, 47, 64
Candace, S., 129
Candy, P.C., 156
Carnine, D.W., 4, 13, 28, 174–175
Carpenter, S.L., 48, 64
Carr, R.W., 17, 100, 104
Carta, J.J., 13, 175
Carter, C.M., 51, 64
Carter, D.B., 15, 162, 165, 169
Carver, C.S., 6, 27
Cash, M.E., 67, 86
Castles, E.E., 143, 149
Castro, L., 173

Cavalier, A.R., 17, 51, 63, 166
Cavin, M., 49, 63
Center on Education Policy (CEP), 108, 127
Chadsey-Rusch, J., 16–17, 161–162
Charman, J., 16, 169
Chiang, B., 13, 177
Childers, J.H., 16, 168
Childs, K.E., 17, 171
Chiron, R., 49, 63
Christie, 16
Christy, M.D., 15, 174
Ciminero, 15
Clarke, S., 17, 68, 85, 171
Cleary, C.P., 15, 164, 169
Clement, P.W., 16, 19, 27, 173
Cole, C.L., 16, 166
Coleman, M., 16–17, 172
Coleman, R.S., 16, 20, 27, 49, 63, 162
Collet-Klingenberg, L., 17, 162
Colletti, G., 15, 49, 63, 168
Columbus, M.A., 21, 27, 162
Colvin, G., 17, 172
Connis, 15–16
Conti-D'Antonio, M., 47, 63
Cook, 16
Cooke, N.L., 110, 127
Copeland, A.P., 16, 159, 162
Copeland, S.R., 16, 48, 61, 63, 68, 85, 91, 104, 171
Corno, L., 6, 27
Cottingham, L., 5, 7, 28
Coulter, W.A., 13, 177
Cowart, C., 16, 163
Cox, P., 67, 86
Crandall, V.C., 7, 173
Crandall, V.G., 7, 173
Creedon, C.F., 16, 141, 143, 149, 168
Cross, T., 110, 127
Crouch, D.P., 16, 159
Crownover, C., 110, 128
Cummings, 16
Curtiss, K.A., 7, 169, 173
Cushing, S.S., 107, 113, 127
Cuvo, A.J., 17, 167

D

Dalton, T., 17, 57, 63, 166–167
Danoff, B., 17, 162
Darch, C., 13, 174
Darch, G., 175
Davis, 17

De La Paz, S., 17, 162, 169
deBaca, P.C., 5, 7, 28
Decenteceo, E., 15, 163
Deci, E.L., 69, 85
Decker, P.J., 16, 164
Deer, M., 16, 166
Deno, S.L., 13, 27, 176–178
DePerczel, M., 68, 85
DePry, R.L., 128
Derry, S.J., 17, 162
Deshler, D.D., 16, 115, 129, 162
Deutchman, 16
Devany, J., 171
D'Huyvetters, K.K., 16, 168
Dickerson, E.A., 16, 141, 143, 149, 168
Digangi, S.A., 17, 166, 170
Diggory, J.C., 15, 172
Dimino, J., 4, 28, 91
Dirks, M.J., 15, 160, 164
Ditrichs, R., 15, 173
Dodd, J.M., 17, 167
Doegel, L.K., 17, 170
Donley, C.R., 13, 175
Doorlag, D.H., 3, 5, 28, 91
Doren, B., 115, 127
Douglas, V.I., 15, 162
Drabman, R.S., 15, 162
Drew, C.J., 5, 28
Drouse, J.P., 13, 176
Dubey, D.R., 15, 75, 87, 141, 149, 165
Dunlap, G., 16–17, 68, 85, 170–171
Dunlap, L.K., 16–17, 170
DuPaul, G.J., 17, 55, 63, 166, 168
Dweck, C.S., 17, 162

E

Edwards, 17
Egan, M.W., 5, 28
Ehren, B.J., 17, 169
Eisenberger, J., 47, 63
Elias-Burger, S., 16, 169
Ellis, E.S., 16, 19, 27, 31–32, 42, 44, 162
Ellis, J., 17, 20, 29, 167
Engelmann, 13
Engelmann, S., 5, 7, 27, 174
Engelmann, T., 5, 7, 27
Englert, C.S., 17, 159, 162
Epstein, R., 15, 20, 27, 163
Erickson, A.M., 17, 20, 28, 167
Ersner-Hershfield, R., 15, 49, 63, 168

Estrada, M.T., 16, 162
Etzel, B.C., 15, 163
Evans, S.E., 13, 176

F

Fagen, S.A., 15, 163
Fantuzzo, J.W., 15–16, 19–20, 27, 30, 49, 64, 68, 76, 87, 163, 165, 173
Fanzini, L.R., 15, 164, 169
Faw, G.D., 16, 160
Fear, K., 17, 159, 162
Feldman, S.E., 15, 173
Ferguson, C., 13, 177–178
Ferretti, R.P., 17, 51, 63, 166
Ficzere, S.A., 17, 170
Field, S.S., 112, 127
Finch, A.J., 15, 164
Fink, W.T., 13, 174
Firman, K.B., 17, 166
Fish, M.C., 16, 160
Fisher, D., 48, 50, 63
Flexer, R., 15, 168
Floor, L., 15, 172
Flowers, C., 115, 127
Flynn, J.M., 15, 173
Fodor-Davis, J., 16–17, 49, 64, 159, 166–167
Fodor, I., 15, 161
Fowler, S.A., 16, 170
Fowler, S.E., 61, 63
Fowler, S.F., 16, 166
Franzini, L.R., 15, 164
Frazier, E.S., 22, 29, 67, 86, 118, 121, 128, 169
Frea, W.D., 17, 167
Fredericksen, L.W., 15, 173
Frederiksen, C.B., 15, 173
Friedling, C., 15, 160
Friend, M., 5, 27
Frietas, 16
Frith, G.H., 16, 170
Fry, P.S., 15, 160
Fuchs, 16
Fuchs, D., 13, 17, 168, 177–178
Fuchs, L.S., 13, 17, 20, 30, 168, 177–178
Fuchs, S., 4, 27
Fuerst, J., 17, 20, 29
Furman, W., 15, 172

G

Gajar, A., 16, 170

Gallagher, J.J., 5–6, 28
Gallanter, E., 7, 29
Gambrell, L.B., 16, 170
Gardner, W.I., 16, 166
Garff, J.T., 17, 166
Garfield, C.A., 67, 85
Garfield, G., 22, 27
Gargiulo, R.M., 5, 28
Garner, N., 115, 129
Garner, R., 16–17, 163
Garson, C., 15, 162
Gast, D.L., 17, 171
Geller, M., 15, 164
Geller, S., 15, 164
Gentry, 13
Gerken, K., 49, 63
German, G., 13, 178
German, S.L., 117, 127
Gersten, 91
Gersten, R.M., 4, 13, 28, 174–175
Gettinger, M., 16, 163
Gickling, 13
Gilberts, G.H., 50, 53, 61, 63, 170
Glass, C.R., 143, 149
Glenwick, D.S., 15, 160, 163
Globerson, T., 16, 165
Glomb, N., 17, 166
Glynn, E.L., 15, 141, 143, 149, 163, 173
Glynn, T., 16, 160
Goetz, E.M., 15, 163
Goff, Chauncey D., 106
Goldfried, M., 15, 163
Gomez, A., 68, 85
Goodman, J., 7, 15, 161
Gorman, J., 17, 167
Goss, C.M., 15, 20, 27, 163
Gottman, J.M., 15, 170
Grace, N., 16, 163
Graham, S., 16–17, 160, 162–163, 165, 168–170
Granzin, A., 13, 174
Graves, A., 17, 170
Greenebaum, 16
Greenwood, C.R., 13, 175
Greer, R.D., 13, 47, 63, 175–176
Gross, A.M., 166
Grossi, T.A., 17, 20, 30, 56, 63, 68, 86, 165, 172
Grusec, J.E., 7, 170
Guess, D., 44
Guevremont, D.C., 16, 160
Gutkin, J., 13, 175

H

Haddox, P., 13, 174
Hale, C.A., 16, 162
Hall, 13, 15
Hallahan, 16
Hallahan, D.P., 5, 28, 171–172
Hallahan, M., 110, 114–115, 128
Halpern, A.S., 115, 127
Hamad, C., 68, 87
Hamby, R., 17, 170
Hamelett, C., 17, 168
Hamlett, C.L., 13, 177–178
Hamner, W.C., 15, 169
Hanawalt, D.A., 68, 86, 126, 128
Hanel, F., 16, 169, 173
Harchik, A.E., 17, 166
Hardman, J.L., 5, 28
Haring, 13
Haring, K.A., 16, 64, 167
Haring, N.G., 5, 7, 13, 28, 49, 176
Harmer, M.L., 17, 141–142, 149, 160
Harrell, K., 15, 163
Harris, K.R., 16–17, 160, 162–165, 170
Harrower, J.K., 51, 64
Hartig, M., 15, 160
Haskins, R., 164
Haughton, E., 13, 176
Hay, R.L., 171
Hayes, S.C., 16, 171
Haywood, 15
Heins, E.D., 16, 171
Heistad, D., 4, 29
Helland, C.D., 15, 173
Hemmers, N.S., 17, 174
Hemmes, N.S., 17, 172
Hendrickson, J.A., 16, 171
Henker, B., 164
Herbert, F., 15, 159, 162
Herr, C.M., 115, 127
Hershfield, S.M., 15, 49, 63, 168
Heshusius, L., 4, 13, 28
Hetherington, E.M., 15, 165
Hetzroni, O.E., 75, 86
Heward, W.L., 5, 13, 17, 20, 28, 30, 56, 63, 68, 86, 165, 172, 176
Hewett, F.M., 5, 7, 28
Higa, W.R., 15, 160
Hildebrandt, D.E., 15, 173
Hill, Napoleon H., 28, 67, 86
Hilliard, 16

Hinshaw, S.P., 17, 164, 171
Hiss, 16
Hoff, K.E., 17, 55, 63, 166
Hogan, 17
Holland, J.G., 5, 7, 28
Holman, J., 15, 171
Holombo, 15
Holstein, R.B., 15, 165
Home, L., 7, 28
Homme, A., 5, 7, 28
Hopman, M., 16, 160
Hopper, C., 166
Horner, R.H., 16, 20, 29, 172
Howard, 17
Howley, T., 68, 87
Hrydowy, E.R., 16, 173
Huber-Marshall, L., 67, 86, 108, 110, 113–115, 117, 121, 127–128
Hughes, C.A., 16–17, 20, 28, 46–50, 54–55, 61–65, 68, 75, 85–86, 91, 102, 104, 141–142, 149, 160–161, 165, 167, 170–171
Hughes, W.M., 110, 127–128
Humphrey, L.L., 15, 167, 173
Hundert, J., 15, 172
Hunt, N., 5, 28
Hurley, C., 17, 167
Husch, James V., 22, 29, 67, 86, 118, 121, 128
Hwang, B., 63, 171

I

Ingham, P., 13, 175
Ironsmith, M., 15, 20, 30, 165
Irvine, B.A., 17, 20, 28, 167
Israel, A.C., 15, 160

J

Jackson, H.J., 6, 28
James, V.L., 164
Jeffrey, D.B., 6, 28
Jenkins, J., 13, 176
Jenson, W.R., 68, 87
Jerman, P.A., 110, 127–128
Johnson, 108
Johnson, E.P., 16, 169
Johnson, M., 16, 160
Johnson, M.B., 16, 160
Johnson, M.R., 159
Johnson, S., 141, 143, 149
Johnson, S.M., 15, 162

Johnston, 16
Jones, E.D., 4, 13, 15, 28, 176
Jones, R.T., 15, 173
Jorgensen, C., 48, 63
Joyce, B., 91, 104
Juniger, J., 15, 172

K

Kahana, B., 7, 161
Kameenui, E.J., 13, 174–175
Kanfer, F.H., 6, 15, 28, 50, 160, 164–165, 169, 173–174
Kapadia, S., 49, 64
Karlan, G.R., 16, 159
Karniol, R., 15, 161, 164
Karoly, P., 15, 160, 164, 167, 169, 173
Katkovsky, W., 7, 173
Kaufman, K.F., 15, 143, 149, 172–173
Kaulfman, J.M., 5, 28
Kazdin, A.E., 15, 169, 171, 173
Keating, T., 13, 175
Kebbeh, A.S., 21, 28
Keel, M.C., 13, 176
Kelchner, K., 115, 129
Kelley, M.L., 68, 86
Kendall, P.C., 15, 160, 164
Keogh, D.A., 16, 160–161
Kern, L., 17, 171
Killian, D.J., 17, 141–142, 149, 160
Kim, J.S., 15, 169
King, R.P., 13, 178
King-Sears, M.E., 4, 17, 28, 48, 63–64, 91, 104, 167
Kiresuk, T.J., 100, 104
Kirk, S.A., 5, 28
Kirschembaum, D.S., 15, 167, 173
Klausmeier, 13
Klein, M., 15, 173
Klein, R.D., 16, 168
Klukas, N., 15, 172
Knapp, 13
Kneedler, R.D., 16, 172
Knivila, 15
Koegel, L.K., 17, 51, 64, 167
Koegel, R.L., 17, 51, 64, 167, 170
Kompik, J.J., 16, 167
Koorland, M.A., 13, 176
Korinek, L., 17, 167
Kosiewicz, M.M., 172
Koslow-Green, L., 171

Krantz, 17
Krause, J.P., 4, 28
Kuehnle, K., 13, 176
Kunzelman, 13
Kuperis, S., 17, 170
Kurtz, P.D., 15, 164

L

Lagomarcino, T.R., 16, 49, 59, 64, 161, 167
Lamm, N., 13, 176
Landrum, 16
Latham, G.P., 16, 169
Lattin, D., 65
Lawrence, M., 115, 129
Layman, R.D., 15, 172
Layne, 15
Leal, D., 5, 30
Leavell, A., 17, 170
Lecklitner, G.L., 15, 164, 169
Lefebvre, D., 17, 173
Leggett, E.L., 17, 162
Lehmann, J.P., 107, 113, 127
Lenz, B.K., 16–17, 19, 27, 162, 169
Leon, J.A., 16, 161
Leonard, 17
Lepper, M.R., 15, 165, 169
Lessen, E., 4, 27
Lewis, R.B., 3, 5, 28, 91
Liberty, K.A., 13, 17, 176
Liebert, R.M., 7, 174
Lindsey, O.R., 5, 29
Lindsley, O.R., 7, 13, 176
Lipinski, D.P., 15, 171–172
Litrownik, A.J., 15–16, 164, 169
Lloyd, J.W., 13, 16–17, 164, 167, 171–172, 175
Locke, E.A., 16, 169
Lockery, M., 13, 175
Lodhi, S., 13, 176
Loesch, C., 108, 113, 128
Long, N.J., 15, 163
Lovett, D.L., 16, 49, 64, 167
Lovitt, T.C., 5, 7, 15, 28, 107, 113, 127, 167, 169, 173
Loyd, R., 17, 166
Lozanoff, 16
Lund, S.H., 100, 104
Luria, A.R., 6–7, 29, 161
Lyman, 15

M

Maag, J.W., 17, 166, 170
MacArthur, C.A., 16–17, 160, 168
MacDuff, 17
Maggs, A., 13, 175
Magnusson, 13
Mahoney, K., 15, 164, 173
Mahoney, M.J., 15, 164, 173
Malott, R.C., 13, 59, 64
Malott, R.W., 16, 167, 176
Mandinach, E.B., 6, 27
Mank, D.M., 16, 20, 29, 172
Mar, D.K., 68, 86, 126, 128, 170
Marchand-Martella, N., 17, 57, 63
Marchard-Martella, N.E., 166
Marquardt, P., 16, 20, 30
Marshall, K., 5, 16, 28, 108, 118
Marston, D., 13, 177–178
Martella, R.C., 17, 57, 63, 75, 85, 159, 166
Martin, A., 15, 168
Martin, G., 169, 173
Martin, G.L., 16, 168, 173
Martin, J., 67, 87, 100, 105
Martin, James E., 7, 9, 16, 22, 29, 32, 44, 47, 52, 56, 63–64, 67–68, 86–87, 91, 105–106, 108, 110, 112–115, 117–118, 120–121, 127–128, 161, 164, 166, 169, 179, 217
Martin, M.E., 86
Martinez-Pons, M., 20, 30
Martino, L.R., 17, 169
Marton, P., 15, 162
Masters, J.C., 7, 15, 172–174
Mastropieri, M.A., 17, 75, 86
Matson, J.L., 16, 163
Matuszewski, J., 108, 113, 128
Maxson, L.L., 110, 114–115, 127–128
Maxwell, 16
Maxwell, L., 13, 178
Maxwell, S.E., 161
Mayhall, 13
McAdam, D.B., 17, 167
McCall, C., 17, 172
McCarl, J.J., 17, 49, 64, 171
McClannahan, 17
McCorkle, N.P., 13, 175
McDade, C.E., 13, 176
McDonald, M.E., 17, 172
McDonough, S.H., 47, 63
McDougall, D., 17, 19, 29, 167, 171
McElroy, K., 17, 170
McFall, R.M., 15, 170
McGahee-Kovac, M., 115, 128

McGonigle, J.J., 16, 173–174
McGreevy, P., 13, 176
McKee, M., 16, 161
McKenzie, T.L., 15, 171
McKinley, C., 17, 20, 27, 162
McKinney, J.D., 16, 20, 30, 164
McLaughlin, T.F., 16–17, 171
McLeoud, M., 15, 163
McMahon, C., 16, 20, 30
McNally, R.J., 16, 167
Meacham, J.A., 15, 161, 169
Mechling, L.C., 17, 171
Meichenbaum, D.H., 7, 15, 159, 161, 164
Meinberg, D.L., 17, 52, 64, 167
Melloy, K.J., 76, 87
Melnick, S., 17, 171
Mendola, L.R., 16, 160
Menlove, F.L., 7, 170
Mercer, A.R., 13, 176
Mercer, C.D., 13, 176
Meyer, L.A., 13, 175
Miller, 15, 17
Miller, D.L., 68, 86
Miller, D.T., 15, 161, 164
Miller, G.A., 6–7, 29
Miller, R.J., 112, 127
Miller, W.B., 17, 20, 29, 167
Milstead, M., 16, 162
Miner, S., 17, 171
Mirkin, P.K., 13, 27, 176–178
Mischel, Walter, v, viii, 7, 15, 164, 170, 174
Misra, A., 17, 20, 171
Mithaug, Deirdre K., 7, 9, 20–21, 29, 31, 47, 56, 64, 66–69, 86–87, 91, 105, 108, 118, 128, 130–131, 133, 137, 149–151, 164–165, 179, 217
Mithaug, Dennis E., 3, 7, 9, 16, 20–22, 27–29, 31–32, 42, 44, 47, 54, 56, 64, 67–69, 73, 76, 86–87, 90–91, 100, 104–105, 108, 118, 120–121, 126, 128, 131, 137, 149–151, 161–162, 164–166, 169–170, 179, 217
Mitts, 15
Monahan, J., 15, 161
Montague, M., 17, 170
Moore, 15
Moore, J., 4, 13, 29, 175
Moore, S., 16–17, 159, 166
Moore, S.C., 16, 49, 64, 167
Morgan, D.P., 16, 20, 29, 168, 172
Morgan, T.K., 16, 161
Morningstar, M.E., 108, 113, 128
Moura, N.G.M., 15, 173

Moxley, R.A., 17, 171
Mungas, 15
Murphy, M.J., 17, 51, 63, 166
Murphy, R., 17, 51, 63, 166

N

Neisworth, J.T., 15, 164
Nelson, 15
Nelson, J.R., 17, 52, 64, 167–168, 172
Nelson, R.C., 171
Nelson, R.E., 15, 173
Nelson, R.O., 16, 171–172
Nelson, W., 161
Nelson, W.J. Jr., 15, 161, 174
Newbery, J., 15, 168
Newman, B., 17, 52, 64, 167, 172, 174
Niarhos, F., 17, 141–142, 149, 160
Ninness, H.A.C., 17, 20, 29, 167
Nowakiwska, M., 15, 172
Nowinski, J.M., 16, 166

O

O'Brien, 108
O'Grady, M.A., 17, 172
Olander, C.P., 13, 176
O'Leary, D., 161
O'Leary, K.D., 7, 15, 20, 30, 75, 143, 149, 161–162, 165, 172–173
O'Leary, S.G., 15, 87, 141, 149, 160, 165
Oliphint, J.H., 22, 29, 67, 86, 118, 120–121, 128
Ollendick, T.H., 16, 172–174
Olvey, 108
Olympia, D.E., 68, 87
O'Reilly, 13
Osborn, K., 5, 7, 27
Osnes, P.G., 16, 160

P

Pachman, 15
Paeth, 17
Page, V., 17, 168
Page-Voth, V., 17, 169
Paine, 16
Palkes, H., 7, 161
Palmer, S., 67, 87, 100, 102, 105, 108, 115, 128–129
Palmer, S.B., 166
Paluck, R.J., 15, 173
Paris, S.G., 17, 165

Parke, R.D., 15, 161, 165
Parry, P., 15, 162
Patterson, C.J., 15, 162, 164–165, 169–170
Patz, M., 173
Peacock, R., 15, 172
Pear, J., 15, 165
Pearl, R., 16, 165
Pepe, H.G., 16, 161
Perloff, B., 7, 58, 63, 170
Peshka, 13
Peskay, J., 15, 174
Pesut, D.J., 6, 29
Petersen, D., 16, 160
Peterson, D., 4, 29
Peterson, J., 4, 29
Peterson, L.D., 17, 19, 29, 167
Peterson, Lori Y., 67, 86, 106, 110, 128
Peterson, M.H., 17, 20, 29, 167
Peterson, S.K., 16, 167
Phillips, E.L., 5, 7, 28
Phillips, N., 13, 178
Pierce, K.L., 17, 20, 29, 167
Piersel, 16
Polirstok, S.R., 13, 176
Polite, 16
Pollack, M.J., 68, 87
Polloway, 16
Pons (see Martinez-Pons)
Post, 17
Potter, M.L., 13, 178
Poulson, C.L., 17, 172
Powers, L.E., 108, 113, 128
Prater, 17
Pratt, 13
Presley, J.A., 171
Pressley, M., 15, 17, 163
Pribaum, K.H., 6–7, 29
Proper, E.C., 13, 174
Pugach, M., 4, 29
Punzo, 17

Q

Quasebarth, S.J., 15, 162, 169
Quevillon, R.P., 15, 159
Quinn, 16

R

Rachlin, H., 15, 165
Rachline, 173

Rager, A., 13, 175
Ramsey, R.S., 4, 29
Raphael, T., 17, 159, 162
Rapp, N., 17, 173
Reid, D., 16, 160
Reid, M., 16, 165
Reid, R., 17, 163, 170
Reinecke, D.R., 17, 52, 64, 167
Renzaglia, A., 16, 161
Reschly, D.J., 4, 29
Reynolds, M., 4, 29
Rhode, G., 16, 20, 29, 168, 172
Richards, S.B., 13, 178
Rickard, H.C., 15, 172
Rieth, 16
Ringel, B.A., 16, 172
Ripple, 13
Ritts, C., 17, 20, 27, 162
Riva, M., 16, 161
Robbins, Anthony, 22, 30, 67, 87
Roberson, R.L., 128
Robertson, 15
Robin, A.L., 15, 161
Robinson, E.J., 17, 170
Rodi, M.S., 171
Rodriguez, M.L., v, viii
Romanczyk, R.G., 15, 173
Rooney, 16
Rosen, M., 172
Rosenbaum, 15
Rosenfield, S., 13, 178
Rowe, 16
Rubinson, F., 13, 178
Rudrud, 16
Ruhl, K.L., 16, 167
Rumsey, I., 16, 168
Rung, L., 171
Rusch, F.R., 16, 32, 44, 49, 59, 64, 67, 86, 118, 128,
    159, 161, 164, 167, 170
Rushall, B.S., 15, 171
Rutherford, R., 20, 29, 167
Rutherford, R.B. Jr., 170
Rutherford, R.D., 17, 167
Ryan, C.S., 17, 167
Ryan, D.M., 69, 85

S

Saari, L.M., 16, 169
Sabornie, E.J., 16, 19, 27, 162
Sagotsky, G., 15, 165, 169

Sainato, D.M., 17, 173
Sale, P., 117, 127
Sale, R.P., 108, 113, 128
Salent, 17
Salzberg, C.L., 16, 20, 27, 159
Sands, D.J., 47, 64–65, 107, 113, 127
Santogrossi, D.A., 15, 173
Sapona, 16
Sawin, D.B., 15, 161, 165
Sawyer, R., 16–17, 160, 165
Sax, C., 48, 63
Scheier, M.F., 6, 27
Scheuermann, B., 17, 172
Schloss, C.N., 16, 170
Schloss, P., 16–17, 20, 30, 168
Schloss, P.J., 16, 170
Schloss, P.T., 17, 172–173
Schreibman, L., 17, 20, 29–30, 167–168
Schumaker, J.B., 16, 115, 129, 162
Schumm, J.S., 5, 30
Schunk, D.H., 16, 49, 64, 142, 149, 169
Schwartz, C.W., 169
Schwartz, M., 166
Schwartz, S., 17, 168
Schwartz, S.S., 168
Scott, S.V., 17, 167
Scruggs, T.E., 17, 75, 86
Selinske, J., 13, 176
Severson, H., 13, 174
Sevick, B., 13, 178
Sexton, M., 17, 165
Seymour, 15
Shank, M., 5, 30
Shapiro, E.S., 16–17, 115, 128, 166, 168, 170, 173–174
Sharpton, W.R., 16–17, 20, 27, 162, 166, 170
Shavit, P., 75, 86
Shaw, K.N., 16, 169
Shee, S.M., 15, 141, 143, 149, 163
Sheehan, M., 16, 141, 149, 165
Sheldon, J.B., 17, 166
Sheridan, S.M., 68, 87
Sherman, G., 16, 167
Sherman, J.A., 17, 166
Shinn, M.R., 13, 177–178
Shire, M., 165
Shoda, Y., v, viii
Shure, M., 15, 165
Sieck, 15
Siegel-Causey, E., 44
Silbert, J., 13, 174–175

Simmons, D.C., 13, 175
Simon, 15
Sinclair, T., 49, 61, 63
Singer, G., 17, 20, 28, 167
Sitlington, 49
Sivage, C., 16, 162
Skiba, R., 13, 178
Skinner, B.F., 5, 7, 28, 58
Smiley, L.R., 17, 169
Smith, A.C., 115, 127
Smith, D.D., 5, 30
Smith, D.J., 16–17, 52, 64, 167–168, 172
Smith, S., 5, 30
Snow, K., 17, 46, 63, 161
Snyder, E.P., 115, 128
Solomon, G., 16, 165
Soukup, J., 115, 129
Sowers, J., 16, 141, 149, 165
Spates, C.R., 15, 165, 173–174
Spence, 16
Spitalnik, R., 15, 162
Spivack, G., 15, 165
Springer, C.J., 16, 172
Srikameswaran, S., 16, 168
Stahlberg, D., 17, 20, 28, 167
Stahmer, A.C., 17, 20, 30, 168
Stancliffe, R.J., 105
Stebbins, L., 13, 174
Stecker, P.M., 13, 17, 20, 30, 178
Stein, B.S., 91, 104
Stein, M., 13, 175
Stevens, D., 17, 159
Stevenson, H.C., 16, 19–20, 30, 49, 64, 68, 76, 87, 165
Stewart, M., 7, 161
Stokes, T.F., 15–16, 160
Stone, 16
Storey, K., 17, 166
Stowitscheck, J.J., 16, 20, 27, 159
Strain, P.S., 17, 173
Stright, M.H., 170
Stump, C.S., 108, 113, 127
Sugai, 16
Sullivan, 17
Sulzer-Azaroff, B., 68, 87
Svobodny, L., 17, 49, 64, 171
Swaner, J., 17, 46, 63, 161
Swarts, V., 16, 20, 30
Swartz, C.W., 142, 149
Swatta, P., 16, 20, 30
Sweda, J., 75, 86

Sweeney, M.A., 114, 129
Switzky, 15

T

Tarver, S.G., 175
Tawney, 13
Taylor, F.D., 5, 7, 13, 28
Taylor, R., 174
Taylor, R.L., 178
Templeman, M., 16, 20, 30
Terborg, J.R., 15, 169
Test, D.W., 16, 110, 115, 127
Tharp, R.G., 15, 141, 160, 165
Thierman, G.J., 16, 168
Thinesen, P.J., 20, 30, 172
Thomas, 13
Thomas, G.V., 17, 170
Thomas, J.D., 15, 141, 143, 149, 163, 173
Thompson, C.K., 13, 16, 170
Tindal, G.A., 13, 176–178
Tollefson, N., 16, 169
Toner, I.J., 15, 165
Torrance, M., 17, 170
Townsend, 13
Tracey, D.B., 16, 169
Trammel, D.L., 17, 172–173
Trask-Tyler, S.A., 17, 20, 30, 165, 172
Troia, G.A., 17, 20, 30, 163, 170
Trtol, K.A., 16, 164
Truhlicka, M., 16, 171
Tucker, J.A., 13, 178
Tuntigian, L., 17, 167
Turkowitz, H., 15, 20, 30, 165
Turnbull, A., 5, 30
Turnbull, A.P., 108, 113, 128
Turnbull, H.R. III, 108, 113, 128
Turnbull, R., 5, 30
Turner, A., 108, 113, 128

U

Ueberhorst, P., 13, 176

V

Van Doorninck, W., 15, 159, 162
Van Dycke, J.L., 67, 86, 110, 128
Van Eyk, D., 13, 176
Van Reusen, A.K., 115, 129
Vaughn, S., 5, 30, 75, 85

Verdi, M., 16, 141, 149, 165
Vergason, G.A., 4, 30
Visser, M., 16, 20, 30

W

Wacker, D.P., 16–17, 20, 30
Wade, T.C., 15, 173
Walden, R.J., 117, 129
Wallace, I., 15, 165
Wamre, H.M., 13, 178
Wang, M.C., 30
Ward, M., 112, 127
Watkins, C.L., 13, 176
Watson, D.L., 141, 165
Webber, J., 17, 172
Wehmeyer, Michael L., 7, 9, 29, 46–50, 52, 55–56, 58, 61–65, 67–68, 87–88, 91, 100–102, 104–105, 108, 112, 115, 118, 127–129, 161, 164–166, 170–171, 179, 217
Weil, M., 91, 104
Weinberg, 15, 163
Weinstein, S.M., 15, 161, 164
Wells, 108
Wesson, 13
Wesson, C., 177–178
Wesson, C.L., 178
Wesson, C.S., 178
West, R.P., 16–17, 19, 29, 166–168
Whalen, C.W., 164
Whinnery, K.W., 17, 20, 30, 168
White, 13
White, D.M., 16, 161
White, O.R., 176
White, R., 68, 85
White, W.A.T., 13, 175
Whitman, T.L., 16–17, 20, 27, 49, 63, 67, 87, 159–162, 166
Whitten, M.E., 4, 29
Wilcox, L.E., 164
Williams, 17
Williams, D.Y., 15, 20, 30, 166
Williams, G., 13, 175
Willits, P.P., 13, 178
Wilson, D., 68, 85
Wilson, G.T., 15, 49, 63, 168
Wilson, R., 108, 113, 128
Winograd, P., 17, 165
Wolf, N.K., 115, 127
Wolman, J.M., 21, 29, 47, 64
Wong, B.Y.L., 16–17, 20, 30, 166, 170

Wood, C.E., 17, 20, 30
Wood, R., 15, 173
Wood, W.M., 110, 115, 127
Woodward, J., 4, 13, 28, 175
Wray, 108
Wright, S., 68, 85

Y

Yeager, D., 55, 65
Young, K.R., 16–17, 19–20, 29, 167–168, 172
Young, R.K., 167
Ysseldyke, J.E., 13, 178

Z

Zegiob, L., 15, 172
Zeiler, M.D., 141, 149
Ziarnik, 16
Zimmerman, B.J., 16, 20, 30, 68, 87, 166
Zirpoli, T.J., 76, 87
Zivin, G., 15, 161, 166
Zohn, C.J., 16, 172

SUBJECT INDEX

A

Arc's Self-Determination Scale, 101
Assessment
    ChoiceMaker, 112
    curriculum-based, 12
    scales, instruction and curriculum, 190–191
    self-directed employment model, 118–121

B

Behavior theory (*see* Operant theory)

C

Cards, self-regulation, 76–84
Causal agents, 89
CBA/DI (*see* Direct instruction)
Choice Principle, viii, 154
ChoiceMaker solution, 108–112
    assessment, 112
    choosing goals, 110–112
    materials, 108–109
    and self-directed IEPs, 112–117
    work improvement contracts, 123–124
Choose and Take Action, 125
    cycle, 125–126
    see also Employment
Constructive theorizing, 91
Contracts
    student choice, 143
    work improvement, 121–123
Curriculum-based instruction (*see* Direct instruction)
Curriculum scales (*see* Scales)

D

Delivery, 59
    see also Self-reinforcement
Direct instruction
    conceptual basis, 6
    derivatives, 175–176
    research and sources, 174–175
    vs. self-instruction, 3–27
        empirical data, 12–19
        practical differences, 19–24
        theory, 5–12
    see also Self-instruction
Disabilities, students with (*see* Students)
Discrimination, 59
    see also Self-reinforcement

E

Education of All Handicapped Children's Act
    (1975), 5
Educational supports, 95–96
    see also Self-determined learning
Employment
    self-determined
        Choose and Take Action, 125
        how it works, 123–124
    self-directed
        model, 118–123
        and self-instruction, 118–126
    work improvement contracts, 121–123

G

Gambia, 21
General Problem Solver (Newell and Simon), 91
Goal Attainment Scaling (GAS), 100–102
Goal setting
    education, 110–111
    personal, 111–112
    research and sources, 168–169
    strategies, 67
    teaching, 77–78

I

Individualized education program (IEP), 111–112
    and *ChoiceMaker*, 112–117

self-directed, 113–115
and *Take Action*, 115–117
Individuals with Disabilities Education Act (IDEA,
1975), 110
Instruction
    assessing control and content, 33
    comparison with others, 33–41
    correlations with empowerment, 206–207
    curriculum-based, 177–178
    and functional directedness, 33
    in-class, 141–143
    levels, 74–77
        mnemonic supports, 75
        self-regulation cards, 76–77
        self-talk supports, 75–76
    pedagogy, changing, 41–44
    philosophy statements, 141, 144
    practicum work, effect on, 140–144
    precision teaching, 176
    self-determined learning model, 91–96
        implementation, 96–99
    teaching profiles, 35–39
*Instruction and Curriculum Scales of Self-Determined
    Learning,* 179–217
Instruction scales (*see* Scales)

L

Learner control
    adjusting, 66–85
    beliefs and practice, gaps between, 46–50
        passive engagement, 47–48
        self-control strategies, 48–50
    developing, 45–62
    self-monitoring, 50–54
Learning center, autonomous, 74
Learning (theory)
    directing, 88–104
    discovery, 91
    learning to learn, 19–22
        teaching strategy, 23–24
    models
        instructional, 96–99
        research and sources, 100–103
        self-determined, 91–96
    self-determined, 7–9, 106–127
        instruction and curriculum scales, 179–217
        see also ChoiceMaker solution
    student-directed, 89–91
        role of teacher, 99–100

M

Marshmallow Test, v
Matching Principle, viii, 154–155
Mnemonic supports, 75
    see also Instruction; Self-regulation

O

Operant theory, 5–7, 10–11
    see also Direct instruction

P

Passive engagement, 47–48
    see also Learner control
Pedagogy, changing, 41–44
    see also Instruction
Peer tutors, 53–54
    see also Self-monitoring
Persistence Principle, viii, 155
Pivotal behaviors (see Self-monitoring)
Placement (self-directed employment model), 121
    see also Employment
Practicum work, 133–136, 140–144
    belief indicators, 143–144
    effects of instruction and choice, 140–144
    effects of teachers and choice, 133–136
    results of choice, 136–137, 145–147
    see also Students; Teachers
Predictors (see Scales)
The Pursuit of Knowledge Under Difficulties (1830),
    156

R

Research and sources, 159–178
    curriculum-based instruction, 177–178
    direct instruction, 174–175
        derivatives, 175–176
    goal setting, 168–169
    precision teaching, 176
    self-evaluation, 172–173
    self-instruction, 159–161
    self-management, 166–168
    self-monitoring, 170–172
    self-planning/scheduling, 169–170
    self-regulation, 161–166
    self-reinforcement, 173–174
Retardation, mental, 46–47
    see also Students

S

Scales, instruction and curriculum, 179–217
    Arc's Self-Determination Scale, 101
    baseline, establishing and comparing, 32–33, 39–41
    curricular content, 182
    evaluation of the model, 190–191
    Goal Attainment Scaling (GAS), 100–102
    group differences
        applied skills curricula, 202–203
        basic skills curricula, 201–202
        student directedness, 200–201
        teacher directedness, 199–200
    instructional directedness, 181
    predictors
        applied skills, 188–190
        basic skills, 187–188
        instructional directedness, 213–215
        self-determination, 209–210
        self-efficacy, 207–209
        student directedness, 186–187, 212–213
        teacher directedness, 184–185, 210–212
        teacher empowerment, 213
    reliability, 182–183
    utility, 193–215
        detecting changes in baselines, 203–206
        explaining teacher directedness, 206–215
        identifying differences in ratings, 199–203
        identifying patterns of teachers, 193–198
    validity, 183–193
        correlation analyses, 183–184
        factor analysis, 191–192
        regression analyses, 184–191
School and work (and self-determined learning), 106–127
Self-adjustment
    strategies, 67
    teaching, 82–84
Self-control strategies, 48–50
    see also Learner control; Self-evaluation; Self-monitoring; Self-reinforcement
Self-determination, 46–47
Self-determined learning
    ChoiceMaker Self-Determination Transition Curriculum (*see ChoiceMaker* solution)
    educational supports, 95–96
    instruction and curriculum scales, 179–217
    at school and work, 106–127
    theory, 7–9

Self-Determined Learning Model of Instruction, 89–96, 101–102
    implementation, 96–99
Self-evaluation, 54–58
    combining procedures, 56–57
    research and sources, 172–173
    strategies, 67
    teaching, 57–58, 80–82
    when to use, 54–56
    see also Learner control
Self-instruction
    choosing, 150–156
    vs. direct instruction, 3–27
    research and sources, 159–161
    student-directed, 31–44
    teacher-directed, 31–44
Self-Instruction Principle, viii, 154
Self-management, 166–168
Self-monitoring, 50–54
    discriminative properties, 54
    and peer tutors, 53–54
    research and sources, 170–172
    strategies, 67
    teaching, 53, 79–80
    when to use, 51–52
    see also Learner control
Self-planning/scheduling
    research and sources, 169–170
    strategies, 67
    teaching, 78–79
Self-recording (*see* Self-monitoring)
Self-regulation
    cards, 76–84
    and choice opportunities, 67–73
    instructional levels, 74–77
    research and sources, 161–166
    teaching, 73–84
    teaching tips, 77–84
    see also Learner control
Self-reinforcement, 58–62
    research and sources, 173–174
    student-directed learning, 60–62
    teaching, 59–60
    see also Learner control
Self-talk supports, 75–76
    see also Instruction; Self-regulation
Students
    choice contract, 143
    directing their learning, 88–104
        and inclusion, 60–62
    with disabilities, 20–22, 48, 55

mental retardation, 46–47
and learner control
adjusting, 66–85
developing, 45–62
practicum work, effect on, 133–136
and self-instruction, 31–44
see also Teachers

T

Take Action program, 115–117
Teachers
practicum work, effect on, 133–136
reluctance to choose, 130–149
role in student-directed learning, 99–100
scales, instruction and curriculum
general educators, 193–195
special educators (U.S.), 195–196
special educators (West Indies), 197–198
and self-instruction, 31–44
see also Students
Teaching (*see* Instruction)
Think and Grow Rich (1938), 90
Tutors (*see* Peer tutors)

W

West Africa, 21
West Indies, 33, 36–37, 193
Work improvement contracts, 121–123